The Art of Kamau Brathwaite

The Art of Kamau Brathwaite

Edited by Stewart Brown

seren

seren is the book imprint of
Poetry Wales Press Ltd
Wyndham Street, Bridgend, Mid Glamorgan
Wales

A CIP record for this book is available at the
British Library Cataloguing in Publication Data Office

ISBN 1-85411-092-6
1-85411-127-2 paperback

The publisher acknowledges the financial support of the Arts Council of Wales

Cover photograph: Moira Conway

Printed in Plantin by
The Cromwell Press, Melksham

Contents

Introduction

Born in 1930 in Barbados, Kamau Brathwaite (christened Lawson Edward Brathwaite) is arguably the most original poet yet to emerge from the Caribbean. Certainly, in terms of his technical experimentation with form and language, as well as in the scale and ambition of his work, he has been more adventurous than the other major poet of the West Indies, with whom he is inevitably compared, Derek Walcott. Brathwaite has now published more than a dozen collections of poetry, several important books of cultural criticism, two small volumes of plays for schools and dozens of essays on literary and more broadly cultural issues. He has recently been experimenting with a kind of poetic prose and a volume of his *DreamStories* was published in 1994 — as was his *Zea Mexican Diary,* a searingly honest account of his response to his wife's death in 1986. He has edited several volumes of creative work by other writers, was for many years a contributing editor to *Bim,* the Bajan literary journal, and editor of *Savacou,* the journal of the Caribbean Artists Movement. All this creative/literary work is in addition to his academic publications as a Professor of History. His major historical work, *The Development of Creole Society in Jamaica* (1971) — although it generated its own controversies — has become a standard text. The two strands of his career cannot really be separated in that way however, his poetry includes two major 'historical' trilogies — *Rights of Passage* (1967), *Masks* (1968) and *Islands* (1969) were published together as *The Arrivants* (1973); *Mother Poem* (1977), *Sun Poem* (1982) and *X/Self* (1987) together form the second trilogy — and indeed all his writing, however seemingly 'personal', is underpinned by his sense of history. To borrow Gordon Rohlehr's phrase from his essay in this collection, Brathwaite's poetry represents the "rehumanization" of that history which has been his life's study. Speaking for himself, Brathwaite, asked what his work 'was about', summed it up as:

> The retracing of our people's movement through space and time and the resurrection of their cultural materials[1]

Although scholars, literary critics and — perhaps more importantly — other West Indian writers have been paying attention to Brathwaite's work for at least three decades now, and his ideas are widely discussed (a peek at the secondary bibliography to this volume will confirm the extent of that interest) *The Art of Kamau Brathwaite* represents the first full length study of his work as a whole, attempting to relate the various facets of his activity one to another.

Brathwaite's childhood and background was similar to Derek Walcott's in many ways (not so surprising given that they were both born in the same year, on islands very close to one another); Brathwaite's family was respectable black middle class and he had a 'conventional' upbringing in the circumstances of colonial Barbados in the thirties and forties. He enjoyed/endured a "sound colonial education" and indeed he won a coveted Barbados Scholarship, to enable him to study history at Cambridge, whereas Walcott stayed in Saint Lucia before taking up a scholarship to study at the University College of the West Indies — as it then was — in Jamaica. There is an irony here in that Walcott, the poet who stayed in the Caribbean, writes, in his early verse particularly, in an English that was very much of the centre, the metropole. Brathwaite, on the other hand, who travels away from the Caribbean *to* the metropole, becomes the poet of 'nation language', his work rich with the voices of the *folk*, of the ways of saying of West Indian people. The crucial difference between the two men's early experience, which to some extent at least explains that divide in terms of their literary language, is to do with the linguistic circumstances of their respective islands. For although Brathwaite's middle class/scholarship boy orientation inevitably created a gulf between himself and the *folk* of his island, the language of the folk and the language of his education were not so much at odds as they were in Walcott's St Lucia, where French-creole was/is the language of 'life' but a very formal English was the language of education and government. In Barbados, although the creole of country areas of the island was distinctive and Bajan 'standard' was itself inflected in a distinct voice, there was not so great a divide between the language of literature and the island's 'nation-language' — Brathwaite's term for the languages West Indian peoples actually speak. Brathwaite's work has always claimed the authority of that spoken and heard tongue, which has had much to do with the shape and surge of his poetry off the page as well as embodying his fundamental concerns as a poet. As J. Edward Chamberlin argues in his essay here, "Brathwaite begins with speech". So any account of his work must begin there also, hence the inclusion of Nathaniel Mackey's 1991 *Hambone* interview with Brathwaite at the beginning of this book. That interview is much cited by other contributors to the *The Art of Kamau Brathwaite* and the poet has confirmed that it very much represents his current thinking and "speech".

For Caribbean intellectuals of Brathwaite's generation the luxury of absolute specialisation, even had it been desired, was not available. Brathwaite is, as I have said, an academic historian by profession, and that discipline — in both senses — informs all his literary work. But this book is concerned with the expression of that historical sense in the range of his cultural activities — his poetry, his criticism and his work as a cultural activist, particularly in relation to the Caribbean Artists Movement and his pan-Caribbean sensibility. To understand any of those aspects of his work it is vital to have some sense of the three inter-connected concerns that have most particularly shaped his consciousness; Africa, jazz and the issues around a West Indian poet's use of language. So *The Art of Kamau Brathwaite* includes essays focusing on each of those areas, as well as others which concentrate on particular ideas in his poetry and on his activity, both critical and practical, towards the fulfilment of his vision of cultural alternatives to the given colonial/neo-colonial models.

Brathwaite was writing and publishing poetry from an early age — in the school magazine, *The Harrisonian*, which he co-founded, and later in *Bim*, under the editorship of Frank Collymore, one of the great men of West Indian letters. If Brathwaite's earliest poetry, (much of it collected now in *Other Exiles*, 1975) is as derivative as the work of many colonial poets of his generation's almost inevitably was — Brathwaite has spoken of "the tyranny of the pentameter", of being rigidly schooled in the tradition of Keats and Wordsworth — yet even in those early occasional pieces it is clear that Brathwaite was attempting to find ways to accommodate rhythms and voices that had hardly been heard before in 'English' poetry. T.S. Eliot is his acknowledged master in this early writing but for Brathwaite it is the Eliot of the American south, influenced by jazz and ways of saying that were far from standard English. That interest in jazz is one of the lasting and most significant influences on the shape, sound and content of Brathwaite's poetry, indeed, as Louis James has argued in his essay here, jazz has been the catalyst for Brathwaite's most profound thinking on the creation of "an alternative Caribbean aesthetic".

Those experiments were continued in the years Brathwaite spent in England as a somewhat alienated student, but he only discovered his particular poetic voice — and themes — during his 'return' to Africa, where he worked as an Education Officer, in Ghana, for eight years in the nineteen-fifties and early sixties. The theme of *The Arrivants*, the trilogy of long poems which established his reputation as a poet, is broadly that of re-birth, re-discovery, reclamation of identity for West Indian people through an examination of their roots in the African past. In all his work — as Maureen Warner-Lewis makes clear in her essay here — Brathwaite explores the ways in which an acceptance of those roots will begin to heal the negative self-images established by the experience of middle passage, plantation and colonial life. For Brathwaite the crucial *ground* of that recovery lies in the society's understanding of the confrontation between the languages which enforced slavery and those which endured and overcame it. English was not, of course, the only language of enforcement — Spanish, Dutch and French were heard too, on different islands, at different times, and parallel with Brathwaite's reclamation of the African heritage is his interest in the 'wider Caribbean', the shared experience that was not limited by the antagonisms of the colonizers. As Bridget Jones argues in her essay here, for Brathwaite "the unity is submarine". The concern with Africa and with a pan-Caribbean consciousness have obvious cultural and social implications. Brathwaite was never content to withdraw into the domain of his personal poetic imagination, indeed the vision of the poet that his work depends on is essentially communal, social. At one point in his career he made the comparison between the élite poet of the European romantic tradition — a lone soul investigating his personal angst — and the folk poet, whose role was like that of some west African griots, to find words for the common experience of a community. Brathwaite has seen himself cast — by history as much as by personal choice, he is by nature a very private person — in the latter role. That sense of a communal duty is evident in much of his writing but also in the work he has done at many levels in terms of enabling and promoting the careers of other Caribbean writers and artists, most especially in his work with the Caribbean Artists Movement (CAM) which Anne Walmsley chronicles in her essay here. The interweaving of the various strands of his activity is caught in the remark she quotes Brathwaite as making about his vision of CAM, "I was working on the African concept of the community. I felt it was important".

Such notions have been consistently explored in Brathwaite's critical writing over almost forty years. Indeed it might well be argued that Brathwaite's work as a cultural critic is at least as important as his poetry — although again the two are impossible, really, to separate. In his essay on Brathwaite as a cultural critic in this volume, Glynne Griffith doesn't try to summarize that vast body of work but selects what seem to him some of the most significant ideas that Brathwaite has developed, linking again with the essays that examine Brathwaite's theories on language, his emphasis on Africa and, as Griffith puts it, his over-riding "sense of the necessary connectedness of the literary and the historical". Griffith makes several references to Brathwaite's major essay of recent years, 'Metaphors of Underdevelopment: A Proem for Hernan Cortez'. Several other commentators in this book refer to that essay also, and Brathwaite himself, writing in 1992, says of it that, although it was originally written in the early eighties:

> I am still trying to absorb the world of disequilibrium I disc in that limbe: a kind of prophesay, really ... an important-for-me doc[2]

Although the original essay was published in journals in both Europe and America, it is not readily available, and its importance to both Brathwaite himself and the scholars working on this book — and indeed to the students/scholars/readers who will use this book, makes its re-publication here particularly valuable.

Those essays and the interview provide the context for the five pieces which offer a close reading of Brathwaite's major poetry. These essays follow the two trilogies sequentially, from Mervyn Morris's measured analysis of intersecting journeys in *The Arrivants*, through Nathaniel Mackey's detailed and pointed account of Brathwaite's technique in *Islands* and *Mother Poem*, and Stewart Brown's review of the significance of *Sun Poem* in the architecture of Brathwaite's overall project to Gordon Rohlehr's powerful re-assembly of the cultural and philosophical elements in Brathwaite's work that climax in *X/Self*. Elaine Savoury's essay looks at Brathwaite's most recent poetry collection, *Middle Passages*, which re-formulates and re-focuses some of his earlier work in light of the Columbus quincentennial 'celebrations' but also anticipates, in his development of the "sycorax video style" manipulations of the word processor's possibilities, his experiments with a kind of 'dream prose'. Her essay also explores the issues around the publication — or non-publication — of Brathwaite's work and the — often ill informed — critical reception it has generated.

It will be interesting to see what critics make of such radical seeming developments as the form of his *DreamStories* or the harrowing content of *Trench Town Rock*. What the essays in this volume demonstrate is that the shape and content of the *DreamStories* can, in fact, be seen to have evolved — if not inevitably then certainly logically — from Brathwaite's earlier practice and ideas. The concern with dream, with possession, with trance, is one that is explored in various ways — and in various forms — throughout his work. Often such states of mind are associated in Brathwaite's work with the confrontation — willing or otherwise — of the *unspeakable*, be it the horrors of the middle passage or the re-discovery of a submerged/forbidden consciousness of Africa or in the approach to God that occurs in the trance of possession. The descent into an abyss of social despair and personal grief that seems to inform many of the *DreamStories* and particularly *Trench Town Rock* perhaps represents another kind of *unspeakableness* which the Sycorax video style and the dreamstory format attempt to address.

Together the pieces in *The Art of Kamau Brathwaite* provide an account of the writer's work and concerns which will enable students and future reviewers/critics of Brathwaite's work to approach his writings from a more firmly grounded perspective. Approaching his sixty-fifth year, Brathwaite's achievement is cause for celebration; the accolades and prizes his work is beginning to attract — most recently the prestigious Neustadt International Prize for Literature — suggest that the literary world has begun to acknowledge the genuine importance of his life's work. If this book can enable a more informed, serious, reading and response to his poetry and ideas, that would be the most effective celebration that he — or we — could wish for.

References

1. On the cassette interview *Edward Kamau Brathwaite: an interview with Yolande Cantu*, London, British Council, 1980.
2. Private correspondence, from Kamau Brathwaite to Stewart Brown, 1992.

Nathaniel Mackey

An Interview with Kamau Brathwaite

Mackey: You've now completed your second trilogy, with *X/Self* in 1987. I'm wondering if you could speak to the issue of the trilogy as a form, an organizing principle, in your body of work, how you came to settle on the trilogy as the way in which your work would proceed. How does it inform the process of writing? Is there some kind of overarching design to the trilogic form as you employ it?
Brathwaite: Judging from the experience of the first trilogy, it was really a matter of raising an issue, replying to that issue and trying to create a synthesis. In other words, the first question, which is in *Rights of Passage*, is: How did we get into the Caribbean? Our people, the black people of the Caribbean — what was the origin of their presence in the Caribbean? And the antithesis to that was — well, the answer to that which emerged was that they came out of migration out of Africa, so that the second movement in the trilogy was the answer to that question. We came out of Africa. Hence, *Masks*. And then, we came out of Africa and went into the New World. Hence, *Islands*. So the trilogic form is based upon the question, an answer and resolution of that answer into a third book. And the same thing happens in the second trilogy. Where were you born? The nature of your landscape? *Mother Poem*: the mother, the coral, limestone. Then, is that your only source of influence, power, aura? The answer was no, there was a male element as well, your father. *Sun Poem*: light, air, in addition to water and ocean. And then the third movement, the resolution into myself, into *X/Self*. That is how it is structured. It is not really conscious. It is not that I have any conscious sense of creating a form of that nature. It is just that my experience and my method of proceeding is always to try to answer the question raised and then try to see how it resolves itself into a third movement.
Mackey: You mentioned in conversation the other day that you were working on a splice between *Sun Poem* and *X/Self* ...
Brathwaite: I was considering a splice.
Mackey: You were considering a splice. What is it about the transition from *Sun Poem* to *X/Self* ...
Brathwaite: It's abrupt, you see. The nature of *X/Self*. X itself, suggests an abrupt transition anyway. But I was wondering — I

haven't settled on that — if, to make it easier for the reader, some more carefully placed transition from *Sun Poem* to *X/Self* might not be a good idea. It's something I'm thinking of, but I'm not certain. In other words, it might even involve the abandoning of the notion of three and making it four, you see, because I have no fixed, no real, overall, absolute, fixed idea about these things. But it is only an idea and I think the publishers are happy with the three as they are.

Mackey: So you don't necessarily see that three as a closed set?

Brathwaite: No, the three isn't closed. In fact, the nine poems which I imagine myself to write — I can see them being juggled. I mean, it doesn't follow in fact that — for instance, there is an order in which *Masks* could be placed as a splice in the centre of *Rights of Passage*, so that when I say, "But I returned to find Jack / Kennedy..." — that could come after *Masks* is finished, right? And in the same way, *X/Self* could come before *Mother Poem*. So that until the nine poems are completed I don't think the form of them will be completed either.

Mackey: How much does the notion of a progression forward inform and determine your sense of that form?

Brathwaite: No. It doesn't. It's not a linear movement, except in the sense of thesis-antithesis-synthesis. That is an overall idea. But since I started that it has been superseded with the idea of tidalectics, which is dialectics with my difference. In other words, instead of the notion of one-two-three, Hegelian, I am now more interested in the movement of the water backwards and forwards as a kind of cyclic, I suppose, motion, rather than linear. So that the trilogy form might well undergo some changes during the process of writing it.

Mackey: That leads into another question I wanted to ask. What is your sense of the continuities between *The Arrivants* and this new trilogy? What's your sense of their differences?

Brathwaite: The continuities are there in the sense that the first three are archetypal. They deal with the outlines of the subject, the genesis and the outlines of the subject. They deal with the communities that give rise to Caribbean peoples and their problems. In the second trilogy, it is the grounding of that whole thing into person. It's about my mother, it's about Barbados, it's about myself within the family context. And you can see now that the third trilogy will be what you could still call a synthesis of those two. In other words, how does my self now go forward into that wider community again, seeing it now from the point of view of a new personal baptism into unexpected areas of loss and the hopeful reconstitution of all this once more into the psycho-natural elements of wind, water, metal fire, green history?

Mackey: Is this the move signalled by the greater emphasis on early Mediterranean history, for example, in *X/Self*? It seems to me that the screen widens beyond the Caribbean in a much more extensive and sustained way.

Brathwaite: And the Amerindian as well. Yes, I think that is what is happening there. It is my widening sense of history, of the influences that make up not only the biological history of the Caribbean but the personal one, the intellectual history. *X/Self* is a biography of my history, if you can put it that way. It is how the things that influenced my own growing up — not the physical aspect of the growing up — in a sense it is a Calibanization of what I have read, the things that informed my growth in terms of ideas.

Mackey: One of the recurring lines in *X/Self* is "Rome burns / and our slavery begins". One senses in reading it that it's packed, that it's a densely packed motif. Could you unravel some of what's packed in there?

Brathwaite: Well, the basic idea is one of equilibrium, right? That if an empire collapses a vacuum is created and new forces rush in. What I'm saying there is that Rome created some kind of law, order, structure, for the ancient world and with Rome's fall mercantilism, commercialism and materialism, unbridled materialism, rushed in to fill that gap. And that included eventually the alterRenaissance, the business of selling us, selling people, selling Africans, the slave trade. That is how the thing works out. The Roman Empire, the *civus* of Rome, gives way to the mercantilism of western Europe. The death of Rome signals the beginning of western expansion, which includes slavery and the slave trade and resultant disequilibriums throughout the world and within, therefore, the word. As Mt Blanc rises, Lake Chad and Kilimanjaro sink and the desertification of Africa begins.

Mackey: Yes. It seems to me that one of the things in the second trilogy is that the agitation or the perturbation at the linguistic level is so much more intense, denser than in *The Arrivants*. And it reminds me of a much-quoted statement of yours, originally in *The Development of Creole Society in Jamaica 1770-1820*, where you say: "It was in language that the slave was perhaps most successfully imprisoned by his master and it was in his (mis-)use of it that he perhaps most effectively rebelled. Within the folk tradition language was (and is) a creative act in itself." Those linguistic turns and detours and fragmentations and neologisms and so forth that you call Calibanisms would be in the tradition of that kind of folk/slave rebellion?

Brathwaite: Right. Yes. It is also, I think, a surrealization of x/perience which we first saw in Césaire's *Cahier*.

Mackey: Yes. But I'm wondering what you think of the caution issued by George Lamming in *The Pleasures of Exile*, where he writes: "Prospero lives in the absolute certainty that language, which is his gift to Caliban, is the very prison in which Caliban's achievement will be realized and restricted."

Brathwaite: The very prison?

Mackey: Yes. "... the very prison in which Caliban's achievement will be realized and restricted."

Brathwaite: I don't know if I understand that fully. What Lamming is saying there is that Prospero creates a prison of language in which he traps Caliban. I presume that's what he's saying, although Lamming's own work doesn't do it that way either. Well, if Prospero creates the prison in which Caliban is trapped, Caliban's responsibility is to break his way out of it. The only way he can break his way out of it is to return to the language of his mother, Sycorax, and that is what these poems are trying to do. Instead of Caliban revolting even against the language of Prospero he is really trying to hack his way back to the language of the forgotten, submerged mother, Sycorax. He doesn't have to be in a prison at all, as long as he recognizes that he did have a mother and does have a mother and therefore in relocating her, rediscovering her, he is already free of anything that Prospero can spin around him.

Mackey: Does that mean that Caliban's language doesn't have to be a reaction to Prospero's, doesn't have to be a curse hurled at Prospero's language, but is actually a move through that curse to a...

Brathwaite: Back to his own mother, who has her own cosmos. Yes. In fact, even looking at Shakespeare, I'm never concerned with Caliban's so-called curse. In fact, the person who claims that Caliban curses is Prospero, but actually Caliban, though he repeats this, does not himself do any cursing as far as I remember. He has the most beautiful lines in the whole play, you know. But that is what I'm trying to do there, not to conceive of Caliban as a binary opposite of Prospero or anything like that, but to see Caliban as a gateway to an alternative which Prospero has recognized but censored out of Shakespeare's consciousness.

Mackey: Is that what you mean in *X/Self* when you say, "not fe dem / not fe dem / de way caliban // done // but fe we"?

Brathwaite: Right. Yes.

Mackey: Is that a critique of Calibanism as we understand it?
Brathwaite: Yes. It's a critique of the Caliban that has come down to us as this primitive rebel, as a person who really, well, basically fails in the revolt because he doesn't go far enough. The traditional Caliban does not go far enough, he's a would-be rebel. He is a would-be rebel because he never connects back with that mother.
Mackey: I think the point that Lamming is also making is that revolt has to take place in some arena other than language to be effective.
Brathwaite: Yes. Fair enough. Yes. I would think that the revolt has to be total in order to achieve anything. The language helps to inform the thought and the thought helps to inform action, be it political or whatever. But I don't think you can separate the various kinds of revolt. Revolt tends to be total whenever it comes. Revolts that are successful, like the French Revolution and the Haitian Revolution and, in a sense, the Russian Revolution — they all had a gestalt element about them. It was not simply that people were hacking down or destroying the Bastille of words, but they were also destroying physical and ideological Bastilles as well.
Mackey: Yes. There is, though, a special emphasis that you place on language and that's due, perhaps, to the fact that you're a poet.
Brathwaite: Right. I couldn't do it any other way.
Mackey: In the quote I just quoted —"It was in language that the slave," etc — there is a prioritizing of language there that...
Brathwaite: Which can be extended to education though, don't forget. And ideas. I mean, it doesn't only mean language in terms of verbs and sentences, but the whole business of the structures, the ideological structures that are built to control the colonial, to control the slave, to control the underclasses of the western world, to control the mind. That is what Prospero constantly attempts to do, be it through television or through comic books or through the books you have in school. But it is the responsibility of Caliban, of the colonized, not only to revolt against that imposition but to discover his own coral, his own roots.
Mackey: Another sense of direction that I get in my reading of the two trilogies is that in the recently completed one there tends to be less of a sustained narrative or strands of narrative than in *The Arrivants*. There seems to be less presentation of a determinate scene or location. There is more shifting and in some way more fragmentation, in some way — you could call it drift. In fact, the title of the last poem in *Mother Poem* is 'Driftword', that coinage which seems to suggest some kind of embrace of fragmentation, of

instability, of flux, of a kind of animate debris. If that's the case, how did you come to that? Or how would you rephrase what I've said to make...

Brathwaite: It probably is that, although there is an internal core constantly trying to create integration. But it hasn't come yet and that's perhaps because it's the middle trilogy. What happens is that in the first trilogy the narrative is much clearer because it is history, it has happened, and therefore I can recall it confidently as having happened. We know things started, shall we say, in the year 2000 B.C. and moved to 1492, right? But when it comes to the personal trilogy it would have to be in prismatic form if not in fragmented form, because my own experience has not been objectivized in any way. It's impossible for me to do that. What I'm doing is discovering myself in, as Eliot calls it, shafts of sunlight, little intuitions. And I try to overlay, one on top of the other, and interleave them wherever possible. But it is an effort there to try to perceive some coherence out of the various shafts of intuition. There's not much more, then, that one can do there. You'll find that the moments of coherence come when it is no longer personal meditation. Anytime the mother comes into it, or in the case of *Sun Poem* that long section on the slave trade, starting in Africa and coming right through to the arrival of the giants, the Igbo people, on the coast of Barbados. There you have a flow and that is because it is once more a narrative which has had an objective reality. But then it is quickly followed by these fragments, these pebbles, these offshoots of that particular boulder. And that is very conscious form. I don't want it any other way. The challenge of the third trilogy will be to see what can be constructed out of a personal history when it is put once more into the effort to reintegrate into community.

Mackey: Does this envision an end to fragmentation? I spoke earlier of an embrace of fragmentation. Is it an embrace that's trying to work through fragmentation? Do you see or wish there to be a coherence on the other side of it?

Brathwaite: I would expect so. I don't know the nature of that coherence but one hopes that the coherence will be observable. I mean, what I am learning from looking at myself through mother, looking at myself through father, looking at myself through history, education, whatever you find in *X/Self* — that that will lead to a structure in the third trilogy which will seem more like the coherence of the first. That is a vague model that is there, but I have no evidence or proof or guarantee that it will come that way. The thing is entirely open-ended. And I think it's also a test of my own integrity. I mean, assuming that fragmentation suggests some uncertainty, some caution, some — well, all sorts of things which are not coherent anyway, which is part of the modern sensibility — but, assuming that that is what the second trilogy suggests, one hopes that as one becomes more self-aware, as one has worked through the history of self, the auto-anthropology, really, of the self, one will return to forms and to lines which suggest much more the coherence of, say, *Masks* or *Rights of Passage*.

Mackey: Though even in *The Arrivants* there is the recognition of fragmentation and a willingness to dwell in it. At the very end of *Islands*: "now waking / making // making / with their // rhythms some- / thing torn // and new". That kind of...

Brathwaite: Yes. And *Islands* itself is much more fragmented than *Rights of Passage* and *Masks*. That is because it's reflecting the physical and geo-psychic fragmentation of the *Islands* themselves. What we really want to see, I suppose, is what kind of aesthetic comes out of fragmentation.

Mackey: Can't one say we already have it in such a work as this?

Brathwaite: I don't know. You see, I'm not aware enough of the effect of that work, of what it really has achieved, to be certain. I'm aware of an increasing interleaving of experience rather than a linear movement, but whether that is in fact the result of a fragmentation aesthetic I can't say.

Mackey: Well, if, as you say in 'Mid/Life' in *Mother Poem*, "the child / is born to splinters // broken islands / broken homes // driftwood of beaches," how could you hope to arrive at coherence?

Brathwaite: Yes, that's what I don't know. I mean, it might well be that one can't go any further. I think the coherence now would come more in the effect of the poem, you know. In fact, to be able to write a poem which is built up on fragmented slivers but still has an overall archetype of coherence — something like that, like the form within music, that you might break it down into movements within the overall form, but that the overall form is very confident and certain. But again, that might not be the direction that one is moving into, because, you see, the nature of the poetry is so intuitive. It is not based on any predetermined pattern. That's the difficulty of speaking about it. Until the poem is written you cannot really say what it meant, in a sense. The meaning comes in the doing of it and then the reflection on what has been done — to me that becomes the meaning. So I can't really say that this is how I plan to do any one thing.

Mackey: Is your interest in creation myths related to this question of the co-existence of coherence and fragmentation?

Brathwaite: It could well be that, you know. In fact, we feel — at least, I do and, I think, many of us in the Caribbean are very — we feel the absence of creation myths. We know that in a situation such as ours there should be some presiding organon for us, but it is often not there. We don't really deal in archetypes. We tend to deal in stereotypes, unfortunately. And I suppose my interest in creation myths is to see how other people did it and to see if anything that I might come across reflects what I intuitively perceive in our own landscape. Up to now I have never found anything that seems to correspond to what we have. Perhaps it is not our responsibility to deal with creation myths in that form at all. I don't know.

Mackey: Have you felt any impulse to go to the Arawak and the Carib mythologies as does someone like Wilson Harris?

Brathwaite: Yes. Still, it's for me not comfortable. Wilson does it, I suspect, because he comes from Guyana, on the mainland. He himself, I suspect, has part origins in that area, you know, and he has done it remarkably easily and naturally and with consistent, almost awesome deconstructive creativity. I myself have not been able to relate to any of that comfortably up to now. Like Lamming, perhaps, and, well, most of the people on the islands, one feels that you'll have to struggle with self-creation, the creation of a myth out of our own landscape, out of our own modern landscape, out of our own post-Amerindian landscape. That's how it seems.

Mackey: And the importation of African creation myths would not...

Brathwaite: Very important, but, still, you see what I did in *Sun Poem*. I brought them across the water to explain how those rocks in Bathsheba were created. That's the nearest I have come to it. I have Legba, but Legba is a war veteran. And, you know, that is perfectly within the Haitian form but it is still not a creation myth and is still not used centrally. The only central effort is the Legba people, the coming across the water from Africa to the east coast of Barbados.

Mackey: I asked about the Amerindian in part because of the last poem in *Sun Poem*, 'Son': "Water went / they say // land was not / they say // breath only then / they say" and so forth. Isn't that from a Meso-American creation myth?

Brathwaite: Could be. I don't know. That was *mine*.

Mackey: Oh, really?

Brathwaite: Right. So you see, I don't know. I mean, I have seen similar things, not only Meso-American but Pacific Islander, that kind of thing. There's a form of that which I was touching on and that is my own. But even so, that is a coda. To me that is something after the thing has been finished and you're making a final comment. It is not a central concern, it doesn't create the form of the poem. You see, the form of that poem still comes from the experience of that boy growing up on the beach, is actually created out of the light, shadow, glints, sands, suns of that environment. It doesn't come from anything outside of it. Creation comes from his own sense of splash and glitter, like when he sees the wall, the sea throwing its messages on the wall of his room. That is his creation myth. Nothing more than that. No god or divinity behind it.

Mackey: So it's in the moment...

Brathwaite: Yes, yes. It is in the moment...

Mackey: And in the body, that sense of the body as "the castle of my skin"...

Brathwaite: Yes, could be, yes...

Mackey: No monumental myth, no monumental history, only the...

Brathwaite: What you sense. Sense and sensibility. So far. But one is haunted that there is more there. I mean, whales inhabit my imagination. Underground and under the water there are larger forms which have deeper resonance and we haven't yet reached them.

Mackey: Yes. Does that line of Walcott's, "The sea is history," mean much to you?

Brathwaite: I know that one. Yes.

Mackey: Are you getting at that kind of sense of some depth that has yet to be plumbed?

Brathwaite: Well, yes, that's one of the things. I mean, that is a basic thing, that we have to go deeper, we have to go deeper.

Mackey: I was struck by your use of the term "magical realism" in the notes to *X/Self*. First of all, because I rarely see that term applied to poems. It's mainly, almost exclusively, at least in my reading, applied to narrative fiction. I'm wondering how you come at that term, how you see it. I mean, it's a term that everyone seems to have his or her own definition of.

Brathwaite: Yes. Well, "Rome burns / and our slavery begins" is that too. It is, you see, a magic lantern. It is the conversion once more of the deterioration of images from one thing into another, the transformation of reality — because it's not only images — from one thing into another. I'm very much aware that in this second trilogy that is what is happening to me, that gardens become corals and corals wither away or transmute themselves into light. And, you know, that is the kind of thing which I call magical realism. How the metaphors and images interlock and interweave and interpenetrate each other, so that increasingly you have a seamless — in fact, it's a seamless kind of poetry, increasing without punctuation, where images inform, flow and influence each other. It is a kind of surrealism as well, but magical realism, I think, is nearer to it, because it is the transformation of reality into this prism of imagination and light.

Mackey: *X/Self* seems to proceed, in many of its moves, by way of what one might call historical rhymes. Certain disparate events or persons in history, separated in time and in space, are brought together.

Brathwaite: Magical realism again. That is my application of the notion of creolization. What I'm saying in *X/Self* is that whenever two empires meet or two people, like Herodotus and Herod, meet, the result of their *frisson* and fusion is a creole event. And that they can live together in the same space, even if they come from two different time centres. I mean, you increasingly can bring all sorts of people together to participate in a new, magical event, because they share this business of osmosis. Their cultures are informing each other, exchanging information.

Mackey: That's so much a creolization of the word or by the word, via the word, 'Herod' being the first five letters of 'Herodotus', you know, that I'm wondering...

Brathwaite: But it is not only in that kind of thing, the playing on the words. You find it also in how Hannibal comes from Africa and colonizes the northern Mediterranean. You find it in the Romans going to Britain and creolizing Vercingetorix. That to me is interesting, the number of black people that come up — Severus, Socrates, Othello, Saladin, Solimann Africanus — that's why the Mediterranean is so important to the poem — that come up from northern Africa and colonize the imagination of Europe. And Cortez going to Mexico and becoming a postage stamp — he is absorbed back into the underground of that culture. To me that is what I'm getting at. So that "Rome burns / and our slavery begins". Rome in fact becomes like the metropolis of the modern Caribbean. Nero could have been any of the slave-masters who were dancing in the Caribbean at that time.

Mackey: What we've been talking about touches on the relationship of poetry to history, the interrelationships between the two. Being a historian as well as a poet, you're in a special position to address an issue that has certainly been critical to a number of major

U.S. poets — Ezra Pound talking about the epic being "a poem containing history," T.S. Eliot seeming to have thought that he could never learn enough history, the same thing, or, if not the same thing, a related thing in Charles Olson, his "special view of history," his concern with being a poet and being a historian, and so forth. I'm wondering, first of all, how familiar you are with those writers and their concerns with history and, second, how you see your own practice as poet-historian related, if at all, to those concerns.

Brathwaite: You see, first of all, I have to confess that I don't know very much about them. You're dealing here with a situation where my own development has come about, almost, through my own struggle with the various elements of it. For instance, I still don't know Olson's work. I don't know if it's a good thing or a bad thing, but I have never yet felt the need to come to grips with it. Now that you've mentioned his concern with history perhaps it will be easier for me to make a connection. Pound I've always found hard to read. He deals in what I call real fragments. I've never found Pound able to reconstitute elements. It seems as if he was breaking them down and therefore I've found the poetry dry, arid, hard to get to. Eliot I was always attracted to by his speaking voice, as I've said over and over again, but I find him, again — well, I suppose it was a post-war expression of his — too much concern with the ruins, living among these beautiful ruins, if you like, but not really, again, reconstituting the elements of it. Whereas, you see, as a Caribbean person, we start with the ruins and our responsibility is to rebuild those fragments into a whole society. We have always been concerned with the rediscovery of source, the revitalization of origins. To me that has been such an entirely different concern from those of the U.S. poets that you mention. I cannot say I've been influenced by them, I don't know them well enough. Nor do I know of any other Caribbean writers whom I could say have been. And I think there is a reason for that. I think that the concerns are on a parallel line. They have not really crossed over into our concerns. The influence has not been there. I find that, for instance, we're influenced much more, say, by the Bible, which is another example, you know, of people trying to deal with fragment, if you like, with destitution, with things stripping away — but underlying it always the effort to in-gather, to restore. I think that's why the Bible has been such a powerful influence on so many of our writers. The other big influence, of course, for me is history, as you say, the history of the sense of migration, the constant movement of peoples over the landscape of the world and how, from the very beginning, people

have by their very contiguity influenced each other. That creolization, that interlapping of experiences — to me that has been the big thing. So that when Africans come into the Caribbean one is very much aware that they have not only brought their own culture with them — they have not come naked, as people usually say — but that that culture begins to relate to the culture of the European, the conquistador, the Amerindian, and right away we are at the threshold of a new kind of social structure, a new kind of cultural imagination.
Mackey: Which North American writers, if any, do you feel a consonance with?
Brathwaite: You ask me these embarrassing questions.
Mackey: We'll cut it. [Laughter.]
Brathwaite: You know, I can't, I can't — none of them has ever done anything significant for my guitar strings, as it were. And in this I don't mean to imply no arrogance or undue ignorance, though I'm afraid there is a colonial? Third World? non-Metropolitan? element of that in here too. But, you see, like here in California I can feel the dry, very ancient wind blowing up from Mexico, from the Aztec and the Inca, as it were. Your clouds reflect in blue the Easter Islands rising out of the Pacific. And there is desert even by the waters here, but very different, kind of Nile, of Niger, and a cold Polar imprint too — Alaska Borealis — and a vocabulary of volcano, fire and earthen stutter, earthquake, your gravity almost if not always on the verge of disequilibrium, as it were — which I love, the whole sweep of it, which I recognize now that I am here, but which, you see, I knew nothing of before, heard no rumours of even in the U.S. writing I was reading, though no doubt it's there. But it couldn't have connected with me, been constant or consonant simply because your trade winds (in all their senses) don't blow our way and so my guitar strings aren't touched or tightened. Or take again Lowell's gray boulders of pentameter — as he might say, pantameter — along the Northeast world of Ahab's whales, those Dry Salvages. Take Hawthorne's scars and scarlet savages, those perfect sixteenth-century villages like Amherst, Salem wood and carpenters becoming Shakers, gray howlers like Manhattan. Hart Crane's great hurricanes of stone and glass and girder wire are not from Africa, from harmattans like ours. "An octopus of ice / deceptively reserved and / flat" excites and haunts me, yes, but Marianne and Dickinson and Plath speak flattened fifths so different from Damballa. And what I'm saying too is that there can't be any singing influence upon the strings, the lyre, kora, lute, my sonophone, unless and until there is real x/change, until the

disequilibriums equal out, as it were: Mt Blanc and Kilimanjaro, Sahara/Prairie/Arizona all the way from Chad to Zacatecas, Atlantically balanced, Mississippi blowing south like Walcott's "Glory Trumpeter," if you see what I mean. It gets easier, at least for me — more confluence? — with the sound of Frost and Edwin Arlington Robinson, *Spoon River* too. But why not *Paterson*? What keeps me back from all those *Cantos*, all that *Maximus*? But it is only when — and now — that I can talk like this — see them within integument like that, that I can talk of "influence," of "congruence," of "con*flow*ence" that leads perhaps to "conference" and "flowers". But perhaps I boom X/Self too down with "canon" when I — we — yes — when certainly *I* — certainly — should be saying "Harlem," "Basin Street," "Ogotemmeli" and listening to worksong, Louee, Pharoah Sanders' "Sun Ship," Tom Dent's New Orleans whispers, Baraka, Mother Brooks and Sterling Brown, though even these I come to later, later, later, even if not too too later. But not too early neither, like when we were learning pebbles, syllables and "*pick-up-sticks*". So that I should be speaking more easily now of Langston Hughes and Kubayanda's drum poetics and welcoming the miracle — not really miracle but natural phenomenon of nommo — of Margaret Walker's voice, of Alice Walker's vision, Yemajaa Margaret Danner's in/chanting of the Caribbean sea: "This Painted Lady is a small African / butterfly, gayly toned orchid or peach / that seems as tremulous and delicately sheer // as the objects I treasure".

Mackey: Well, let me, to add to that, read you a piece of literary lineage-making and see what you make of it. This is from Edouard Glissant's *Caribbean Discourse*: "Whereas I feel that Brathwaite revives thirty years later Aimé Césaire's discourse, he places it actually in a new context: the concrete and diverse realm of lived experience. Brathwaite's link is not as much with Césaire's poetics as with the broken rhythms of Nicolás Guillén or Léon Gontran Damas. The written becomes oral. Literature includes in this way a 'reality' that seemed to restrain and limit it. A Caribbean discourse finds its expression as much in the explosion of the original cry, as in the patience of the landscape when it is recognized, as in the imposition of lived rhythms".

Brathwaite: Yes, he puts it very well. Thanks for letting me hear that. There — if people want to — yes, that's the lineage: Césaire, Brathwaite, Guillén, Damas. Yes, to some degree, not widely acknowledged, perhaps, part of our disequilibrium, I suppose, but there is a kind of continuity of concern and the way the poetry enacts that concern that the francophone Glissant and anglophone Caribbean critics like, say, in particular Gordon Rohlehr, for instance, and Maureen Warner-Lewis have recognized, though in general there is a kind of meanness and animus and shall we say cultural/personal politization of our literary criticism which isn't really doing our culture, us — I won't say 'literature' — much good. The point that I'm still trying to make is that too much of our work is achieved without the benefit of critical benefice, of tradition, of a sense of *accretion*, of the conscious accumulation of shared experience both of 'xperience' (the harshing of our people) and the shared experience of how we have counterveiled in terms of defense/survival communities, but also in the sense of how we have discovered the word/forms to say that this has been happening, like when, for instance, I talk about in "The stone had skidded / arc'd and bloomed into islands" how long it took me, in my isola, my? colonial isolation, to discover the genius and perhaps genesis of our islands in the language of calypso and how that calypso, in my verse, is related to water and sun and pebble continent and song and kinesis and an ever-widening unlocking of a central atomic *name* or *mane* or *nyam* or *nam*. What I am saying here is that I did not discover Césaire until after *Rights of Passage* was well underway. My echo of Césaire, "we who have achieved nothing," I had just — in fact, I had thought of translating Césaire and Zea Mexican was in fact on a first draft at about the time when I was "starting" *Rights*, though I didn't have a chance even to look at it until after *Rights* was kind of 'over,' so that although there are coincidences and correspondences on many levels and critics have pointed these out, I was, in fact, ignorant of what Césaire had done in the *Cahier* even though it had been written when I was nine years old and living in the same backyard of his sea. In any case, it was not available in translation (hence Zea Mexican's decision) and the original was as rare as a genie in a bottle in our Caribbean of that time. Similarly, Guillén did not really 'collide' with us until around 1975 when he visited Jamaica when Cuba and Jamaica were on 'diplomatic relations'. Before that, one had heard on the BBC 'My Two Grandfathers' or 'Sensemaya', but no more. I mean, we were not aware of Guillén's work either. And the anthologies gave you a little Damas and you knew of the Négritude movement in a kind of vague way, but we did not have any direct, intimate connection on a personal or intellectual level with any of them. Same thing with Langston Hughes. Linton Kwesi Johnson speaks about when he begins to write and about the dub poets of the Caribbean writing in the early eighties — it is only *then* that they discover Langston and Césaire, you know. It is a very late development for all of us. It's a sign of our isolation and of the poor nature of our education. And our own lack of curiosity. We have to blame ourselves too. We were content to live in this Garden of Eden in the Caribbean without enough curiosity to find out what was out there. Even if it's not in the schools, there's no excuse why you should not set up your antenna and discover what is there. For some reason, very few people even did that.

Mackey: Your early poems, those in *Other Exiles*, show a clearer jazz influence. Your more recent work seems to be more discernibly influenced by reggae and Rasta music, by calypso and so forth. I was wondering how you see yourself in relationship to dub poetry and such people as LKJ. I've read somewhere that you're a kind of father figure to some of them.

Brathwaite: Some say that, some say not. Some say nothing at all. There has been no overt thing, but I would've thought that the work I did through *The Arrivants* certainly would have given them the kind of start which I did not get since I didn't know Guillén or Langston Hughes in the kind of way that they now know me. I mean, my readings and public lectures must have influenced, in some way, the development of "dub". In the sixties we had Yard Theatre with Marina Omowale Maxwell in Jamaica and I was reading many of my poems with Count Ossie on drums. A lot of people who became dub poets, I think, would have been present on those occasions and therefore I think that, since I was the only person — I'm not blowing my own trumpet by any means, but I knew I was the only person because it was a very lonely experience — and since I was then the only person introducing drum rhythms into poetry it would have connected with them and they could have carried it on. I mean, I started with jazz and with train rhythms and so on. They then went straight to the local music, the local popular music, ska, rock steady, reggae, and they transferred their verse immediately into the sound system. But they did have a stepping stone in the kind of thing that I was doing. This is how I would see it, but there hasn't been any critical account of this.

Mackey: What about personal relationships with people like Mutabaruka, LKJ or reggae singers like Burning Spear? I mean, do you know them personally, do you hang out with them?

Brathwaite: Yes, I know them. No, I don't hang out. But the musicians — that's another clan again. I can't say I know many of them. Only one or two I've gotten to know over time. Not the reggae people, but like Cedric Brooks (jazz/folk/Rasta), Count Ossie and the Mystic Revelation of Rastafari, Brother Single, Bongo Jerry,

Miss Queenie and some of the kumina musicians, Chalkdust (Trinidad kaiso), the bongo drummer Mackey Burnett who I ran into teaching pan in Providence, Rhode Island, a few years ago, and, of course, Olive Lewin and Rex Nettleford who has visibilized our music into dance. In Barbados there is a whole range of musicians: El Verno del Congo and Ernie Small and Gabby and some of the tuk band people and the Landship and people into Bajan folk and folk music research like Elombe Mottley and Trevor Marshall. All over the Caribbean — St. Lucia, Belize, Haiti, Cuba, St. Vincent, Bahamas — one has these encounters, pro/tacts. The dub poets, of course, yes. Some of them, anyway. LKJ — okay — is a friend. I've known him from the Caribbean Artists Movement in London and over the years, me going to London and him coming to Jamaica. I was also quite close to Michael Smith and perhaps you know the poem, 'Stone,' that I wrote after he'd been stoned to death on Stony Hill in Kingston soon after he returned from what John La Rose described as his short brilliant meteoric career in Jamaica and briefly in London (Book Fair, BBC TV, the LP *Mi Cyaan Believe It*, Paris, UNESCO, etc, etc, etc). In his early days we used to hang out together a lot especially at the School of Drama where he was a student and I a part-time tutor in 1977-79 when "dub," you might say, was coming into its own in Jamaica with Mikey and Oku Onuora and Jean Breeze and Claudette Richardson and the "Godfadda" Noel Walcott, whose poem "A pat wah dat" forms the cover of *Savacou* 14/15, which really is the first dub poets anthology, though there are other things in that there also. Mutabaruka was not so much around at that time. I think he was ital on the North coast farming and fishing at the time and had not fully developed. Or shall we say he was then developing his own now very characteristic "dub" style. Never really got close to him, but that's probably a personal thing. He calls me Mr Brathwaite and that puts me off. [Laughter.] As if — I get the feeling with some of the dub poets that — in fact, when they started, when dub poetry started, there was this — this thing happened that they thought that they were the first and only poets, that nothing had happened before them, etc, etc, as if here at last was Genesis, etc. And it was, in a sense, it was such an exciting time, such a wonderful breakthrough back into oral tradition, but so too was the Harlem Renaissance and the 1960s/70s out of which they came — my point being, again, disjuncture, lack of continuity, ignorance of that continuity, the really longer lines of complexity of their tradition. But their blocking of others off — that doesn't help to creolize. That doesn't help to interculturate.

[Laughter.] In my view, there has not been enough mixing of the two things. Sometimes I wonder if they really do know about my work and if it means anything. But these things will probably, you know, change as things go along. I've read with Muta. I remember there was a great thing at the London Black Book Fair in 1984 with Baraka, Muta, myself and LKJ, which I really wish that they had recorded and published, as they had published the earlier poetry festival. That was, to me, extraordinary. The four cadences of expression were quite remarkable that evening.

Mackey: Have you done any reading to reggae accompaniment?

Brathwaite: Yes, yes. A lot of the poems in *Black & Blues* were influenced by reggae and have been read to reggae — I have some tapes somewhere, I hope, of these and with Cedric Brooks and his group in the Yard Theatre in the seventies.

Mackey: The early poems show the impact of jazz, as I've said. How much of that has to do with a sense of it as a kind of outlaw music?

Brathwaite: Could be. It's a sense of alternative anyway and it was the music that made sense to *me*. That was the music I grew up with, music that I personally discovered — let's put it that way — and it immediately made sense to me. But don't forget that this is in the absence, in Barbados, of folk music, of the living enjambment of folk song. And what you see in the early work is this alternative music giving me an alternative riddim, as it were, but as I get to know more about the Caribbean the emphasis shifts from jazz to the Caribbean, to calypso, to reggae, to our folk music, to the (religious) music connected with the *hounfour*, so that it appears to be a moving away from jazz, as it is, in one sense, and an effort to explore more fully the nature, the musical patterns, of the local scene, though one can't "move away" from jazz or any of the forms of Black Music as long as one's aesthetic and can we say *ethic* (?) is/are rooted there.

Mackey: Well, by outlaw music I guess I'm thinking about your early experience as a jazz deejay in Barbados and...

Brathwaite: Well, yes, alternative or outlaw if you like. It was regarded as devil music in Barbados, especially bebop, which I grew up on in the fifties there. We had a radio program as schoolboys — Harrison College, you know, the élite school of the island — and when we went on the air that first evening, the one and only evening, the people flooded the station with phone calls demanding the incarceration of the perpetrators, the, as they saw us, *cultural traitors*. Instead of Mozart or Rogers and Hart we were playing,

I think, 'Oop Bop s'Bam' or 'Shaw Nuff' or 'Ornithology,' certainly something hard by Dizzy and Bird, followed by Thelonious Monk — I mean, even that man's *name* was unbelievable and phone calls began coming in about *that* — with some walkin' sixths in 'Criss Cross' or 'Evonce' or 'Misterioso,' followed by an "overdose" of Boyd Raeburn for good measure goodness sake. Can you imagine what was going on at the station — and *out/**side**?* Well, in fact the station — they didn't turn us off, they didn't even turn us *down*, as was to happen many years later in another island — I find that they were very good that evening. They let us play it out to the bitter end. But the Man, the manager said politely (he was English!) that there wouldn't — couldn't — be a second such xperience. And you can imagine me upon the carpets of the various drawing rooms around the island afterwards: how I had let the "side" upside down (a partial cricket metaphor — Barbados is the HQ of Cricket) and "Harrson" College (Harrson/Harrison College is the HQ of Caribbean Education) and "Cdear Eddie mahn, you int got no *Shame*," etc, etc, etc, as if I was some slave rebel like Bussa.

Mackey: Well, coming very rapidly back to the present — earlier you alluded a little bit to a third trilogy. Is there anything more you want to say about that?

Brathwaite: No.

Mackey: What are some of the other projects that you're involved in right now? What can we look for in the future from you?

Brathwaite: The first thing is that I look forward to getting publishers because I'm finding it increasingly difficult, with the kind of work I'm developing, to find publishers who are consonant with it, who are really sympathetic. My feeling is that it's always an act of terror nowadays to deliver anything to a publisher, because you get, as you know, these kinds of remarkable rejection slips of letters that, you know, the work is either inaccessible, though it even ain't Joyce or Derrida, or it don't have — like my present publishers in England have sent back these things about "We haven't got a public for this, for this kind of thing. There is no market for it, no interest in this kind of thing and" — best of all —"why don't you write a different book?" So, as we go on exploring the Caribbean experience...

Mackey: These are poems they're talking about?

Brathwaite: Poems and prose things, ideas, things like a book called *Missile and Capsule*, which tries to look at Caribbean history in terms of those two icons. People in the United Kingdom are not interested, I'm told, in ideas of that kind. I don't know why, but I suspect it's because the ideas come from Caliban. That is how I see it, but I may be wrong. But to get back to your question: I'm now working on, among other things — there has been since 1972, believe it or not, this massive, indeed monumental — which is what it really is in reality — and in intention — celebration of Caribbean poetry. I wanted to celebrate the fact that I was a member of a whole group of people and in 1972 after Carifesta in Guyana I thought I would make a list of the poets of the Caribbean in English as a start. I assumed that this would be an afternoon's work and then I thought it would be a weekend's work and now I've been on it since 1972, which is a long fifteen years or whatever. So that is my big lifework project now and I continue to work on this even though there is not even a publisher or, it seems, even a *prospect* of a publisher, one of your U.S. publishers having abrogated my 1975 contract on it on no pretext whatever, just suddenly let us have it, all the way from the Caribbean in 48 hours or *hellse*, and another, more recent, suggesting that I might want to convert this whole thing into a bio-bibliography not of *Caribbean* poetry but of *all* Caribbean literature in English (French, Dutch, Spanish too?).

Mackey: This is an annotated bibliography, with commentary along the way?

Brathwaite: Yes, annotated. And with quotations. And it comes right through from Marvell's sixteenth-century poem about the Bermudas to the present. It includes translations, it includes working anthologies — that alone is massive — and resource materials, what things people have written on the poetry of the Caribbean — Arnold's book, books on Guillén, the books that people have done on dub poetry. And then there is a volume on recordings on tapes and discs. And then performances, because since oral performance is so important a thing I try to keep an eye on clippings and newspaper when I — this is only a smattering, that aspect of it — but I want to respect also the performances that I've come across from poets. That is that big project. Then I'm also working on a book on slave rebellions and, before that, a book on slave control — the control of the slave followed by the rebellion of the slave. So those two books go together. And currently I'm completing a massive thing on Caribbean women during the period of slavery called *One Haan Cyaan Claap*, plus several things on slave revolts, including an alter/native look at Toussaint L'Ouverture, and I've just started a study of Sparrow's kaisoes. So, as C.L.R. James once too unkindly, I thought, quipped ("and I hear he's working hard"— which after all is and has to be pretty true of all of us down here in the sea salt mines and minds), I'm busy. So, wish me luck, nuh?

(This interview took place on April 5, 1990, in Santa Cruz, California, during Brathwaite's stay as Regents' Professor at the University of California, Santa Cruz.)

J. Edward Chamberlin

The Language of Kamau Brathwaite

Kamau Brathwaite is a poet of crossings. Not just ocean crossings, but cross-roads, contradictions, cross purposes. The intersections of his poetry are thematic — the Middle Passage, Europe and Africa, slavery and freedom, home and away. But they are also schematic, reflecting his preoccupation with territorial (and typographical) boundaries — defining and connecting, opening and closing, limiting and liberating, insular and national, phonetic and semantic. Most of all, these intersections make up Brathwaite's language, uniting peoples and places and poetic traditions within a legacy of disconnection, dislocation and dispossession, and negotiating between the prerogatives of art and life.

His work brings into new focus a very old question: whether the language of poetry is different in kind or in degree from ordinary language; and whether the difference is formal or functional. Recent theories of language have shifted attention from what language *is* to what it *does*, from language as structure to language as social process; and this shift has moved discussion away from essential characteristics — and essential differences — to an analysis of the way language works in specific discursive communities. But Brathwaite, for all his commitment to the social situation of language — the speech acts that constitute poetic intercourse — still looks fondly back to an older fashion that insists on the fundamental difference between poetic and ordinary language.

And he plays on this difference, with a sure sense of how it gives purchase to the rhetorical devices and figurative strategies of poetry, including some of its distracting ironies and disconcerting paradoxes. Advocating the particulars of a nation language, Brathwaite celebrates the universals of a new internationalism. He demonstrates the authenticity of local languages by underwriting them with the authority of literary texts. He has an extraordinary presence as a performer, but often disappears in the masking and miming of his poems. His outrageous puns and made-up phrases reflect a deep seriousness about the ways in which words determine our representations of self and our perception of others. And always, everywhere, in everything he writes, Brathwaite displays the complementary allegiances of poetry to reality and the imagination.

At the base of his craft is a very simple, very powerful, set of relationships, often concealed by a proliferation of referential gestures — the names and places and events with which he fills his pages. These sometimes make his poetry seem much more casual, much less structured, than it is. But Brathwaite makes the axes around which poetic language turns — the similarities of metaphor (this is that) and the contiguities of metonymy (this is put for that) — mirror images for the elements of difference and displacement that are such important features of West Indian life and literature; and he makes them a framework for his expressions of identity and authority. These axes provide him with an opportunity to relate the metaphoric exchanges (between verbal and nominal forms, for example) that characterizes his poetry with the metonymic conventions of history. They also give him a way of grounding his work in two venerable notions of language: as communication, the rational functionalism of what the English poet Peter Redgrove calls "crossing the bridge", a promise of connection; and as magic, the powerful irrationality of Redgrove's "older tongue called wallow", a locus of passion and power. We often recall these distinctions in our apparently contradictory definitions of poetry: on the one hand as clear, precise and economical; and on the other as obscure, mysterious, extravagant. But we usually forget how fundamentally different they are. Brathwaite reminds us. And he also reminds us how they are connected. The right words in the right order taking off the tops of our heads.

Brathwaite begins with speech. The idea that speech comes first is a durable and democratic one, sustained both by everyday experience and by a stubborn belief that the learning of language by children replicates its development by human beings. Theories about the development of human societies — Giambattista Vico's three ages (the mythic, the heroic and the vulgar) being the most influential as far as language is concerned — have also helped entrench the idea that speech precedes and informs written language. Most philologists and anthropologists and literary critics in the late nineteenth and early twentieth century based their attitudes towards language on this hypothesis. It was called the law of recapitulation — "ontogeny recapitulates phylogeny" was how the natural scientists put it — and although it is now generally discredited, it has had a stubborn persistence. Brathwaite routinely draws on it to conflate some of the qualities of childhood language — a patterning of sounds, a play of nonsense, a fondness for namings and neologisms, a love of excess — with the origins of poetic language in speech. There is a complication here, however. Most people know that speech is not a bit more 'natural' than writing, but just as arbitrary and artificial as any other form of language. And yet the continuing disdain for local language — language spoken in the streets or in casual company or whatever — by custodians of propriety reinforces a popular sense that common speech is less civilized, less cultivated — which is to say, more natural — than the written variety.

Performance provides a conflation of these categories of naturalness and artifice, centred as it often is (certainly in the case of Brathwaite's performances) in a written text that ripples out into story and song on the one hand, and into sign and sound on the other. Performance also highlights the tacit agreements between speaker and listener that are part of almost all conversations, agreements that certain things will be taken for granted and certain questions will not be asked. In doing so, it replicates an old-fashioned sense of the political — a politics of community and place — as well as a kind of ethic — an openness, a welcoming, a commonality that contrasts with the élite mysteriousness of the written text. This notion of an ethical contract is admittedly very elusive, for it was the elitism of particular performances — priestly ones — that led to the production of some written texts (such as the Bible) in the vernacular. Also, persuasion and pleasure figure largely in our sense of performance, and they often bring a negative connotation that is inconsistent with the idea of an ethical exchange. And performance introduces notions of intention that are problematic. And yet it does invoke an admirable sense of the text as always potentially present, always enacting its meanings.

Furthermore, it draws on some of the ambivalences of speech, stylized and spontaneous by turns, exclusive as well as inclusive, binding people together by its difference and by the same token setting them apart. And performance links language with what we call an oral tradition, to which speech is only an introduction. In the West Indies, this tradition includes highly refined forms of story-telling and song, along with various forms of dispute, a collection of boasts and insults, and a kind of credit union of proverbial sayings. There are a couple of attitudes towards oral traditions that illuminate some important relationships between language and poetry. One holds that they are less imaginatively complex and therefore less worthy of critical attention than written expression, because the circumstances of composition and performance make the story or the song or whatever seem unsophisticated and lacking in subtlety. This is the generous version. The less generous one is that these traditions are typical among people who have no sophistication or subtlety anyway. This is nonsense, as anyone familiar with the rich tradition of secular and sacred celebration in oral forms around the world will know. But it is stubborn nonsense, which Brathwaite is determined to dispel.

Another rather different attitude is that written texts have lost the authenticity of speech, which is supposedly exemplified (in quite contradictory ways) by its ostensible realism, on the one hand, and on the other by its figurative vitality. But dead metaphors abound in the clichés of speech as much as in any conventions of writing. And neither writing nor speech has any monopoly on dullness. In fact, it is precisely out of a determination to enliven language that poets like Brathwaite combine spoken and written forms, hoping to refresh each through the resources of the other. And in Brathwaite's case, hoping also to bring the traditions of African (and older European) performance into the foreground, and to illuminate the complex elements of both.

The idea that performance, in some sense representing speech, revives the figurative qualities of language goes back in European intellectual history at least to the eighteenth century, when Johann Gottfried von Herder outlined the contrast between what he characterized as living language — exemplified for him in folk traditions, especially folk songs — and dead verse. He also emphasized the ways in which speech and performance create a collective national spirit. This was not unlike what his contemporary William Blake called a "firm persuasion" — which for Blake was what the imagination was all about. "Does a firm persuasion that a thing is so, make it so?" he asked. "All poets believe that it does, and in ages of imagination this firm persuasion moved mountains; but many are not capable of a firm persuasion of anything." For Brathwaite, as for Blake, the task of the poet is to regenerate that capability.

As I have suggested, there is always something conventional, not to say conspiratorial, about linguistic intercourse — presumptions of certain rules and acceptable behaviour, of previous communications (within a speech community or a literary tradition), of current codes. These presumptions — and the codes that confirm them — are usually unmistakable when language replicates speech. Many of Brathwaite's poems do just that, from the unqualified (but highly stylized) street talk of 'Folkways' ("I am a fuck- / in' negro, / man, hole / in my head, / brains in my belly") to the social formalities of 'The Dust' ("Evenin' Miss / Evvy, Miss / Maisie, Miss / Maud.

Olive, // how you? How / you, Eveie, chile? / You tek dat Miraculous Bush / fuh de trouble you tell me about?") and the colour commentary of 'Rites' ("So Gullstone went in. / You could see he face whitenin' // under he tan an' you know // that that saga-boy frighten: bat / tappin', feet walkin' 'bout like they talkin' // wid ants; had was to stop meself axin' / meself if he ever play cricket on Brown's beach before"). Brathwaite also represents a more elaborate but still notionally conversational gambit, in this case in the style of a modernist traveller — self-conscious, self-centred, self-important — in poems like 'Didn't He Ramble' ("So to New York London /I finally come / hope in my belly / hate smothered down / to the bone"), 'The Emigrants' ("So you have seen them / with their cardboard grips, / felt hats, rain- / cloaks, the women / with their plain / or purple-tinted / coats hiding their fatten- / ed hips") and 'Islands' ("So looking through a map / of the islands, you see / rocks, history's hot / lies, rot- / ing hulls, cannon / wheels, the sun's / slums: if you hate / us. Jewels, / if there is delight / in your eyes.").

All of these are from *The Arrivants*, the gathering of the trilogy *Rights of Passage* (1967), *Masks* (1968) and *Islands* (1969) which first appeared in 1973. In his next books (*Mother Poem* [1977], *Sun Poem* [1982] and *X/Self* [1987]), there is still the presumption of speaker and listener, but the relationship has become more formalized by the developing conventions of his poetry (and presumably also by a developing contract with his readers and audiences). That is, a certain artifice has become conflated with the naturalness of voices — voices at the intersection of languages (African and European), of registers of language (the literary and the local; and within each, the formal and the casual), and of genres (lyrical, dramatic and narrative). These voices take on a kind of family resemblance, as their naturalnesses and artifices become indistinguishable — and eventually, inseparable.

They also join the voices of contemporary poetry well beyond the West Indies, displaying not only the avant-garde allusiveness and intertextual homogenization of modernism but also a new focus on language that crosses boundaries and hovers between determinants in the discourses of poet, poem and reader, as well as of the street and the salon. Brathwaite's wide-ranging notes to his own poems, and his extensive critical commentaries about poetry and performance generally, underlines this interplay of relationships, and of poetic traditions.

But what about the specific relationships between the poet, the poem and the reader? The truth of a poem is first of all the poet's truth. Or is it the poem's? Something of both. It is spoken in the poet's voice, which is to say the voice of the poem; and heard by the reader, who is expected to believe it. This is where things get very complicated — which is why a lot of attention has focused on the specific situation in which poetic statements are made, including the circumstances of publication and distribution as well as of performance; and on readers and audiences, which may constitute anything from what Brathwaite calls a "democracy of witness" to a small élite.

Telling the truth and being believed are two sides of the same coin. Poets make believe; readers suspend their disbelief. And they do so for various reasons. When a poet's language is what the Jamaican poet Bongo Jerry called a "strange tongue," readers sometimes give a special kind of credit to that strangeness. On the other hand, a familiar idiom has the advantage of — well, of familiarity, for a start.

Credit means simply "he or she believes," and ultimately readers have the choice. A poet of course tries to leave them no choice, by making it all seem inevitable. There is a totalitarian streak about assumptions of authority, poetic no less than political. But credibility is not an absolute, nor is it simply located in the text itself. The poet tells the truth — sometimes by lying; and readers believe it — or not. Credibility hovers between the poet, the poem, and the reader. And in the West Indies it shuttles between the prerogatives of European and non-European traditions of expression.

Poets have often been accused of lying. Plato called them untruthful, and therefore immoral. Others have been even less generous. But poets, for the most part, have embraced these accusations, welcoming them as a signal of their freedom from the distorting prerogatives of utility and morality. And yet poets never claim freedom from an obligation to tell the truth, insisting only that they do so in their own way, with the authority that comes from having nothing to gain, and nothing to lose. Of course, that's not quite accurate either, for poets typically are both interested and disinterested parties, claiming at most a special sort of immunity from compromise, a kind of privilege of the imagination, and contending that if they are vulnerable to influence, it is influence of a higher order.

The question of what to believe, and whom, has preoccupied literary criticism for a very long time. In different forms, it preoccupies members of *any* community every time they try to determine the truth. And so they establish some criteria for passing judgement, and develop some consensus (or conspiracy) of sympathetic understandings. In the case of poetry, this question is complicated by an endemic uncertainty about whether we believe the poet or the poem, the teller or the tale. It is an ancient uncertainty, embedded in the language we used to talk about all of this. The word *witness,* for instance, is both a noun and a verb, with the noun referring to the testimony given as well as to the individual giving it. The habit of identifying truth with the teller is reinforced by a variety of associations, some of them linked to the importance of individual testimony in oral traditions. There are other associations, too. In the Bible, the Greek word for which *witness* is the usual translation is the root of our English word *martyr.* On the other hand, the etymology of the English word *witness* centres around notions of memory and knowledge and wisdom, which brings us a bit closer to the authority of texts rather than individuals. The hovering certainties of the Gospel according to St. John, where the concepts both of witness and the word are most prominent, provide a notable example of the contingencies of truth-telling, as Brathwaite underlines in his use of the rhetoric of the Word.

The abiding importance of literary criticism — and in this case, of his own critical enterprise — is that it focuses our attention on the relationships between the credibility and the conventions of language, relationships that have very wide significance. The balance between spontaneity and style we ask of those bearing witness in church or in court, for example, has close and clear analogues in literature, specifically in the balance between naturalness and artificiality that we admire in the language of a poem. (The Trinidadian educator John Jacob Thomas, who took on James Anthony Froude so passionately in *Froudacity* (1889), wrote his creole grammar specifically to assist those working in local churches and courts, so that they would hear and understand the truth about people's experiences when they told it in their own words.) A poem or a witness is believable when their language is accepted both as an expression of the tradition within which belief has become customary, and as (in some sense) the poet's or the witness's own words.

And so authority and authentiticy become dancing partners, like truth and beauty. Brathwaite exemplifies this throughout his work. Take, for instance, the opening of 'Nam' (*X/Self*; first published separately [under the title 'Soweto'] in 1979, and later in *Middle Passages* [1992]).

Out of this roar of innumerable demons

hot cinema tarzan sweat
rolling moth ball eyes yellow teeth
cries of claws slashes clanks

a faint high pallor

dust

oceans rolling over the dry sand of the savanna...

out of this dust they are coming
our eyes listen out of rhinoceros thunder
darkness of lion

the whale roar stomping in heaven
that black bellied night of hell and helleluia
when all the lights of anger flicker flicker flicker

and we know somewhere there there is real fire
basuto mokhethi namibia azania shaka the zulu kenyatta the shatt
erer the maasai wandering into the everlasting shadow of jah

A whole set of associations are invited here, in rhetoric that runs from Revelation to Rastafari, and from heightened to grounded language. It also runs from poet to poem to reader, like ground or maybe cloud cover. And it shares much of its strategy with other contemporary writing. Here is an excerpt from 'They Feed They Lion' (*They Feed They Lion*, 1978), by the American poet Philip Levine. It is about the Detroit uprisings of 1967, and it shows something of this commonality. (Levine has described how its form came to him by way of the Spanish poet Garcia Lorca, writing a series of poems titled *Poet in New York*.) One of the ironies of contemporary criticism is the way in which it isolates poets and publics, ignoring the relationship between the politics and practices of language in poetry across regional and national boundaries, as well as those of race and gender and class. And ignoring too the relationship between the politics and practices of language outside of poetry.

Out of burlap sacks, out of bearing butter,
Out of black bean and wet slate bread,
Out of the acids of rage, the candor of tar,
Out of creosote, gasoline, drive shafts, wooden dollies,
They Lion grow.
                    Out of the gray hills

Of industrial barns, out of rain, out of bus ride,
West Virginia to Kiss My Ass, out of buried aunties,
Mothers hardening like pounded stumps, out of stumps,
Out of the bones' need to sharpen and the muscles' to stretch,
They Lion grow.
                                        Earth is eating trees, fence posts,
Gutted cars, earth is calling in her little ones,
"Come home, Come home!" ...
                                        From my five arms and all my hands,
From all my white sins forgiven, they feed,
From my car passing under the stars,
They Lion, from my children inherit,
From the oak turned to a wall, they Lion,
From they sack and they belly opened
And all that was hidden burning on the oil-stained earth
They feed they Lion and he comes.

There are obvious affiliations between these voices, these languages. Like all good poets, and like Philip Levine and Garcia Lorca, Brathwaite writes at the cross-roads, both within a poetic tradition and outside it.

And yet despite the similarities, Brathwaite's voice is unmistakable. It is especially unmistakable to anyone who has heard him read. There are two issues here. The language of his poetry, over forty years, has become his own — different from the language of speech, and different from anyone else's poetic language. And the many different voices uttering this language in the poems have somehow, in the defiantly illogical way of poetry, become Brathwaite's voice, also different from any other. This is the mark of good poetry, and good poets. And of good criticism to recognize this as it is happening. Certainly, it is common practice as we become familiar with what we call a poet's voice, and sense its consistency, to give it a name — Kamau Brathwaite, for example — and perhaps describe it in other ways as well — a man's voice, a black man's voice, a black Barbadian man's voice, a late twentieth century black West Indian's voice. Soon we find ourselves making all kinds of other generalizations about poetic voices, and describing so-and-so as the voice of the dispossessed, or of male privilege, or of Mexican independence, or the Puritan sensibility, or whatever. But this does raise a number of questions.

What exactly do we mean by Brathwaite's 'voice'? How do we identify it? Do we need to hear its actual sound? That is, do we need more than a sense of the linguistic features of his written language — a sense perhaps of the paralinguistic markers in his speech which are not signalled in writing: the accentual patterns (determining pronunciation, and thus rhythm and rhyme), the emotional tones, the expressive uses? Will just talking do; or do we need a performance? Do we also need a sense of his speech community; and is such a thing notional or actual — is it located, to pick up his own grim question, "in Paris Brixton Kingston Rome?// Here? / Or in Heaven?" ('Postlude/Home') And what then of Barbados, where Brathwaite grew up? Or Ghana, where he went to work? Or Jamaica, where he has lived and taught for several decades? Or New York, where he lives now? Or the wider community of his African, European and American audiences and readers, the community of oral and written traditions within which his work is located?

Soon the questions pick up momentum. Is his language local, or literary? Is it a language of resistance, or a language of recovery? A new and different language, or an old and familiar one? These may be foolish and false alternatives, choices between being isolated in particulars and being overwhelmed by universals, between separation and assimilation, between being marooned on an island and drowned in the sea. But at the same time, these choices are urged on us by Brathwaite himself. He is an extraordinarily gifted performer of his own work, with a physical presence as well as qualities of voice that enhance his poetry in a variety of ways. But *which* variety? It is a question we have to ask, since he plays on it. How do tone and rhythm, or pitch and phrasing, affect our response? Are there changes only of degree, or of kind as well, between the written and the spoken text? Do artifice and naturalness, or familiarity and strangeness, work differently in each? Which is the ur-text, the oral or the written? Is one a paraphrase of the other? A parody? Is one a sort of backing for the other, like the backing of a mirror — or like the backing for a line of credit, or the coins and banknotes that governments underwrite?

This kind of catechism is part of a litany raised by Brathwaite's work as a whole, and is connected to some fundamental epistemological as well as hermeneutical issues. Or not often connected — for Brathwaite is seldom taught in literature courses. There are reasons for this. We have neither the theory nor the practice to read him, or to listen to him. And the polemic of post-modernism and post-colonialism, most of which is preoccupied with prose and given to the homogenization of literary traditions, does not do justice to his work. But these reasons aside, there is a more fundamental problem, having to do with our endemic anxiety about how to reconcile visual and verbal signs, or the different dynamics of showing and telling.

The tension between visual and linguistic signification is exemplified in an old assumption that sound (and speech) are the beginning of language, with sight (and its cognate, speculation) being the beginning of knowledge. Spoken language is thus associated with revelation, and written texts with reflection. The debate about this goes back a long way, and has sponsored longstanding distinctions between proclamation and manifestation, interpretation and vision, allegory and symbolism. It has also generated some troublesome questions. Is there a different set of criteria with regard to the interpretation and evaluation of spoken and written forms? Is one a diminishment, or a betrayal, of the other? Are there words which are untranslatable from speech to writing? Or vice versa? Or from one language to another? Poets have sometimes proposed this; or else suggested, in Robert Frost's phrase, that poetry is what gets lost in translation. Still, poets ply the straits and narrows between languages, and between varieties of language. Indeed, linguists such as the Russian Mikhail Bakhtin insist that this trade is at the heart of all literary discourse, and a good deal else besides. Translations, like traditions, are carryings between time and place, and between peoples. And Brathwaite's belief in etymologies (or a logic of actions, of causes and effects, of contingencies) and ideograms (or a logic of ideas), underlines his sense of the fundamental untranslatability of languages, as does his conviction that certain words have magical power. His poems are full of words that discourage or defy translation, words that seem by their difference to embody a talismanic authority, words that represent both passports into new territory and prohibitions against trespassing. "Traduttore, tradittore", goes an Italian pun. The translator, the betrayer. The Maoris talk about interruptors instead of interpreters.

Images of betrayal, and of trust, are as common in discussions about language as they are in the discourse of trade and of treaties. For Brathwaite, language represents what the Jamaican poet Philip Sherlock once called a "freedom-fortress place". Sherlock was speaking about the stronghold of the Maroons in Jamaica's Cockpit Country, and his phrase suggested other associations also having to do with language. The Maroons were originally slaves who ran away from the Spaniards in the middle of the seventeenth century when the English came to Jamaica — the word comes from the Spanish, *cimarron*, meaning wild; and it came to refer to the wide-ranging resistance they represented. Over the years, the Maroons were joined by other runaways, and became a formidable presence in the mountain areas where they lived. They communicated, especially in times of trouble, by means of the 'abeng', or cow's horn, as well as by drumming; and they spoke a language understood only by themselves, in which words of African origin predominated. 'Dread' talk, or the particular language of Rastafarianism that has developed as part of that community's retreat from an oppressive society, also has many of the characteristics of a 'secret' language. Brathwaite draws on this notion, sometimes masking it as the twists and turns of a trickster, sometimes adopting a pose of primitivism, sometimes claiming the autonomy of improvisation, and sometimes (as in his use of derogatory terms like nigger and bongo man) invoking irony. These strategies are in some measure implicit in every discourse, for language always has codes that function both to facilitate communication within the given circle and to frustrate communication beyond. A recent account of the language of blacks in London, for example, talked about a "breach in the linguistic barrier" when police were given a phrase book; and James Joyce once said that the value of English was that it gave the Irish a language not to write in. In its resistance to appropriation by the centre, especially in circumstances where communities feel themselves under seige, language often paradoxically confirms the marginality against which it is a protest.

Brathwaite draws upon these alternately progressive and reactionary tendencies of language. Images of coercion, like those of community, are surprisingly common in discussions about language, though they are often muted by the niceties of linguistic jargon. So are the conditions of paranoia that language portrays and promotes. Brathwaite has raised the stakes by bringing the political logic of nationalism to bear on the issue. Nation language, his term for local or regional language practice (not necessarily along national lines), brings with it the ideology of loyalty and treason that we usually associate with national solidarity. And so the principles of language converge with the politics of who we are and where we belong.

And yet this sort of analysis of language can encourage a very reductive replacement of one set of politics for another. Language takes sides in a much more complex way, as part of a negotiation between two basic premises: that language determines thought, or that language conveys thought. The latter view, in its simplest form, holds that language was invented for the purpose of communicating; and that language use is to be judged accordingly, as in Alexander Pope's famous commendation of "what oft was thought but ne'er so well express'd". This was the most familiar eighteenth-century attitude towards language, with debate centering around whether linguistic invention was what we might call semantic or pragmatic: that is, whether it involved the revelation of meaning, or the production of effects (which is to say, thoughts in the minds of listeners through speech acts and other signs and gestures).

In the nineteenth century, there was considerable discussion about the alternative view, in which language in some measure precedes, creates or conditions thought and shapes our perception of reality. Early in the twentieth century, the American linguist Benjamin Lee Whorf argued persuasively (mostly by reference to the differences between what he called Standard Average European languages and those of aboriginal Americans, especially the Hopi) that differences in behaviour and thought, including different concepts of space and time and matter, are a function of differences in language. Language, that is to say, represents an attitude towards reality and towards others. This view influenced arguments about how language (and of course literature) encodes not only perspectives but also privileges; and we can sense it behind Brathwaite's celebration of a word like "nam" as an embodiment of a whole way of life, a way of being in the world, a reconstruction of history and possibility in what he calls "crucial areas of the psyche" where invention and discovery converge in the development of a new world consciousness.

The notion of linguistic relativity that is represented here drew on a tradition of speculation about language stretching from Willhelm von Humboldt in the 1830s to Franz Boas and Edward Sapir a century later. It became very popular during the 1930s and 1940s; and it also came under considerable attack. In its radical form, the proposition that language determines thought and culture implied the impossibility of communicating from one particular language to another — the essential untranslatability of languages, and ultimately of experiences. Anthropologists in particular were very troubled by this; and many linguists too, some of whom turned instead to a search for universals, especially universal grammars. One argument to discredit Whorf ran this way: if linguistic determinism is true, it should be impossible for anyone to break free from the categories of his or her native language to understand the categories of another; and yet this is precisely what Whorf claimed to have done in demonstrating the *difference* in Hopi. Whorf's response was that there were still a wide range of possibilities for communication and understanding across language and cultures, but that we needed to be aware of the limitations before we could truly understand the possibilities. To use Brathwaite's image, we need to recognize that we are imprisoned before we feel the need to break out. This is especially true, Whorf and others argued, of what Nietzsche called "the prison-house of language". All of this has a positive side, of course, which we see in Brathwaite's account of the development of creole language and a creole society; and in Frantz Fanon's comment that "every dialect is a way of thinking".

Brathwaite's poetry, for all its apparent commitment to the fundamental determinism of language, is deeply involved in a negotiation between these two propositions. He relies on the sense that words have inherent meanings which will be obvious — indeed "natural" — to the initiated; but he also assumes that these meanings could be available to the attentive. He provides glosses to enhance this availability; while insisting that a word will not disclose its full meaning and value until it has become part of the reader's or listener's consciousness, hard-wired as it were into their way of being and believing. There is nothing particularly unusual about this ambivalence on his part, and indeed it reinforces the ambivalent allegiances of his poetry not only to speech and writing but also to art and life.

Poets draw strength from both. In between, as Derek Walcott once said, they find their own voice. Actually, what he said was that they often lose it. He also said that poets cultivate a schizophrenic gift, trying to combine the naturalness of being themselves with the artifice of being a poet. A poet's voice never seems to be quite there. Listening to literary critics talk about poetic voices is like listening to nuclear physicists talk about atomic particles. First they describe them in detail; and then they tell us they've never seen them. They talk about what they saw a moment ago. Look, they say, that's where it hit something, or combined with something else, or broke up.

But like those who watch for evidence of atoms, readers of poetry are sure that there is something called for convenience (and out of long habit) a poet's voice. We are sure, as physicists are sure, because we feel its effects, the way it hits us. Especially if we hear it in performance. At the same time, we recognize that poets talk not only *to* us but also *within* the tradition (of conversation, literary or local) of which they are a part. Speakers speak within certain conventions, and listeners listen. Outside of those conventions, listeners hear nothing at all, or just noise. The conversations that literature initiates have a wide range of features, one of them being that speakers take on different roles — or what we sometimes call masks or personae — in order to say what they want to say. And yet for all this impersonation, we still recognize — or want to be able to recognize — the person, and the personality, of the actor.

Poets are notoriously impatient about all of this, nobody more so than one of the most important influences on Brathwaite, T.S. Eliot (whose voice recordings apparently inspired a wide range of West Indian writers). The original title of Eliot's *The Waste Land* was 'He Do the Police in Different Voices'. But when it was suggested to Eliot that the poem — or its voices — spoke for an entire generation, he responded that it "was only the relief of a personal and wholly insignificant grouse against life... just a piece of rhythmical grumbling". When it was then suggested that the poem perhaps expressed a sense of disorder and despair that reflected his own intensely personal (and intensely depressing) circumstances, he turned to the French symbolists and loudly proclaimed their ideal of the impersonality of poetry.

The line between personality and impersonality, or at the extreme, between presence and absence, is a fine one. Poets typically speak in a literary voice which is identifiably their own, but in a literary form that is shared. These are not disconnected categories. But they are separable, the way an individual's signature is separable from the conventions of handwriting. This distinction has sometimes precipitated a dispute between literature that derives its power from real places, including the language of those places, and literature that locates itself on Parnassus, in an ideal place far away from here and now. These are not clear alternatives, for attachment to place often becomes a literary formula. We can see the relationship between these traditions, and between the artifice and naturalness they court, in the Greek and Latin words for 'poet' — the one a maker, whose imagination shapes the poem; and the other a diviner, locating sources of inspiration in the everyday. Dante framed the issue in terms of vernacular languages; Castiglioni carried on the dialogue with arguments about linguistic purity and local poetry; and the entire tradition of literature in English sometimes seems to have been dedicated to keeping this discussion alive. In the early years of this century, the poets who described themselves as Imagists called for poetry "to use the language of common speech and to employ always the exact word, not merely the decorative word". A hundred years earlier, William Wordsworth had denounced what he termed "the arbitrary and capricious habits of expression" which only "furnish food for fickle tastes and fickle appetites". He was referring to the elaborate refinements of eighteenth century literary fashion, which seemed to him both impotent and irrelevant; and to the kind of attitude exemplified by Thomas Gray's remark, typical of its time (and of arguably the most popular poem in the English language, his 'Elegy Written in a Country Churchyard'), that "the language of the age is never the language of poetry". Instead, Wordsworth called in his 1800 preface to the *Lyrical Ballads* for "a selection of the real language of men in a state of vivid sensation", conveying "feelings and emotions in simple and unelaborated expressions". In a nice irony, he called for the purity of language by appealing to the impurity of speech. But he was really calling for poets to court the language of their people, and to bring back into their poetry the power of language which supposedly derives from simple speech, rejecting the deliberate preciousness of fancy phrases and elaborate diction.

It was not a simple-minded crusade, for Wordsworth admired the poetry of many of his predecessors. His interest was in the universality and permanence of this language, rather than in its particularities; or at least, in the ways in which its particularities exemplified universal qualities, for he knew that a particular dialect, just like the literary language of a particular period, may sound out of place in another context. He also knew that the language of a poem is, in a sense, a language never heard before or since, and that its referential allegiances are as much to the world of other poems as they are to particular people and places. His own poetry displayed a respect for some of the artifices of poetry, especially rhythm, which he said "heightens and improves" its pleasure. But he sought the illusion of naturalness, and a style that would seem as plain as life.

Brathwaite, too, seeks an illusion of naturalness within the artifice of poetry; and he seeks a heightened sense of personality through the impersonality of literary tradition. Just as Walt Whitman broke the monopoly of the pentameter for American poetry, and William Carlos Williams tried to establish a new footing for poetry rooted in American speech, so Brathwaite assumes responsiblity for rhythmic innovation inseparable from the language of his world, and his people. And like Whitman and Williams, he has a problem. Brathwaite's language is English, but his speech is not. So he embraces an environmental and hereditary determinism in which the rhythms of Africa and the melodies of Europe merge with the social, economic, political and physical geographies of the Americas; and in which the nationalisms of race and region also converge (albeit in ways that take less account of gender, for example, than of geography). For Brathwaite, the land shapes the language. We are possessed by what belongs to us, our language most of all.

And our literature too; for Brathwaite also acknowledges another legacy in which literature exemplifies both the ambitions of language and the achievements of communities. This rather problematic idea, which had wide currency in the nineteenth century, coincided with the emergence of the European ideologies of nationalism. Its influence is almost as widespread now, and it certainly informs our commonly held view that black literature, or women's literature, or any other literature construed as the product of a particular community, should be taken as an expression of its collective identity, signalling and certifying its accomplishments. The ideology of post-colonialism, which identifies national character with national literature, sometimes seems to do so in a colonial imitation of an imperial habit of mind, and often with more than a trace of the high Victorian view that people without national status — colonial people — will only develop what James Anthony Froude called "a character and purpose of their own" when they either take up the national literature and language of their master or develop ones of their own. The dichotomy at work here is not between naturalness and artifice, but between the raw and the cooked, the barbaric and the civilized. And it is a dichotomy that Brathwaite uses, often ironically, for poetic as well as political purposes. More than most poets, Brathwaite reminds us of the origins of poetry in what Northrop Frye called babble and doodle; and he also draws on its sources in riddle and charm.

Other dichotomies, such as the one that we began with — between words as things (or signifiers of things) and words as events (or enactments) — Brathwaite employs with no irony at all, mostly to advance the power of naming as both referential and rhetorical. For Brathwaite, language defines a boundary not so much between stages of human development as between some human beings and others, and between all humans beings and the natural world. For all his subversive instincts, he is surprisingly comfortable ignoring the dominion this presumes, celebrating the poet as a namer who creates the world in his or her own image, bringing into being what used to be called momentary gods, metaphoric or metonymic representations of encounters and relationships. He has lots of company in this, and a long history of literary predecessors. But it is arguably a significant concession to the imperialism of language, and its super-power insistence on boundaries of its own devising. There are contemporary poets, including the Jamaican Anthony McNeill, who (following the lead of the American W.S. Merwin) have recognized rather different limits, and tried to use language itself — usually very difficult language — to subvert the hegemony of its own namings.

But Brathwaite also constantly reminds us of the most notorious dichotomy of all for West Indian poetry, between obedience to and defiance of the conventions — or notional 'standards' — of language. These are arbitrary, and often imperious; and he has been eloquent in discounting them. The idea that there is a standard form of a language is a powerful fiction, representing a hierarchy of prestige and a presumption of familiarity, for the strange is by definition non-standard. (This is an important element, because although English written by West Indians may *look* standard it will always *sound* different, or non-standard.) Standard language tends to have some corner on power. And it does generate resistance, uprisings against the government of the tongue. That ambition not to be standard, that sense of the need to decentre oneself, is both a fundamentally poetic instinct and a venerable strategy for those who are determined to get out from under the shadow of imperial governments, linguistic or otherwise. It is also why those from the centre often assume that those who sound different are somehow inherently poetic. And while it is in a sense true that standard English is a language never spoken by anyone — Thomas Hardy referred to it as "the governess-tongue of no country at all" — this ubiquitous governess seems to have shuttled about the world with formidable Britannic zeal over the past couple of centuries, waving a grammar book and talking like the Queen. Or to put it in the grimmer terms that Brathwaite proposed in his history of the development of a creole society in Jamaica, "it was in language that the slave was perhaps most successfully imprisoned by his master, and it was in his (mis-)use of it that he perhaps most effectively rebelled".

This rebellion, of course, was almost by definition an uprising of the barbarians. The only alternative to a civil society was always assumed to be a barbaric one. The simple meaning of barbarism was — and still is — what other people do, those who are different, them who are not like us. The word barbarian originally meant "one who does not speak Greek"... to the Greeks, of course. But it soon came to mean all those people out there, beyond the walls of the city. This was the way the issue was joined during the confrontation that followed the publication in 1971 of the *Savacou* anthology edited by Brathwaite, when Eric Roach castigated him for turning his back on "culture in the traditional aesthetic sense, meaning the best that has been thought, said and done". As Matthew Arnold (whose words Roach echoed) would say, the choice is simple: culture or anarchy. Both sides agreed, in George Lamming's words, that "English is a West Indian language", capable of its own range of expression. But when Lamming called for a language of expression "no less immediate than the language of drums", some folks started to get nervous. After all, Arnold might be right. The alternative to transported English culture might be homemade West Indian anarchy. And a shift to local standards might merely signal a drift to a new set of cultural mandarins.

Brathwaite, who performed his poems with the great Rasta drummer Count Ossie and published them with Oxford University Press, has negotiated ground for himself between these territories with remarkable diligence and determination. Like Ananse, whose image he conjures up in the following passage ('Ananse', *Islands*), his poetry is shaped by the implacable conundrums of craft.

he squats on the tips

of our language
black burr of conundrums
eye corner of ghosts, ancient his-
tories;

he spins drum-
beats, silver skin
webs of sound
through the villages

Maureen Warner-Lewis

Africa: Submerged Mother[1]

I

> The ancient watercourses of my island
> echo of river, trickle, worn stone,
> the sunken voice of glitter inching its pattern to the sea
> 'Alpha', *Mother Poem*

Thematically, these lines speak of replication, even as their phrasing recalls other Brathwaitian lines pertinent to the signification of Africa in his poetry. "Dust glass grit / the pebbles of the desert... silica glitters", and the evidence of past watercourses in"dry river / beds" constitute the setting which starts *Rights of Passage.* There the poet traces the Saharan and Sahelian origins of the West African savanna and forest peoples whose descendants were forcibly kidnapped for the lands across the Atlantic. Here, in *Mother Poem*, the sunken river beds and coral limestone are geological references to Barbados, the poet's birthplace. Barbados and the Sahel become mirroring sites of genesis.

These mutually resonant passages reveal the writer's insistence on anchoring place, persona, and action in historical context.

> hannibal heavily crossing the alps
> was his father my father setting out in his
> mental canoe
> 'SPQX', *Third World Poems*

This concern with genealogy and history has been a universal and ancient tradition; but, as far as Africa is concerned, it is one which negrophobia has sought to deny African descendants in the West Atlantic. For despite the unmistakable historical and physiological link between African and Caribbean populations, influential approaches to Caribbean cultural analysis have strenuously sought to question African influence on Caribbean life. However, inspired by the cultural parallels between Africa and the Caribbean which he had observed in the Gold Coast/Ghana, Kamau Brathwaite set himself the goal of re-integrating Africa into the paradigm of

Caribbean history, culture, and academic concern.

This consciousness of the Atlantic, not as "a divider", but as a bridge, is one of Brathwaite's reiterated visions. "[B]ridges of sound" originating from elephants of the East African Rift Valley — humankind's putative matrix — extend across continent and ocean to Havana and Harlem. Community, in the form of "a dark skin", is "a chain" ('Jah', *Islands*).

Just as the sea and the people connect the two hemispheres, so do the winds from the Sahara bringing harmattan weather to West Africa and an analogous cool, dry season of 'Christmas breeze' in the Antilles:

> This is the drought.
> It is a fine haze.
>
> On clear days
> lifting from Africa
> it is the desert's gift
>
> of Christmas.
> 'Naming', *Islands*

Besides repeatedly establishing the geographical and demographic connections between the Caribbean and Africa, Brathwaite seeks to deconstruct the ignorance and negative images of Africa — factors which have led to the excision of Africa from paradigms of West Atlantic history and culture. That 'dark' and 'savage' Africa had, as Hegel had decided, and as so many others had concurred, no place within the annals of human civilization — a case of the first being relegated to the last, surely!

> there were tribes there of scarecrows
> hunters of heads who ate human bones
> crink skull and cavicle
>
> big buttock women who preferred to mate with baboons
> orangoutangs who ate oranges like well trained
> children in our zoos
> 'Twine', *Third World Poems*

They muttered "langridge", their poetry was "godderel", their musical instruments "manimal membranes". Against this degrading fiction the poet devotes the epic, *Masks*, to consideration of the Africa-Caribbean nexus within a poetic exposition of an African society, that of the Akan of Ghana. It is a multidimensional depiction, recreating and alluding to landscape; history; sociopolitical structure; philosophy; oral, musical and visual artforms; foods; and rituals of social etiquette, religion, kingship, and lamentation. It marks a pioneering achievement in the West Atlantic literary treatment of Africa, a product as much of a sensitive personal response to a lived environment as of an intellectual immersion in documentation of Akan art and customs.[2]

Other *alter ego* personae augment the burden of trans-Atlantic ties carried by the omniscient narrative voice. Most often, these are the voices of enslaved Africans. They moan "farewell, farewell to the land":[3]

> It will be a long long time before we see
> these farms again, soft wet slow green
> again: Aburi, Akwamu,
> mist rising
>
> 'New World A-Comin', *Rights of Passage*

In foreign lands, "despised and rejected",[4] such positive memories allow them subversively to affirm pride in that lost world: they

> ...dare to remember
>
> the paths we shall never remember
> again: Atumpan talking and the harvest branch-
> es, all the tribes of Ashanti dreaming the dream
> of Tutu, Anokye and the Golden Stool, built
> in Heaven for our nation by the work
> of lightning and the brilliant adze
>
> 'New World A-Comin', *Rights of Passage*

In the Western world, the memory of this and other legends will fade; but later descendants will re-discover this past, with its glory and shame. One such voice succeeds that of the observer-commentator which has already declared the "reduction" of the imprisoned African Jamaican in the twentieth century for whom:

> gospel was a great wind freedom of savannas
> gospel was a great mouth telling thunder of heroes
> gospel was a cool touch warm with the sunlight like
> water in claypots, healing...

As the poem progresses, the objectified victim speaks his own pedigree:

my authority was foot stamp upon the ground
                    the curves the palms the dancers
my authority was nyambura: inching closer
                    embroideries of fingers silver earrings:
                        balancers
'Kingston in the Kingdom of This World', *Third World Poems*

The past presented through romanticised cultural activity and imposing culture heroes such as kings and griots is the narrative mode of nostalgic or self-asserting reminiscence. This mode typifies the recall of an idealised pre-colonial Africa imaged in rounded and cyclic shapes, savoury flavours, and all-embracing astral and terrestrial references:

the world was round and we the spices in it: time
        wheeled around our memories like stars:
yam cassava groundnut sweetpea bush

and then it was yams again

birth child hunter warrior
and the breath which is no more
        'The Visibility Trigger', *Third World Poems*

The voice here is like that of the masked spirit of the ancestral dead. But in a work more concretely anchored in historical detail, the consciousness of an African descendant born of slave plantation ancestors re-enters the African continent

Back
through Elmina,
white granite stone

stalking the sun-
light, the dun-
geon unbars. I hear

the whips of the slavers,
see the tears
of my daughters...
        'Korabra', *Masks*

The present, though, appears innocent, belying the experience that "time was evil":

> Mammies crowded with cloths,
> flowered and laughed...
>
> well have you walked
> have you journeyed
>
> welcome.
>
> 'The New Ships', *Masks*

Yet, the "stranger / after three hundred years" is prey to bewilderment: "Whose / brother, now, am I?... Whose ancestor am I?" These problematic questions arise because trans-Atlantic slavery forced the intermingling of multiple African and European ethnicities, creating ethnic identities whose complexity defies classification: "new soils, new souls, new / ancestors" ('New World A-Comin', *Rights of Passage*).[5]

By contrast, the ghosts of enslaved Africans had no hesitation in asserting their kinship ties with Africa. Indeed, their sense of belonging was unequivocally asserted when they travelled the return route to Africa to intercede with their "ancestors" and "grandfathers of old" on behalf of the living they had deserted ('Wake', *Islands*). All the same, their insistence on this return sprang from the view that death was "a welcome release from the calamities of life, and... a passport to the delightful, and never-to-be-forgotten, scenes of their nativity". As such it restored them "to the society of their dear, long-lost relatives of Africa".[6] With psychological realism, though, Brathwaite empathises that they too, like their future descendants, harboured anxieties over successfully reintegrating with their past. Hidden in the dark of the same underdecks into which they had been unceremoniously crammed for the passage out of Africa, the souls of dead slaves huddled on the journey that would cancel their dislocation:

> there are shadows about me
> eyes like mine
> pores sweating fears like mine...
>
> there is no grey on the sea
> with wind
> there is no grey in the sky
> with rain
>
> 'Wake', *Islands*

The use, then, of an omniscient commentator and surrogate voices actualizes the poet's own conscious reclamation of blood and cultural heritage. But himself a product of the "amnesiac blow"[7] of slave "seasoning" and colonial moulding, and therefore aware of his own earlier deficiencies, Brathwaite grapples as well with subconscious and unconscious levels of Africa awareness as manifested by Caribbean people.

II

> my mother is a pool
> 'Alpha', *Mother Poem*

The constellation of ideas and impressions which Brathwaite ascribes to "pool" may be found in his attributions to Lake Chad:

> This sacred lake
> is the soul
> of the world;
>
> winds whirl
> born in the soul
> of this dark water's world...
>
> no peace in this world
> till the soul
> knows this dark water's
>
> world.
> 'Chad', *Masks*

Lake Chad, then, may be understood as a metaphor for mother, island home, and Africa. The lake or pool thus represents both the subconscious and the unconscious presence of that mother in the personal and ethnic psyche. One mechanism for re-connection with this pool of submerged consciousness is the ritual possession of the living by African deities and ancestral dead. Brathwaite dramatizes possession rituals in *Islands* and *Mother Poem*, recreating the horse's[8] utterances and fragmented visions of ritual objects: glasses of water for libation, water also being the element of powerful spiritual force; metallic bells which vibrate the spiritual energies of air:

> you must pour
> you must pour

you must pour me out
so the god can enter the silver
so the god can enter the river
'Shepherd', *Islands*

Possession in neo-African and Afro-Christian religions of the Caribbean serve as rituals where African and Caribbean world views converge. This convergence is largely subconscious because adherents of *vodun, santeria/lucumi/shango/kele/etu, koromanti play/winti/kumfa, nation dance* and *kumina*; Zion, Revival, Pukumina, Shouter, Shaker and Spiritual Baptist, belong to them less out of loyalty to Africa than for the spiritual and emotional support these religions offer. However, since the possessed devotee's personality is replaced by that of the supernatural 'power' — as encoded in dance, face and body gesture, held or worn insignia, the artistic imagination can harness these mystic performances as symbols of socio-cultural and political renewal. The violent explosiveness of revolution is conveyed in the long lines, resonant polysyllables and forcefulness of the deities invoked to yield up:

...the graven Word
carved from Olodumare
from Ogun of Alare, from Ogun of Onire
from Shango broom of thunder and Damballa Grand Chemin.
'Vèvè', *Islands*

While Olodumare is one of the names of the Supreme Deity among the Yoruba, Ogun is their patron deity of war, iron, and metallic instruments; Shango is god of the thunderbolt and lightning; while Damballa is the Aja-Fon (Dahomey) python god symbolic of change and motion.

On the other hand, evolution and subversion are represented by the Legba-Ananse symbols so frequently invoked in Brathwaite's poetry, either directly or by allusion to their iconography. Among the Akan of Ghana and the Ivory Coast, Ananse is the culture-hero of intelligence and commonsense, and therefore of the ability to triumph over disabilities. This wit was entrusted to him by Onyame, the Akan Supreme Divinity. Thus folktales — capsules of wisdom — belong to Ananse. Himself the chief character of his tales, he displays his intelligence as a trickster in spider form who symbolises the principles of ambivalence, ambiguity, paradox, deception, and chance. As trickster, he fulfils, through artifice, roles which society normally considers anti-social and disruptive. At the same time, his spider persona suggests magic, balance, order, creativity and artistry. Brathwaite associates him with images of light, wholesomeness, transparence, cognition, stillness, and nonentity. The poet thus seeks to rehabilitate the significance of the lowly creature, so that creativity and innovation should not "[burn] to a spider" ('Jah', *Islands*), but rather become an icon charged with transformative potential.

he stumps up the stares
of our windows, he stares, stares
he squats on the tips

of our language
black burr of conundrums...

and he sits with the dust, desert's rainfall of soot
plotting a new fall from heaven

threading
threading
the moon
moonlight stories
'Ananse', *Islands*

The allusion to lameness is a reference to Eshu Elegbara (Yoruba)/Legba (Aja-Fon), regulating deity of communication between humans and gods, patron of metamorphosis, transition, and uncertainty. In the mythology, he functions in part as a morally ambivalent trickster who can distort appearances or delay information. Thus Eshu-Legba manifests in *vodun* and *santeria* as an aged, lame, hunch-backed or one-legged god. Ironically, however, physically defective spirits are more powerful than sound ones. Thus the Eshu-Legba "horse" eventually metamorphoses into an agile medium, symbolising the god's power to change and rejuvenate. C.L.R. James, writing *Black Jacobins* out of a Eurocentric intellectual background in Trinidad of the 1930s, attributes the genesis of the Haitian Revolution to French Jacobin ideology; on the other hand, Brathwaite, like Alejo Carpentier in *The Kingdom of This World*, emphasizes the catalysing force in this singularly successful enterprise of the *loa* (*vodun* deities) — "limp- / in angels" ('Conqueror', *Third World Poems*), "a lame old man on a crutch" ('Legba', *Islands*). In addition, Eshu-Legba's quintessential location at transition points of time and place accounts for the poet's frequent allusion to crossroads. The following lines are infused with images integrating slave rebellion, Ananse, "anthills of the [African] savannah"[9] landscape, Christianity, Eshu-Legba, and Zaka, apotheosis of the Haitian peasant: [10]

> where the slave at the crossroads was a red anthill
> eaten by moonbeams, by the holy ghosts
> of his wounds
>
> the Word becomes
> again a god and walks among us;
> look, here are his rags,
> here is his crutch and his satchel
> of dreams; here is his hoe and his rude implements
> 'Vèvè', *Islands*

So intimate indeed are the links between her "lost children" ('Fever', *Mother Poem*) and their mother, Africa, that vocabulary like "ooona", "kukoo", "okro", "conkies","booee" occurs appropriately in the Barbadian contexts of *Mother Poem* and *Sun Poem*. The poet himself is sufficiently at home with the forms and rhythms of African oral poetry that he can deploy them not only in *Masks*[11] but also in the 'Irie' section of *Third World Poems*; and can coin idiosyncratic terminology like *nam*, meaning soul-source, secret essence, out of diverse lexical items like *Nommo* (Dogon) — creative force; *Nyame* (Akan) — Godhead; *nyam* (Wolof, Fula) — eat. These various instances attest to the nativization of Africa in the Caribbean — a testimony both of Africa's intrinsic presence in the fabric of Caribbean life as well, ironically, of her unrecognized continuity in the present:

> The streets of my home have their own gods
> but we do not see them
> they walk in the dust...
>
> The streets' root is in the sea
> in the deep harbours;
> it is a long way from Guinea
>
> but the gods still have their places;
> they can walk up out of the sea
> into our houses
> 'Shepherd', *Islands*

Notes

1. Brathwaite's term. See his *Contradictory Omens: Cultural Diversity and Integration in the Caribbean,* (Mona: *Savacou* Publications, 1974), 17.
2. For an analysis of elements of Akan culture utilised in *Masks,* see my 'Odomankoma 'Kyerema Se...', *Caribbean Quarterly* 19:2, 1973, 51-99; also in Maureen Warner-Lewis, *E. Kamau Brathwaite's Masks: Essays and Annotations* (Mona: Institute of Caribbean Studies, 1992), 35-53.
3. Phrase at the end of George Lamming's *In the Castle of My Skin* (1953).
4. Phrase from a Negro spiritual.
5. Which is why the "past exerts, in different ways, an almost obsessive influence upon the creative imagination of the West Indian writer". But this concern constitutes "not so much an awareness of history as an awareness of self..." Mark McWatt,'The preoccupation with the past in West Indian literature', *Caribbean Quarterly* 28:1&2, 1982, 12.
6. Robert Renny, *An History of Jamaica* (London: J. Cawthorn, 1807), 169.
7. Phrase from Derek Walcott, 'Laventville' (sic.) in *The Castaway* (1965).
8. The medium possessed by the supernatural force. The relationship of the former to the latter is expressed as that of a horse and its rider.
9. Title of Chinua Achebe's 1987 novel.
10. For elaboration on the African religious background to Brathwaite's poems, see Maureen Warner-Lewis, 'The meaning of religious metaphor in Edward Brathwaite's *Islands*', *West Indian Poetry* (St. Thomas: College of the Virgin Islands, 1986), 183-194.
11. See Samuel Asein, 'The concept of form: a study of some ancestral elements in Brathwaite's trilogy', *African Studies Association of the West Indies Bulletin* 4, 1971, 9-38.

Louis James

Brathwaite and Jazz

"Honey", said Louis Armstrong when a reporter asked him for a definition of jazz, "you tell 'em if they gotta ask, they ain't ever going to know."[1] The same is true of Brathwaite's interest in jazz. Jazz is central to his poetic method, but the nature of its presence is hard to define. His interest in jazz goes back to days when he was a sixth former in Harrison College, Barbados; an enthusiasm which brought him into conflict with the taste of the island hierarchy. When he and some schoolfriends presented a jazz programme on the local radio, this was greeted by protests, and the series was immediately stopped.[2] He may have had this in mind when, in 1961, proposing a jazz aesthetic for the West Indies, he declared "I am trying to outline an alternative to the English Romantic/Victorian cultural tradition that operates among and on us" ('Jazz and the West Indian Novel', 39). 'Jazz and the West Indian Novel', given as a talk at a Caribbean Artists Movement meeting in London, 1967, and expanded into three essays in *Bim*, contains some of Brathwaite's most cogent statements on creating an alternative Caribbean aesthetic.

It may be helpful to begin by exploring the elusive concept of 'jazz'. Historically, the form emerged in the nineteen-twenties from the black culture of New Orleans. Brathwaite has contrasted this with the earlier 'blues' of slave culture. Jazz, he wrote, "is not 'slave' music at all. It is the emancipated Negro's music: hence its brash colouring, the bravado, its parade of syncopation, its emphasis on improvisations, its *swing*" ('Jazz and the West Indian Novel', 275). Its African roots survive in such elements as the continuous bass rhythm and in the flattened third, fifth and seventh 'Blue notes', which Gordon Rohlehr has identified as "the result of Black musicians hearing ancestral scales under the superimposed and well-tempered Western ones, and tunnelling back to the ancient non-diatonic scales of West Africa".[3] Marshall Stearns in *The Story of Jazz* (1956) and LeRoi Jones in *Black Music* (1963) examined jazz as the historical and sociological expression of the black experience, and Brathwaite was to develop this approach in relating the history of the African diaspora to its music.

Jazz is also a *release* from history. Brathwaite has emphasised that it was a *new* form, a "brilliant amalgam of the late nineteenth-century New Orleans musical culture: the French quadrille, the tango tinge, Catholic liturgical harmonies, brass band and military music, boat songs, shanties, sankies, traditional Euro-American fiddle tunes, all superimposed on African rhythms and the Afro-American slave blues musical scale" ('Jazz and the West Indian Novel', 275). Transported north to New York, it became a focus for the Harlem Renaissance; it flourished in Paris in the thirties; it attracted white as well as black musicians.

Jazz, then, varied with the context and the players, becoming Swing, Boogie-Woogie, Bebop, 'Cool', 'Formal' jazz, until it might appear a general term for modern urban popular music. Brathwaite's poetry however focuses on specific aspects of jazz which I venture to summarize as follows:

(1) *Jazz is at once 'folk' and modern.* It has the features of folk music; it is accessible, and colourful; it has popular roots and draws on the music experienced in common life, in religion, work, dance, contemporary in its dissonance, flatness, fragmentation, restless syncopation, its clashing of scales and instrumentation.

(2) *Jazz is not content so much as style.* Jazz omnivorously adapts diverse melodies, musical forms, and periods of music, transforming them through the method of performance into 'jazz'.

(3) *It is dependent on performance.* Some jazz has been transcribed, but it is not the score that creates the jazz experience, but the actual moment of playing.

(4) *Jazz is continually creative.* Improvisation operates both individually and within the ensemble. Ralph Ellison writes of "the give and take, the subtle rhythmical shaping and lending of idea, tone and imagination demanded of group improvisation".[4] It is particularly there in the 'breaks' in which the individual plays extempore, exploring the resources of his instrument and his individual vision. "Jazz," Brathwaite wrote, "has been from the beginning a cry from the heart of the hurt man, the lonely man", adding "its significance comes not from this alone, but from its collective blare of protest and its affirmation of the life and rhythm of the group" ('Jazz and the West Indian Novel', 276-7).

Because jazz is style rather than content, it has interacted from the beginning with other media. In December 1929, Vachel Lindsay's discovery of Langston's Hughes's poems 'Jazzonia', 'Negro Dancers' and 'The Weary Blues' established 'jazz' poetry within the Harlem Renaissance. Hughes explored the literary possibilities of different forms of jazz; he read his poems in night clubs to jazz, and poetry was popularly declaimed to music through to the Beat poets of the fifties and sixties. Contemporaneously, Elsworth (Sheake) Keane from St Vincent, himself a musician, also experimented with jazz verse.

Jazz also influenced the novel. Ralph Ellison took the Fats Waller 1929 composition 'Black and Blue' as a motif for his own fractured, jazz-style novel, *The Invisible Man* (1953). In 1966, *The State of Black Desire* by the Jamaican Lindsay Barrett (later, Eseoghene) linked the West Indies to Africa through jazz, and in 1967 he wrote his own jazz novel, *A Song for Mumu*. More recently, Toni Morrison's *Jazz* (1992) took the genre as a motif for Black consolation and identity.

Brathwaite's achievement, then, was to specifically introduce the concept of jazz, already revolutionizing Black culture in the United States, to disrupt the hegemony of British culture in the British West Indies, and open the way for a new developments in indigenous culture. In exploring this we can distinguish four aspects of the genre: jazz as form; jazz as history; jazz as performance; and a Caribbean jazz.

1. Jazz as form.

In 1967 Brathwaite declared that "There is no West Indian Jazz" ('Jazz and the West Indian Novel', 271). Although indigenous music, such as the Jamaican 'ska', was emerging, he believed that the current forms of Caribbean folk music were "essentially collective"; lacking an individual voice, much of it was simply "for dancing" ('Jazz and the West Indian Novel', 277). The statement was deliberately polemical. Later, in *History of the Voice* (1984), Brathwaite was to write of the "Jamaican ghetto/culture hero" Don Drummond as "a jazz musician of genius" in the fifties and sixties.[5] But in his essay he was making the general point that the Anglophone Caribbean had failed to find an expression for its Black culture, as the American South had discovered one in jazz. It is difficult, now, to conceive how rigidly most Caribbean writing was trapped within the hegemony of the British tradition at the time. The subsequent acceptance of indigenous voices such as those of Linton Kwesi Johnson and Mikey Smith indicates a changing cultural environment in which Brathwaite was a pioneer and mover.

Secondly, Brathwaite asserted that "*Words, then, are the notes of this new New Orleans music*".[6] While the Harlem renaissance started with music and poetry, Brathwaite believed the Anglophone

Caribbean discovered its roots through narrative prose. This did not come *directly* through the influence of jazz. In his 1968 essay, he gives his most extended examination of the 'jazz novel' to Roger Mais's *Brother Man.*[7] Yet the aspects on which Brathwaite focuses — the chorus of yard-dwellers, the counterpointing of scenes and character, the dialogue interweaving like the voices of different instruments — are shaped firstly by Mais's love of European music and Greek classical drama, which only then interact with the rhythms of Jamaican speech and yard life. Brathwaite was identifying jazz not as a direct influence, but as an eclectic attitude to artistic creation that freed Mais to explore the roots of Jamaican culture in the folk. He was to follow this approach in his own work.

2. *Jazz as cultural history.*

The poems of *The Arrivants* (1973) explore the history of the African diaspora through forms of black music, from work songs and blues through to jazz and calypso. This has been successfully staged with music and dance[8], and this progression has been well charted by Gordon Rohlehr in *Pathfinder* (1981), where he gives a 'Black/ground' list of the many specific musical references. Brathwaite brilliantly employs the resources of sound and rhythm to create contrasting musical styles, with a broad range he has identified as one of the characteristics of jazz. "Jazz", he has declared, "does not get stick to a single statement but has a series of statements."[9]

The wistful rhythms of plantation blues are set against the discordant anger of the emancipated blacks; the Jamaican Rastafarian speaks through the mounting drum-beat of a cult ceremony. Another passage images the riffs of boogie-woogie blues:

> ...black
> boogie-
> woogie wheels
> fat
> boogie-
> woogie waggons
> rat tat tat
> on the flat-
> out whispering rails
> *Rights of Passage*, 32

as the syncopation of honkey-tonk jazz animates

So went the black
hatted zoot-
suited watch-
chained dream
of the Panama boys
and the hoods
from Chicago
Rights of Passage, 38

Musical cross-references abound, as when the section title 'Wings of a Dove' refers to a ska lyric that comments ironically on the Rastafarian's island-locked aspirations; or when in the closing moments of *Rights of Passage*, the reference to Coltrane's jazz solo 'After the Rain' adds poignancy to the words:

Rain drips
From the trees
in the dawn...
Rights of Passage, 85

Words make music in their own right. In the 'Prelude' to *Rights of Passage* they create a cascade of sounds, melodious, dissonant, playing on the weight and textures within words:

Here clay
cool coal clings to glass
to glass, creates
clinks, silica glitters
the children of stars.
Rights of Passage, 4

Yet, sounds link with sense. As Rohlehr has shown,[10] the recurring 'clink' in the passage quoted from above associates water, chains, and sand turned to bright, fragile glass by heat and pressure; 'cool' both denotes peace, fertility, and, as in jazz, relaxed control. Later, in the section 'The Dust' (*Rights of Passage*, 63-70), Brathwaite's sensitive evocation of Barbadian speech interweaves the voices of Barbadian villagers into a rhythmic exploration of the nature of human suffering. The words again have alternative meanings. "Dust" is the "May dust" of the erupting Mount Pelee, it is the drought of the hard peasant's life, and mortal flesh itself, "dust to dust".

A further dimension is created by the visual effect of the words on the page. This can work against the oral rhythms, creating syncopation as above, or splitting open words to reveal inner meanings, puns or nuances — "among the dead- / ly follies" (*Rights of Passage*, 38) "coursing his own / man- / ouvres" (*Rights of Passage*, 37). A list of names can eddy down through the fragmented lines like a caravan trailing through the sands:

> E-
> gypt
> in Af-
> rica
> Mesopo-
> tamia
> Mero-
> e
>
> *Rights of Passage*, 34

The visual effects of poetry on the page has become increasingly important in Brathwaite's verse, and, although for reasons of space it cannot be explored here, it creates visual patterns of rhythm, dissonance and repetition that have clear correlations with the jazz style. Mervyn Morris has suggested that Brathwaite's punning, often emphasised by typography ("so the boy now nigratin' overseas..." [*Rights of Passage*, 49] or "My new boss / has no head / for [female] figures" [*Rights of Passage*, 54]) has an effect similar to the calculated discords of the musical 'Blue' notes.[11]

Finally jazz grows out of the 'jam session', where the musicians interact with the audience, building up to a climax of shared emotion. Brathwaite's poetry, too, characteristically goes beyond the conventional 'oral' verse in evoking a ritual enactment, as those fortunate enough to hear the charismatic first reading of *Rights of Passage* in the Cochrane Theatre, London, (3 March, 1967), became aware. One suggested origin for the 'jam session' is the religious rituals within which African music is performed, and Brathwaite's *Arrivants,* both in specific movements, such as 'Wings of a Dove' or 'The Stone Sermon', and in its conceptual framework, is a ritual exploration involving both reader and audience.

This becomes explicit in *Masks*, which begins with African ceremonies dedicating the drum (an image for the poet, and also for the deracinated African, the hollow form waiting for possession), and involves the reader in a vision of African history unfolding back to the corruption of the Ashante empire, in the seventeenth century, by political power and by gold. It is this vision that modifies the poem from *Rights* (1967) to the final *Islands* (1969), where plaintive rhythms of the villagers in the early 'The Dust' change to the aggressive assertions of 'Cane', and the rhetoric of 'Wings of a Dove' intensifies to the angry assertion of the secret god-carver in the later 'Ogun'. The process is one of appropriation and self discovery. If *Rights of Passage* ends with echoes of the American Coltrane, *Islands* ends with the Caribbean pulse of the Carnival 'Jouvert':

> bambalula bambulai
> bambalula bambulai
> *Islands*, 11

3. Jazz as performance.

In the Autumn of 1959, Brathwaite wrote seven poems on jazz themes and read them, against recorded jazz tracks, on tape.[12] The history of these poems illustrates the way in which he, like the improviser in a jazz session, continually reshapes familiar material into new patterns, for they were republished no less than five separate times, each version with variations in the titles, selection and arrangement, punctuation, layout and, at times, basic text.

If we look at the sequence as printed as 'Blues' in *Other Exiles* (1975), the six poems refer to the major formative figures in instrumental jazz. Count (William) Basie (1904-84) was the exponent of the 30s 'swing' jazz, with Duke Ellington pioneering the big band style of jazz. He modified his piano playing in a powerful balance to the massed sound of the instrument, where the

> brash boogie-woogie hordes come
> burgeoning up from hell,
> blind and gigantic.
> *Other Exiles*, 12

In Brathwaite's jazz aesthetic, Basie represents the tension between the individual player, "the lonely one" (*Other Exiles*, 276), and the community of the group. His 'big' sound is contrasted with that of the drummer. By referring to George E. Clarke (1911-) by his nickname, 'Klook', he points to Clarke's characteristic 'klooks' or off-beat accents on base and snare drum, played against the base rhythm. This parallels Brathwaite's interest in the creative discord between African and European musical patterns, and this is itself reflected in the counterpointed rhythms of:

> he controls the jumping rumble
> using simple shock and cymbal

his quick sticks clip and tap, tattoo
a trick or two that leaves you

prancing...
Other Exiles, 12-13

Klook's two-dimensional (percussion) sound is like 'quattrocento patterning' to the subtle 'exotic fragrance' of Basie's melodies.

Miles Davies (1926-92), trumpeter, follower of Charlie Parker, was a brilliant technician and constant innovator, restlessly moving from 'cool jazz' in the late forties, through bop, to a modal jazz style. Yet underlying his experimentation, Miles Davies's playing is characterised by a relaxed, often deceptive melodic and harmonic simplicity, a slow yearning evoked by the measured rhythms of Brathwaite's 'Miles':

he sees
nothing
cares
nothing.
he reaches to the sky
with his eyes closed...
Other Exiles, 13

'Miles' is in turn counterpointed by 'Trane', the name taken by the tenor and soprano saxophonist John (William) Coltrane, (1926-1967). This section takes on a wistful tone. Coltrane's gift was as an improviser, playing his own discordant vision against the band, and Brathwaite identifies his playing as wrung from the sense of black uprooting and homelessness:

he pours into the curved and silver horn
his old unhappy longing for a home
Other Exiles, 14

'So long, Charlie Parker' takes the note of sadness further, focusing on Parker in 1955, when, crippled by drugs, mental imbalance and debt, he faced his death. The verse embodies a tension between the expanding, life-seeking, rhythm of the long lines:

he wished to hold the night from burning

and the constriction of:

and life
is short
and breath
is short ...
Other Exiles, 14

The final section of 'Blues' is named 'Bass'. The name of the (imaginary?) player, Bassey, reinforces the theme, but also combines male player with the great female jazz singer Shirley Bassey, the "lovely lady" of the poem. The 'bass' — the irreducible lowest line of jazz — the rhythm, the heart-beat, the echo of the African drum, plays on:

beat by boom
they build this beauty

bassey and his lovely lady
Other Exiles, 16

'Jazz Poems' have been criticised by Michael Dash[13] for attempting to recreate the sound of jazz, and inevitably failing, for words are not music. But the poems make no attempt to directly reproduce sound effects, nor do they give a conspectus of the achievement of jazz. The actual art of two of the most complex and innovative players — Coltrane and Parker — is barely represented. The sections do not exclusively represent individual artistes. There is no evidence that Miles Davies was, as 'Klook' indicates, "a failure in every trade but this", Coltrane was not an unknown player as is suggested in "this crowded bar ... holds all the fame and recognition he will ever earn".

In fact, names do and do not indicate actual jazz players. 'Klook' is both Davies, and every lean, ecstatic drummer, American or West Indian, following Davies in an attempt to overcome an underprivileged life by music. Parker is every artist who has blazed against a life cut short by tragedy. The short sequence itself is a miniature, verbal jazz sequence; the interplay of different tones, voices and rhythms and the play of creativity against the constrictions of poverty, failure and death.

4. *A Caribbean Jazz*

In 'Blues', Brathwaite explored his own perception of jazz through a medium that was still, at that time, largely Afro-American in origin. But this was to change both as his own appreciation of Caribbean music extended, and as indigenous West Indian music gained increasing recognition. "And what you see in [my] early work", he has declared, "is this alternative music giving me an alternative riddim, as it were, but as I get to know more about the Caribbean the emphasis shifts from jazz to the Caribbean, to calypso, to reggae, to our folk music, to the (religious) music connected with the *hounfour*..."[14] In his volume of 1986, *Jah Music*, Brathwaite retained the same opening and closing poems, 'Basic Basie' and 'Bass', using them now as a parenthesis within which to claim a range of black music now firmly established also within the Caribbean. The shift from 'jazz' to 'Jah' made it both indigenous and universal, the music of God.

Jah Music is in some ways a reprise of all Brathwaite's writing to 1986. It incorporates the vision of *The Arrivants* that through music the Caribbean can touch African roots: thus we have passages adapted from the earlier trilogy ('Tano', 'Atumpan', 'Negus'). Its widening perspective also takes in themes from the second trilogy, *Mother Poem* (1977), *Sun Poem* (1982) and (though published after *Jah Music*) *X/Self* (1987). Poems now reinterpret jazz in terms of the contemporary Caribbean. Marjorie Whylie, the talented Jamaican jazz composer, pianist and drummer, Director of the Jamaica National Dance Theatre, takes her place in the sequence of poems, between Charlie Parker and Miles Davies, with 'Birds'. The poem 'Circles' is written for the American jazz trombonist Melba Liston who played with reggae bands in Kingston: the circles of the title refer to her eddying riffs of music, and the spreading circles of sound that link Alabama and Kingston, Jamaica:

> bringing out riddim home
> it is the deep lagoon inside your slide trombone
> *Jah Music*, 18

Indigenous Caribbean music is indicated in 'Negus' from *Islands*, dedicated "to Count Ossie the everlasting [Rasta] drummer", with whom Brathwaite had performed his verse.

As Brathwaite turns to the shanty towns out of which blue beat, ska and reggae emerged, the poetry, the dissonance of the jazz idiom, takes a dark tone. 'Springblade for the I-Three and The Wailers' forms a link with Rastafarian music, and the genius that breaks out of the Kingston slums:

> and the drei gully

> that once in its season stirs
> with stone
>
> the stone. into gush
> and glitter
>
> water
> the water. into voice
> *Jah Music*, 32

If in the earlier 'Twist' (*Rights of Passage*, 40), the shanty town dancers could "twist the music out of hunger", the reggae music of 'Springblade', as the punning title suggests, erupts in violence.

> she will kill you tomorrow in a passion
> of wicks. She will toss the first brick the first stone the
> first yaaaaaaaaaaaaaaaaaaaaaaaaaaaaaaaaaaaaaaaaaaa
> *Jah Music*, 31

The central poem (eleventh out of twenty-one) is 'Stone', a dirge to the Jamaican dub poet Michael Smith, who both drew on popular rhythms in his verse and experimented with reading to a musical background. 'Mikey' was stoned to death in 1983, and the disordered lines evoke a terrifying descent into the disintegration of death itself. As in the title poem, 'Jah Music for the children drowned in the Newmarket cloudburst 1979', 'Stone' is also in form a spiritual, moving from terror and despair to a vision of a transcendent reality. It recapitulates the paradox broached in the earlier poems 'Pebbles' (*Masks*, 39) and 'The Stone Sermon' (*Masks*, 97-100), that the stone is both death and the endurance of life: it is Mikey's resistant courage that both killed him and gave his work a life beyond death.

> i am the stone that kills me
> *Jah Music*, 26

Mixed despair and hope clash discordantly through many of the later poems. Lacking melody and surface coherence, they are a score to a reading that can tax the reader to the extreme. Brathwaite experiments with patterns on the page, sometimes building up rhythms through long columns of short, repeated sounds, sometimes writing paragraphs that collapse in on themselves. There is little capitalization or punctuation, save for stabbing periods that break up the flow in an angry syncopation. Words are chopped, stranded in white space between paragraphs. They break under the strain. Mikey Smith's own characteristic extended word, in 'Stone' trails into a '*lawd*' seventy-seven letters long, an agonized note prolonged to the end of the poet's breath, in both senses of "end of breath".

Here, both in the oral and visual word patterns, we see the increasing influence of the word processor on Brathwaite. Electronic composition might appear to be in conflict with the aural effects of jazz, but Brathwaite has claimed the opposite. For him this 'writing in light' (on the screen) allows a continuity, an immediacy, that is akin to the medium of performed sound. "You don't have to be able to type, you can make mistakes and correct them or leave them, you can see what you hear. When I said 'writing in light' that is the main thing about it — the miracle of that electronic screen means that the spoken word can become visible in a way that it cannot become visible in the typewriter, where you have to erase physically."[15] The flexibility to change print size, emphasis and visual effect also parallels the violently shifting patterns of harmony and discord characteristic of jazz.

The effect of Brathwaite's more recent verse (I write in 1992) is hard to describe, and impossible to illustrate, for any excerpt loses the meaning found only within the whole. It is illogical to complain that Brathwaite is attempting the impossible, using the printed page as if it were sound. All written poetry is a raid on the border between the inner and outer voices, what is heard and what remains in the mind. In these brave, profoundly disturbing poems, Brathwaite pushes to the limits the jazz concept in poetry to express the cycle of destitution and protest of the Caribbean peoples.

Yet jazz does not only express discord. The joyful 'Bass' ends *Jah Music* as it did the early 'Jazz Poems', and now it is extended, bouncing on in the sheer pleasure of sound and rhythm:

bit by boom
        they

        blu
        blu
        blu
        blu
        blu
        blu
        blu

blu

bloo bli doo
bloo bli doo
bloo bli doo

blu
bbassey
&& his llovely llady

For Jazz is both discord and consolation.

Notes

1. Quoted in Scoles, Percy A., *The Oxford Companion to Music* 10th ed., 1970, 534.
2. Brathwaite, private communication: Gordon Rohlehr, *Pathfinder* (Port-of-Spain: private publication, 1981), 4-5; 'An Interview with Edward Kamau Brathwaite', *Hambone* 9, Winter 1991, 57-8.
3. Rohlehr, *Pathfinder*, 77.
4. Ralph Ellison, *Shadow and Act*, (London: Secker and Warburg, 1967), 189.
5. Brathwaite, E.K., *History of the Voice* (London: New Beacon), 41.
6. 'Jazz and the West Indian Novel', *Bim* 44, 1967, 281. My italics.
7. 'Jazz and the West Indian Novel', *Bim* 46,1968, 115-124. Later developed as the Preface to the Caribbean Writers Series edition of Roger Mais's *Brother Man* (1974), v-xxi.
8. *Rights of Passage* has been read against a soundtrack of Blues and jazz (Jamaica, 1967); dramatised by Brathwaite (Jamaica, January 1971); 'Dust' was performed by a Barbadian dance group (Carifesta, Guyana, 1972); Derek Walcott's Theatre Workshop dramatised 'Wings of a Dove' and 'Dust' (Trinidad, 1973). See Rohlehr, *Pathfinder*, 68-9.
9. Stewart Brown, 'Interview with Edward Kamau Brathwaite', *Kyk-over-Al* 40, December 1989, 84.
10. *Pathfinder*, 64.
11. Personal communication.
12. See Doris Monica Brathwaite, *EKB: His Published Prose and Poetry 1948-1986* (1986), 89.
13. Michael Dash, review of *The Visibility Trigger* and *Jah Music* in *The Journal of West Indian Literature* 1:2, June 1987, 87-90.
14. Nathaniel Mackey, 'An Interview with Edward Kamau Brathwaite', *Hambone* 9, Winter 1991, 57.
15. Stewart Brown, 'Interview with Edward Kamau Brathwaite', *Kyk-over-al* 40, December 1989, 87.

Glyne A. Griffith

Kamau Brathwaite as Cultural Critic

The critical and creative writing of Kamau Brathwaite forges a connection and foregrounds the idea of a continuum between African and West Indian "folk" culture. Brathwaite's work emphasizes the strength and resilience of West Indian "folk" culture in its relentless struggle against those ideologies which seek to banish ex-African cultural vestiges in the West Indies to the margins of Western cosmology. Brathwaite's nine year sojourn in Ghana as an education officer provided him with the exposure which facilitated his recognition of African cultural elements in his West Indian homeland. Thus upon his return to the West Indies he was able to locate his exile and return in its historical as well as its artistic context. Brathwaite indicates that:

> I had, at that moment of return, completed the triangular trade of my historical origins. West Africa had given me a sense of place, of belonging; and that place and belonging, I knew, was the West Indies. My absence and travels, at the same time, had given me a sense of movement and restlessness-rootlessness. It was, I recognised, particularly the condition of the Negro in the West Indies and the New World.[1]

Restlessness and a feeling of rootlessness precipitate the quest for a sense of belonging, a belonging with its source in Africa and its urgency of recognition in the West Indies. Brathwaite is at pains to explore an aesthetic which takes full account of the particularities of West Indian experience. He eschews a theory of the aesthetic which purports ahistoricism, and recognizes the political implications of all hermeneutic structures. Locating the raw material of West Indian experience in the tragedy of human and material exploitation, and more importantly in the survival strategies of the oppressed, Brathwaite places the "folk" or common sensibility at the centre of his theoretical explorations.

The use of "common" to characterise what Brathwaite refers to as "folk" sensibility is useful because of its ambiguous nature. The "folk" sensibility as an artistic resource is "common" because it is the collective discourse of West Indian communities in their struggle to assert their West Indianness. However, the sensibility of the "folk" is also regarded as "common" from the vantage point of a bourgeois sensibility which characterises the response of the masses as variously untutored and philistine. It is this implicitly problematic idea of a "folk" sensibility which Brathwaite engages in order to explore the possibility of a Caribbean aesthetic.

As cultural critic, Brathwaite seizes on the ambiguities and paradoxes of the Black West Indian experience to reveal a deep-rooted sense of hope and an irrepressible spirit of survival. Brathwaite's mission, as defined by Gordon Rohlehr in his critique of *Rites of Passage*[2] (but which is certainly applicable to the thrust of Brathwaite's polemic in many of his critical essays) may be understood as contrapuntal to the kind of nihilism and pessimism represented in some West Indian writing (for example, much of the despair and alienation in the fiction of V.S. Naipaul or the type of existentialist despair in Orlando Patterson's *The Children of Sisyphus* (1964). In this sense, Brathwaite's critical stance may be understood as anti-Modernist. It is as though for Brathwaite, the West Indian writer has to acknowledge the positives of West Indian tradition, grounded in "folk" sensibility, before exhausting the potential of Modernism's rejection of tradition. Indeed in the concluding arguments of 'Jazz and the West Indian Novel' Brathwaite indicates that the sort of West Indian novel which he would view as progressive would probably be defined by its contrast to typical Modernist concerns:

> . . The conflicts which give this kind of novel [the West Indian novel] meaning will not be Faustian conflicts of self-seeking knowledge or the Existentialist stoicism of alienation.[3]

The emphasis is placed on a sensibility and a tradition which is communal rather than individualistic. Brathwaite's focus is not on the 'I' of the Freudian ego but on the 'I' & 'I' of communality, such as is represented by Rastafarian consciousness. Indeed, in his espousal of a 'Jazz' theory as literary critique, Brathwaite has highest praise for Roger Mais' second published novel *Brother Man* (1954). In this novel, Mais' protagonist is the Rastafarian Brother Man, and Brathwaite highlights the novel's emphasis on community. In an attempt to elucidate his theory of the 'Jazz' novel, Brathwaite links sections of the novel which foreground community with the dialectic between improvisation and stated theme in Jazz compositions. Although the idea of examining prose fiction in the context of Jazz performance is difficult to promote as praxis, Brathwaite's thesis has merit.

Just as Jazz functioned in North America and elsewhere as a form of cultural resistance and aesthetic counterpoint to mainstream Anglo-American music and the European Classical tradition, the West Indian novel, Brathwaite argues, functioned (and still functions) as an important means of resistance to the hegemonic force of Colonial imperatives in the West Indies. Strategies of resistance, specifically African-American resistance to mainstream ideology in music, and Afro-Caribbean resistance to mainstream cultural ideology in literature, draw these entirely different modes of expression together in Brathwaite's thesis. The correspondence made between Jazz and the West Indian novel might be understood in one sense as an application of the Pan-African theme to forge a link between disparate artistic genres. Such a correspondence which, as indicated above, is problematic as literary praxis is nevertheless coherent at the level of ideology. Just as Jazz may be understood as having grown out of the Black struggle to assert identity in the face of a repressive socio-political reality which denied Black selfhood, so too the 'Jazz' novel may be seen as an assertion of Afrocentricity in the West Indies. This is the ideologically valid correspondence which Brathwaite establishes in 'Jazz and the West Indian Novel'.

Gordon Rohlehr recounts an incident in *Pathfinder* in which the young Brathwaite was upbraided by Thelma Hackett for playing avant-garde Jazz on a Rediffusion programme in Barbados. Brathwaite was visiting with Frank Collymore who was the editor of *Bim* for many years, and Thelma Hackett, also Collymore's friend, criticized Brathwaite's choice of music for the local radio programme organized by the latter. As Rohlehr comments:

> Brathwaite's interest in jazz certainly did survive the disapproval of the culture élite, just as [Derek] Walcott's passion for drama survived the denunciation of St Lucia's Roman Catholic clergy in the same era.[4]

Interestingly, in the resistance encountered by Brathwaite and Walcott we get a glimpse of the two main resistances to the rise of Afrocentric culture in the West Indies; petit bourgeois elitism and Eurocentric religious practice. Brathwaite's effort in his critical explorations may be characterised as a re-evaluation of those ex-African cultural vestiges in the West Indies which have been degraded by Eurocentric ideology and consequently repressed or rejected by mainstream thought and practice in the West Indies. Thus Gordon Rohlehr's comment on the aim and purpose of *The Arrivants* is also true of Brathwaite's criticism; indeed Brathwaite's entire body of critical and creative writing "...can therefore be seen as a work involving the slow reclamation of spiritual ground through the re-education of a Black mind towards the acceptance of its past, its face, and its ground".[5]

The reclamation of this spiritual and ideological ground can provide the West Indian artist with a valuable resource to challenge and overcome his "poetic precursors", recalling Harold Bloom's phrase, and offer some resolution to his "anxiety of influence". The reassertion of African cultural influence in the West Indies destabilizes Eurocentric representations of West Indian ontology and provides the possibility of artistically mediating European hegemony in the region. This is the valuable artistic and ultimately political potential which Brathwaite recognizes in the reclamation process. Without accepting the value of and need for such spiritual and ideological reclamation, the West Indian is doomed to exist in a perpetual twilight zone of 'invisibility' reminiscent of the victimized protagonist in Ralph Ellison's *Invisible Man*. Gordon Rohlehr acknowledges the political and ontological intent of Brathwaite's polemic when he states that:

> The entire point of *Rights of Passage* has been that void and a sense of "nothing" in Black history have been the result of a failure on the part of Black people, including creative writers who function as historians of the sensibility, to place positive value on what has been created. The [Black] remains "invisible" so long as he refuses his own tradition of both pain and craftsmanship.[6]

Thus Brathwaite's continuing emphasis is on the apocalyptic vision, the revelation that in fact refutes V.S. Naipaul's claim[7] and asserts unabashedly that much was created in the West Indies by marginalized peoples, mis-represented in Eurocentric discourse as lack and void.

Rohlehr's characterisation of West Indian creative writers as "historians of the sensibility" is an important point which Brathwaite himself examines in 'Metaphors of Underdevelopment: A Proem for Hernan Cortez'. In this syncretic narrative combining poetry and prose, Brathwaite addresses, among other issues, the question of the West Indian critic's relevance and responsibility to West Indian society. He argues that:

> ...[O]ur literary criticism is really meaningless unless it is grounded in historical psycho-analysis; because what our writers are witnesses of — thanks to their especial sensibilities

> and powers of expression — is the effect of cultural catastrophe on the west indian mind and action... and the point of our literature is that we are describing spectres on a scale of value/movement, without being aware of the total graph or plan. it is this which accounts for our-persisting literary characteristic (which is also our persisting cultural characteristic), the contradiction, the dichotomy, the paradox... so we have lyric slavery, romantic violence, rape as survival rhythm, peace as a hollow silence, howl's opposite. so that as writers, supposedly objective perceivers of the probe and problem, we remain trapped in the maelstrom of frustration, trapped and imprisoned within the detonations of our own fragmented worlds.
>
> 'Metaphors of Underdevelopment: A Proem for Hernan Cortez', 459

I have quoted Brathwaite at length here because the ideas expressed in this section of 'Metaphors of Underdevelopment' reveal his sense of the necessary connectedness of the literary and the historical; Brathwaite, as indicated earlier, eschews ahistorical criticism. Additionally, this excerpt undermines the reification of historical tragedy as trope. In other words, the creative and critical transformation of oppression and marginalization into a signification system that foregrounds its own autonomy through historical disinterestedness, tends to promote the word as fetish. Such creative and critical practice reifies the word as signifier without responsibility to a signified, and represents the word as of the world but not in it.

As Brathwaite argues, in the West Indies, the persisting literary characteristic of contradiction, dichotomy and paradox becomes the persisting cultural characteristic. The ambiguity and paradox promoted by the New Criticism ironically becomes a *modus vivendi* for the people of the putative New World, and a poetics of indecisiveness seeks to diffuse cultural confrontation with the cool detachment of formalism.

Derek Walcott, for example, examines the cultural and ontological schizophrenia of West Indian personality in 'A Far Cry from Africa'. The persona in the poem, trapped metaphysically between Africa and Europe comments:

> I who am poisoned with the blood of both,
> Where shall I turn, divided to the vein?
> I who have cursed
> The drunken officer of British rule, how choose
> Between this Africa and the English tongue I love?[8]

Significantly, the choice is represented as one between a physical Africa and a metaphysical English Language. This New World Caliban curses the Prospero of colonial rule but is unable to motivate himself beyond invective. He thus remains spiritually and epistemologically, a far cry from Africa. Indeed, as long as the historical inter-relationship of Europe and Africa is dichotomized in this way, the West Indian personality will always be spiritually and culturally distanced from Africa and from self-awareness. Brathwaite's theoretical arguments seem to indicate the need within the West Indian personality to view its complex ontology as an aspect of wholeness, rather than fragmentation. Brathwaite's position implies that the fetishization of "schizophrenia" as West Indian literary and cultural trope is in fact a methodological and ontological cul-de-sac. He states:

> what i am saying within this tidal metaphor of historical and cultural equilibrium/disequilibrium, is that the nature of our catastrophe, the effects we feel, have ancient, subterranean but identifiable sources; that our condition: frustration, exploitation, underdevelopment, slavery, colonialism; our very sense of self and literature itself; stems from the original empire on which we impinge, from which the metaphors of our public and official language flow.
>
> 'Metaphors of Underdevelopment: A Proem for Hernan Cortez', 460

Brathwaite sets the West Indian struggle for self-awareness in its psycho-historical context. His argument indicates that there is no progress to be made by privileging fragmentary and "schizophrenic" notions of West Indian selfhood. The persona represented in Walcott's 'A Far Cry from Africa' will always be spiritually and politically paralysed by divided notions of selfhood and misguided notions of impossible choice until he reintegrates the physical world with the metaphysical, and the public with the private. His grounding of selfhood demands recognition of a correspondence between the historical nature of his love for the English tongue and the historical nature of failure in Africa, a failure from which he would turn if he could. The language which Walcott's persona loves cannot be sanitized of its ideological and cultural imperatives for aesthetic purposes. As an aspect of cultural hegemony in colonial Africa it is implicated in the 'horror' of the Continent. Thus the dilemma of the persona in Walcott's poem is not precipitated by the impossibility of choosing between Africa and the English language; it is produced by an unwillingness to acknowledge that Africa's underdevelopment lives in the linguistic unconscious of the English language which he wants to oppose to the tragedy of Africa. He is unwilling to recognize the inter-relatedness of politics and aesthetics, and wishes instead to represent them as thesis and antithesis rather than synthesis.

Brathwaite's emphasis on the historical grounding of literary and cultural criticism leads him to an understanding of West Indian ontology as part of an Old World as well as a New World tradition. Recognising that Africa has been misrepresented as a passive rather than active participant in both traditions, Brathwaite's work attempts to redress the imbalance. Indeed, the process of re-connecting contemporary West Indian social and cultural expressions with their African past undermines the putative "newness" of West Indian "folk" culture. Brathwaite's methodological approach may be seen to parallel Michel Foucault's genealogical studies.[9]

The difference however is that where Foucault's genealogical analyses are concerned with Western epistemologies and the history of Western thought, Brathwaite's studies are concerned with the genealogy of West Indian ontology, the coming into being of West Indian peoples. Since Brathwaite's approach is genealogical, he does not represent the West Indian personality as fragmentary and disconnected. The "schizophrenic" West Indian psyche does not hold the creative promise for Brathwaite that it has held for some other critics.[10] As indicated already, Brathwaite sees the notion of creative "schizophrenia" as problematic at best, if not finally as the debilitating force which it is recognised to be in clinical psychology. Brathwaite states that:

> in the end, the final joke and paradox, (no wonder, then, that some of us begin to emulate the literature of the existentialist absurd), our themes and style become a celebration of the broken word and world; cul de sac indulgences; lacking in historical perspective and therefore lacking in a cultural shape and hope... we accommodate ourselves, therefore, to our own catastrophe; and so we reinforce, not force our psyches out of it.
>
> 'Metaphors of Underdevelopment: A Proem for Hernan Cortez', 459-460

For this reason there is little hope in the notion of a West Indian creative "schizophrenia". This "schizophrenia" is a symptom of the unwillingness and finally the inability to reconcile colonial atrocity with the English (or for that matter French, Spanish, Dutch or Portuguese) tongue which the Caribbean persona loves. The "schizophrenic" West Indian psyche, unwilling and unable to reconcile conflicting personalities eventually destroys and/or self-destructs.

Brathwaite recognises that the history of cultural conflict between Africa and Europe demands a far more politicized literary response from the West Indian critic than the shibboleth of creative "schizophrenia" provides. Diagrammatically he represents European culture in phallic terms:

> ...i characterise that particular kind of culture, a missile culture: its symbols are the castle, spear, arrow, gothic cathedral spire.
>
> 'Metaphors of Underdevelopment: A Proem for Hernan Cortez', 472

African culture and indeed all "subsistence" cultures as Brathwaite calls them, exploited by "missile" culture are represented as "circle, hole or target"('Metaphors of Underdevelopment', 473). The sexual imagery is obvious, and Brathwaite characterizes the context in which phallus penetrates circle as an "...obscure but fatal built-in attraction between the two fields or forces" ('Metaphors of Underdevelopment', 473).

Representing European and African (or indeed 'Third World') culture in this manner may seem to invite the indictment that Brathwaite has oversimplified a complex relationship and resorted to the same stereotypes which were perpetuated by colonialist and imperialist ideology. However, the pejorative connotations attributable to Brathwaite's metaphors derive from a history of abuse of distinctive masculine and feminine characteristics; the characteristic traits are not themselves intrinsically problematic. Thus it is not that Brathwaite has fallen victim to imperialist stereotypes, but rather that a historically overdetermined masculinity and repressed femininity have exploited characteristics which have the potential to be mutually beneficial and supportive. Brathwaite's diagrammatic representation traces historical abuse and exploitation, calcified into stereotype. Indeed Brathwaite's metaphor echoes Rex Nettleford's assessment of a European domination predicated upon science. Nettleford states that:

> ...[I]t was out of this [overdetermined science] that emanated that spirit which sent Europeans into the colonies which were seen as objects to be explored, penetrated, assaulted with

> impunity and mastered. The notion that Nature (the analogy of colonies) could be approached on its own terms, embraced and respected rather than brutalized and dominated, was foreign to that spirit of conquest. That spirit became entrapped in a determinism which all but negated that other side of the scientific tradition which sees exploration of observable data as a liberating influence through the further doubts such exploration creates and the ignorance it reveals.[11]

Brathwaite's analyses as cultural and literary critic are intended to offer the possibility of release for both dominated and dominating spirit, although his emphasis is justifiably on the dominated and repressed forces of Afrocentric culture in the West Indies.

Concentrating on cultural traits, mythologies and memories which were marginalized by Eurocentric expediency, Brathwaite's critiques often privilege the voice. In 'Jazz and the West Indian Novel', the integration of politics and aesthetics in the essay is supported by the essay's deference to the sound of the 'Jazz' novel. In other words, Brathwaite's analysis of Roger Mais' *Brother Man* for example, emphasizes the sound sense of passages in the novel as the essay explores the correspondence between Jazz and this West Indian novel. This concentration on sound, the voice and orality, often marginalized by the efficacy of the literate, is given more detailed treatment in *History of the Voice: The Development of Nation Language in Anglophone Caribbean Poetry*.

History of the Voice addresses the concept of "nation language", an oral/scribal configuration in West Indian poetry, characterized as Brathwaite argues, by a conversational mode of expression which seeks to break out of the pentameter. "Nation Language" as a concept, attempts to redress the imbalance precipitated by Western emphasis on the scribal. Brathwaite's attempt to overcome the imbalance between the scribal and oral may be examined in the context of Frantz Fanon's discussion of native resistance strategies leading up to and following decolonization. Significantly, Brathwaite's concept is grounded in the idea of a 'nation' or national mode of expression; as Fanon argues, the native intellectual must be careful not to obscure national cultural expression in the attempt to subvert colonialist ideology. The tendency to do so results from the particular nature of colonial cultural imposition. Fanon indicates that colonial hegemony did not denigrate individual cultures as it widened its geographical grip, but worked to devalue pre-colonial history on an international scale. Thus, all African culture, or the pre-colonial history of Islam for example, was distorted rather than the individual cultural values of particular colonized nations.[12] Therefore the native intellectual who seeks to redress colonial cultural imbalance by concentrating on an all-embracing African, Islamic or Indian culture for example, runs the risk of being oblivious to the cultural particularities of his own nation and people.

Brathwaite's concept of "nation language" surmounts this difficulty by locating the particularity of "nation language" in the complexity of West Indian registers and dialects, and fixing the commonality of it in regional resistance to colonialism's imperatives. He concentrates on the orality and other cultural practices of the "folk", drawing upon the ex-African cultural vestiges which infuse their West Indian reality.

Although he emphasizes orality in his "nation language" model, Brathwaite is cognisant of criticism's need to find a balance between the oral and scribal. He does not merely reverse the configuration which privileges the scribal over the oral, by fetishizing orality, but argues for a balanced approach:

> To confine our definitions of literature to written contexts in a culture that remains ital in most of its people proceedings, is as limiting as its opposite: trying to define Caribbean literature as essentially orature.
>
> *History of the Voice*, 49

Furthermore, Brathwaite moves beyond purely formal considerations of "nation language" to assert the socio-political nature and revolutionary potential of the model:

> The word becomes a pebble stone or bomb and dub makes sense (or non-senseness) of politics demanding of it life not death.
>
> *History of the Voice*, 50

Thus "nation language" as a literary concept continues Brathwaite's tradition of grounding literary theory and criticism in the socio-historical and cultural reality of the West Indian context.

Brathwaite's role as cultural critic places him in the tradition of Caribbean thinkers such as Walter Rodney, George Lamming, C.L.R. James and Frantz Fanon. He recognizes that the role of literature in the process of cultural de-colonization is of primary importance. Literature, far from being the scrupulously apolitical organism described by the New Critics and the Structuralists, has always been impregnated with the 'taint' of politics. Brathwaite's work as literary and cultural critic details the importance of the Black voice as structural and thematic force in West Indian literature. In addition, his work illustrates the significance of West Indian literature and orature as a catalyst in the formidable task of psychic and cultural de-colonization in the West Indies.

Notes

1. Gordon Rohlehr, *Pathfinder: Black Awakening in The Arrivants of Edward Kamau Brathwaite* (Port of Spain, Trinidad: private publication, 1981), 12-13.
2. See Rohlehr, *Pathfinder,* 53-54.
3. Edward Kamau Brathwaite, 'Jazz and the West Indian Novel', *Bim* 12: 46, January-June 1968, 124.
4. Rohlehr, *Pathfinder*, 5.
5. Rohlehr, *Pathfinder*, 2.
6. Rohlehr, *Pathfinder*, 54.
7. The reference is to V.S. Naipaul's "infamous" claim that "nothing was created in the West Indies". See V.S. Naipaul, *The Middle Passage: Impressions of Five Societies — British, French and Dutch — in the West Indies and South America* (1962; New York: Vintage, 1981), 29.
8. Derek Walcott, 'A Far Cry from Africa', *Collected Poems 1948-1984* (New York: The Noonday Press, 1986), 18.
9. See Michel Foucault, *The Order of Things* (1966; New York: Vintage, 1970); *Madness and Civilisation: A History of Insanity in the Age of Reason* (1961; London; New York: Tavistock/Routledge, 1971); *Discipline and Punish: The Birth of the Prison* (1975; London: Peregrine, 1979).
10. See for example, Michael Gilkes, *Creative Schizophrenia: The Caribbean Cultural Challenge* (Coventry: Centre for Caribbean Studies, Warwick University, 1987).
11. Rex Nettleford, *Caribbean Cultural Identity: The Case of Jamaica* (Kingston: Institute of Jamaica, 1978), 77.
12. See Frantz Fanon, *The Wretched of the Earth,* trans. Constance Farrington (New York: Grove Press, 1968), chapter 4.

Bridget Jones

"The unity is submarine": aspects of a pan-Caribbean consciousness in the work of Kamau Brathwaite

Many key Caribbean thinkers and visionaries have been able to see the region as a whole. Their best insights often spring from rejecting the artificial divisions imposed by colonialism in order to look at the underlying unity, at the continuity of experience within the encircling Caribbean Sea. Some approaches are more political or historical: Fanon was idealistic, hailing the Federation of the West Indies as forerunner of a 'confédération caraïbe' uniting free sovereign states, and using as evidence the common structures of the Creole language family[1]. Trinidadians seem natural cosmopolitans, for example C.L.R. James, who traced continuities from Haitian Black Jacobins to Castro's Revolution[2], or Eric Williams[3]. Almost every poet attempts reconnections, finding metaphors for an arc of islands, a bow turned to Africa, a chain of shackles, a rainbow, a flotilla, rejoining the "dots, in the sky blue frame / of the map" (*The Arrivants*, 205), the confetti, crumpled paper, scattered crumbs, into litanies of singing names. For some the main insight has been to recentre the Caribbean as a hub of the Americas, rejecting ties to Europe. Kamau Brathwaite, both poet and historian, has explored with unique tenacity the meaning of the African connection.

Working as a Caribbean social and cultural historian in the immediate post-Independence years, he was ideally placed to review what the region holds in common: the history of random plundering and mercantile treaties which despoiled the Amerindians and built up colonial empires, the fragile crust of white settlement keeping down a seething brew of African slave labour, imported in unimaginable numbers, and, after Emancipation, endemic migrations and economic dearth. Through this turbulent and tragic past, what values have been created, what emerges to guide and strengthen a scatter of struggling post-colonial societies? or tersely and centrally put in his own Barbadian speech: "What it mean?" (*The Arrivants*, 69). Brathwaite seeks to formulate and tackle fundamental questions like these, with a central insight of a straightforward and instinctively generous democratic kind. The Atlantic slave trade peopled the Caribbean with a black majority of African origin. Africa is the "submerged mother of the creole system" (*Contradictory Omens*, 6), the major force for unity, the vital source.

Brathwaite explores the African dimension with a faith and confidence founded initially not on historical studies but on personal revelation. When he travelled to Ghana to work in education after four years studying in Cambridge, it was a homecoming: "welcome" (*The Arrivants*, 124), a sense of origins rediscovered, a slowly growing certainty of 'roots'. Rational proofs and historical evidence could corroborate but were largely irrelevant to this spiritual certainty: "the bridge of my mind now linking Atlantic and ancestor, homeland and heartland"(*Third World Poems*, 38).

In various dimensions of his work, Brathwaite has developed in somewhat different ways this perception of Caribbean unity grounded in a shared African heartland. With most complexity in his poetry he can create cycles of allusive patterning which reconnect West Africa with the rituals and spiritual traditions on the 'other shore', lending new significance to old gestures, revitalizing through metaphor, dramatisation and especially rhythm. By the end of *The Arrivants,* from all across the archipelago: " ...Santiago / De Cuba, the miles / of unfortunate islands: the Saints and the Virgins, L'Ouverture's Haiti" ('Journeys', *The Arrivants,* 36), fragments of habit and belief have been integrated into a whole. Not a politician's glib regionalism but a vision which honours carnival, vodoun, wood-carving, yam-growing, respect for elders, as facets of a coherent Caribbean culture, much battered but still creative, vitally sustaining.

As a highly prolific and purposeful critic, Brathwaite has mainly commented on writers and artists working within the 'cricket-playing' language area (Rohlehr's phrase) but always tried to incorporate the insights of scholars like Elsa Goveia, Sylvia Wynter, Merle Hodge and Patrick Bryan, who could widen his range of understanding to Spanish, French and Dutch spheres of influence. On topics like religion, the maroons, 'nation language', his bibliographies reveal continued patient additions, valuing contributions from his students as much as from international scholars. It is important not to neglect Brathwaite's personal influence. Over a long career as editor, publisher and educator, his encouragement has proved important in shaping directions of study for many younger West Indians.

However, here it is probably best to give thanks and leave those involved to testify to the influence of a poet-historian whose role could verge on that of spiritual guide or mentor, *houngan* for a flock of *hounsis*, (in Mary Seacole Hall?) seconded by some powerful *mambo* sisters over the course of the years. This essay will limit itself to some more obvious areas of Brathwaite's concern to transcend mental boundaries, those imposed first by island chauvinism, and then by colonial divisions.

As a Barbadian who has worked in St Lucia, spent many years in Jamaica, and is identified with some key moments of consciously Caribbean militancy both among artists and scholars 'exiled' in Britain, and in the regional university, Brathwaite already spans the English-speaking West Indies. However, beyond this 'first circle' are other significant influences and areas, often featured in the talks and discussions of the Caribbean Artists Movement (CAM)[4] and spelt out in the third aim of the launching brochure for *Savacou* magazine: "To help towards the recognition of the whole Caribbean area as a meaningful historical and cultural entity"[5]. The poet-politician from Martinique, Aimé Césaire, has a special place in Brathwaite's work. Haiti and Cuba, in different ways, occupy privileged positions, and many links made at cultural gatherings have reinforced his pan-Caribbean vision.

I

> Aimé Césaire and "his fabulous long poem"
> *X/Self*, 129

From *Rights of Passage* to recent tributes, Brathwaite's poetry honours Césaire as torchbearer, as beacon, and recalls with "conscious acts of reverence"[6] his *Cahier d'un retour au pays natal.* Césaire's poem dates back to 1939, and was translated by 1947 in this earlier version. The revised poem (1956) was then made available in a bilingual text in 1968. Brathwaite encountered Césaire initially through anthologies and references: his student years coincided with the 'second' post-war period of the Négritude movement. Césaire is not among the French-language poets only very occasionally translated in the pages of *Bim* in the 1950s[7], but Brathwaite unmistakably visited postwar Left Bank Paris, when black existentialist sweaters and black intellectuals were both high fashion (*The Arrivants*, 37-39). In 1954 he was browsing in the Présence Africaine bookshop near the Sorbonne.

Whereas in the 1930s the Négritude group had been a smallish circle of predominantly Caribbean student poets, in 1947 *Présence Africaine* magazine began publication, and the next year Senghor produced his anthology of the new black poetry with the crucial preface 'Black Orpheus' by Sartre. Négritude was diversifying fast from a mainly literary and anthropological platform to the much more politicized networks working towards African independence. Brathwaite moved to Ghana in 1955, but must have been aware of the intensifying black consciousness linking writers from all over the diaspora, given focus by the Congresses of Black Writers in Paris (1956) and Rome (1959). He knew George Lamming's paper, 'The Negro writer and his world', given at the first Congress, when Césaire also made an important contribution on 'Culture and Colonization'. *Black Orpheus* magazine began publication in Ibadan in 1957 (edited by Ulli Beier and Janheinz Jahn), and a number of gifted Caribbean writers were working in West Africa during these years (Jamaican Neville Dawes was lecturing in Kumasi, Achimota and later Legon; the Guyanese critic, O.R. Dathorne, was in Nigeria, and his compatriot, Denis Williams, worked on art and archaeology in the Sudan before moving to Ife). Thus, by a paradoxical but quite common process, Brathwaite encountered a wider Caribbean by leaving it.

During the important and very active period when Brathwaite was doing research for his thesis and deeply involved in the Caribbean Artists Movement, John La Rose no doubt helped to amplify contact with the French and Spanish Caribbean. Fluent in both languages, La Rose through his bookselling, publishing, and alert critical sense, was a unique information centre. New Beacon Books (founded 1966) stocked *Présence Africaine* magazine and publications, and La Rose himself several times presented readings and discussions of Césaire's work, especially the *Cahier*.

It is by now a critical commonplace (see Walcott, Ismond, Dash) to make comparisons between Césaire's poetry and Brathwaite's trilogies (though this remains an exercise which many apprentice critics have found quite rewarding).[8] In his essential study of *The Arrivants*, Rohlehr traces points where Brathwaite inscribes Césaire's *Cahier* into his work, for example the celebrated salute to "those who invented nothing". Brathwaite was provoked to contest Naipaul's nihilistic judgement in *The Middle Passage*[9], and transforms Césaire's distanced third person subject 'those', and Naipaul's dismissive impersonal "nothing was created", into a shared lament, a blues, which becomes in itself a creation (*The Arrivants*, 12-16). This poem also incorporates the triumphal 'debout' (rise ... up ... in the sun) phase of Césaire's conclusion, and one facet of 'Tom', the archetypal docile black sufferer, may be that "nègre comique et laid" in whom Césaire had to come to terms with himself.

Brathwaite's interest in the concept of *nommo*[10] is also undoubtedly reinforced by Césaire's example. Featured in Senghor's early poetry as a key technique of African orality, it reinforced Césaire's confidently Rimbaudian or Surrealist sense of the poet as a magus, who has only to name to create (cf. *X/Self*, 98). Vibration of the logos, the living spoken word, the concept shapes Brathwaite's myth of self as poet/prophet and reinforces confidence in a (literally) incantatory approach as one dimension of poetic craft.

There are also fundamental correspondences between *The Arrivants* and the whole project of Césaire's *Cahier*, which, though rooted in the particularity of Martinique, its land, people and plants, extends to encompass the Caribbean, the black diaspora, and reconnects with Africa before returning to base to focus on a dynamic renewal of black pride.

So deep is the pulsation from the Négritude poets, and especially Césaire, that we can understand how Edouard Glissant, the most brilliant of the next generation of Martinican writers, comes to pose the question: is Brathwaite simply reviving Césaire's discourse thirty years later? He concludes that Brathwaite is placing it in a new context: "the concrete and diverse realm of lived experience (...) The written becomes oral"[11]. Many readers would link this to the extraordinary receptivity of Brathwaite's poetic ear, his power to recreate the voices of his 'nation' ('The Dust', 'Rites'): authenticating 'voiceprints' perhaps, for a vision which in Césaire works rather by intense visual and tactile identifications. Both poets respond to the painful heritage of the black Caribbean but where in Brathwaite there is an underpinning of faith, in reconnections, in the witness of many voices, Césaire invigorates with lacerating lucidity.

The other Caribbean poet of Négritude, Léon Damas from French Guiana, does not have as important a role. Brathwaite independently explored the sources important for Damas: black American music, especially the blues. We know that from his schooldays Brathwaite was a very knowledgeable jazz fan, so even when he encountered Damas's poetry (via *Black Orpheus* translations perhaps, or conceivably later when Merle Hodge lectured to CAM[12]), the techniques of poetic syncopation, the interest in improvisational word-play,[13] the poised laments modelled on blues moods, were already within his repertoire. In particular the comparison with Damas's *Pigments* (1937) clarifies the extent of Brathwaite's 'ventriloquism', the fusion of a private voice with a composite public voice, speaking through and for multiple modes and characters, from ska to Akan dirge. With Damas, the topics are often comparable — faith kept with Africa through masks, in the circles of New World huts, the traumas of travelling man and weary blues, but the poetic self remains centrally the same self-mocking and/or self-pitying personal 'I'. Césaire's greater richness, of texture, of poetic intelligence, has proved more nourishing to subsequent generations of Caribbean poets.

II

So on this ground
write

'Vèvè', *The Arrivants*, 265

Césaire had not only hailed Haiti "where Négritude stood up for the first time" in the *Cahier*, but wrote a study of Toussaint L'Ouverture (1961) and in his most successful play, *La tragédie du roi Christophe* (1963), created a multifaceted portrait of the ex-slave and monarch and his monumental citadel at Le Cap. The analysis by C.L.R. James in *The Black Jacobins* (1938) could equally have contributed to interesting Brathwaite in Haiti from an early date, and it is obvious that he studied the approaches and research reports of Herskovits[14] and Courlander. Jacques Roumain's poem 'Guinea' was always a favourite. In the winter of 1968/9 he was able to make a personal visit. The living presence of Africa in the Haitian people, especially their vodoun[15] religion, seems to have inspired a privileged sense of recognition not dissimilar though less intense than that experienced in Ghana (cf. "in the Haitian countryside, the resemblance is quite astonishing — even the West African villages are there", *Contradictory Omens*, 43).

The focal point of his visit was attendance at a vodoun ceremony, not in the least a tourist show, but a three-day gathering in the Artibonite Valley. It is described in his lecture to the third CAM conference in August 1969: the *tonnelle*, the altar table, and especially the feeling of communion among the worshippers, the "patterns of community" in apparently confused or random movement to very complex drum rhythms. In the possession of worshippers by the *loa* (especially Ogun, Erzulie, Legba), Brathwaite finds the most powerful African religious experience in the Caribbean, its vigour and sophistication serving to illluminate more fragmentary rites (pocomania in Jamaica, shango in Trinidad, Cuban santería). He stresses the intense self-identification of worshipper with the divine power as a source of shared "psychological succour" ('Africa in the Caribbean', 36), implicitly that same resistance which overcame the dehumanization of slavery. "On this ground" the gods walk again, "mounting", those believers who have made the Middle Passage and survived to keep faith (*The Arrivants,* 265-6).

Within the pantheon of vodoun divinities, Brathwaite takes a particular interest in the Yoruba creator god Ogun, also associated with iron-working and patron of craftsmen; in Shango the god of lightning, hurler of thunderbolts; and in the Dahomean figure of Legba, lame god of the crossroads, presiding over thresholds between seen and unseen worlds, between life and death, empowered for openings (cf. *X/Self,* 114). These figures recur in a variety of guises in the worship of cult groups of several Caribbean areas, and are appropriated into Brathwaite's work, while Legba is an endlessly productive analogue for the poet's role.

Most particularly, the *vèvè,* the signs which are traced on the dark ground with a light powder (ground chalk, flour, ashes, etc) to consecrate a sacred space for a rite, enter deeply into Brathwaite's imagination. The combination of certain fixed motifs — crosses (compasses) for Legba, hearts for Erzulie — with creative variation resembles that of any artist working within a communal tradition. It allows the poet to see his lines traced on the privileged space of a page as an act of worship which may also attract a succouring (African) sacred power. A *vèvè* drawn by Haitian artist Neamy Jean provided a striking cover for the original edition of *Islands. X/Self* contains a triangular (Ogun) *vèvè,* and closes with a rite to Xango punctuated with the breath of a devotee, spaced out typographically (circles for Shango, crossings for Legba), to reinforce its message of spiritual healing.

The impact of Haiti seems strongly visual, Brathwaite captivated to perceive so much of Africa in the markets, in the style of movement and daily behaviour, admiring also the brilliance of the painters and muralists. Back in Jamaica his feeling for the centrality of Haitian religion was absorbed by those active in theatre in his circle. Dramatic readings of Brathwaite's poetry evolved from more secular experiments with mainly jazz and folk-music accompaniment to attempts to generate for audiences a quasi-mystical experience.[16]

Moreover, although the most significant result of Brathwaite's Haitian experience seems to have been an enhanced perception of Caribbean folk religions as a systematic focus for reinforcing identity, with vodoun as the most fully achieved example of a sustaining theology and practice, there was also a political dimension. To most blacks, visiting Haiti must above all be a pilgrimage to the first nation to free itself from slavery and colonialism. The glory of the Haitian Revolution, the heroic stature of Toussaint L'Ouverture, Dessalines, Christophe still inspire. This is a maroon society on a national scale, where the leadership and military skills of a still mainly African slave population waged a successful war of independence. In comparison, Nanny's stronghold in Jamaica, the Djuka and Saramacca in Surinam, even Palmares in Brazil appear small-scale or transitory triumphs. Thus again Brathwaite can be seen ordering what he sees in and reads about Haiti into the patterns of region-wide resistance (cf."Goin' to burn burn now..." leading into 'Possession', *The Arrivants,* 229). He recomposed a synthesis of psychical and actual 'maroonage' which further post-colonial research into slave revolts has confirmed, since this was obviously an area where official records had a vested interest in suppressing evidence.

Like Césaire, Brathwaite celebrates the achievement of King Christophe in building the Citadelle at Le Cap (*X/Self,* 53-4), its towering walls sufficient refutation of any alleged 'absence of ruins' in the Caribbean. However, he keeps silent over that tragic paradox that few of us have the stomach to face: the material destitution and endemic violence which have persisted in Haiti with little remission since 1804. Captivated by Kenscoff market, by sound-patterns and body language, by all the evidence of African culture, social organization and religious practice persisting despite the forcible transplant to the New World, Brathwaite plays down the painful questions: has Africa endured partly because of deprivation? Has the power of the *houngan* been reinforced by the lowest life expectancy in the Americas, a dire rate of infant mortality...?[17] On the evidence of *X/Self,* as the range of diasporic reference becomes ever more hectic, and Brathwaite tries to face the new threat to identity from U.S. media saturation, the Haitian gods are still seen to dispense a privileged spiritual solace (*X/Self,* 111). However, in one of the recently published *DreamStories,* he responds powerfully to the desolation of Haitian boat-people, drowning victims doomed by the elemental power of the sea, who also, in a complex of associations with Hurricane Gilbert, which for Kamau Brathwaite proved a sombre spiritual experience of dereliction, are condemned by human conspiracies of neglect.

III

Un arcoiris de pueblos, un mismo sol caribeño
Carifesta slogan, Cuba 1979

The encounter with Haiti has to be sited in the context of reactivating lessons from the past: the Revolution, the durability of family and village organization, of vodoun. Brathwaite's personal observations build on anthropological researches of the 1930s and 40s, as well as Price-Mars' *Ainsi parla l'oncle* (1928). For Césaire too, Haiti supplied a numinous symbol, but not a contemporary blueprint to lead Martinique out of dependency. So similarly for progressive spirits in CAM, Haiti pointed the way on to Cuba. C.L.R. James, La Rose and Salkey visited Cuba and publicized the lessons of the Cuban Revolution to anglophone audiences, as in the CAM papers and discussion in Spring 1968 on the Cultural Congress in Havana (Brathwaite was invited but too busy with archival research for his thesis to attend). Following James, Brathwaite hailed the Cuban Revolution as an indigenous Caribbean model for a victorious struggle against "Western mercantilism" (*Love Axe/l*, 54) (the vocabulary suggests the discourse of the historian more than the activist). If the later 1960s saw the undoubted influence of Black Power thinking, adding a more militant political edge to Brathwaite's stress on the Afro-Caribbean majority, another dimension developed in the 1970s, when Cuba entered a period of cultural expansion in the region. In particular Michael Manley's socialist government, which came to power in Jamaica in 1972, facilitated exchanges and visits, for which the Mona campus of U.W.I. was often the focus.[18]

During these intensified cultural contacts of the mid-1970s, when Roberto Retamar, Guillén and the Haitian exile René Depestre visited, recited and lectured, Brathwaite can be seen selecting, responding and incorporating new strands. Retamar, like Lamming, like Césaire, was fascinated by the resonances of the Caliban myth. Nicolas Guillén was honoured as an elder, well known for his Afro-Cuban rhythms and insistence on the African component of Cuba's *mestizaje*.[19] Brathwaite composed a tribute to Guillén for one of several ceremonies or poetic jousts, expressing envy for the revolutionary repossession that is not only poetic but material: "...we learn with you the pleasure / of walking with our roots across the country / owners therein of all there is to see"(*Word Making Man*, and *Middle Passages*, 14).

These contacts were followed up by a personal visit to Cuba (1975). Brathwaite seems to have warmly embraced fellow writers and taken an interest in Cuban scholarship on topics close to his heart, especially the work of Fernando Ortiz, and religious practice, especially the Yoruba societies using ritual chants and dance, but there is little trace of what could have been a serious divergence between his idealism and the materialism of Castro's Marxist state, with its official line that ethnicity was a non-issue since the Revolution and its discouragement of religion. The Cuban Revolution figures in the astonishing apocalyptic hymn 'Dies Irie' (marti / che/ moncadas, *X/Self*, 37-9), but Castro's conquest of an independent Caribbean identity never appears as central to Brathwaite's vision as the lessons of Haiti.

Through such subsidised cultural institutions as Casa de las Américas, with its journal, publishing activity and literary prizes, Cuba during these years provided above all a meeting point and a focus.[20] Brathwaite's volume of verse *Black & Blues* won the 1976 poetry prize, and he was one of the first poets to be recorded for the sound archive series. With his own background of editorial support for *Bim*, work on the CAM newsletter, and then the ambitious activity of *Savacou*, both as journal and publishing house, Brathwaite was well placed to appreciate the difference between state patronage and the endemically precarious funding for the arts in a capitalist economy. It would be interesting to know his views on selection and censorship, since he himself took a quite dominant role in shaping editorial policy for *Savacou*. Not all the guests to Cuba were seduced by the undoubted achievements of their hosts in health and education and their repeated assertions of a society free of all racial discrimination or even racial consciousness. Presiding genially over cultural events, or reading his work to vast stadium crowds, as at Carifesta 1979, Brathwaite maintains what are perhaps some tactful silences and extends his bibliography.

Not a great deal of attention has been paid to these regional cultural gatherings outside the Caribbean, especially Carifesta.[21] They provide a unique forum where enduring links are established, where many practitioners of the arts renew their inspiration, discovering a common heritage as Africa creolizes in symbiosis with so many other varied traditions, from New Orleans to Cayenne, Bermuda to Barbados and Belize, in jonkunnu, cassé-cô, bele, kalinda.... At worst simpering frills and zombified official spokesmen, it is at best the 'fête' of a lifetime. Five festivals have been held: Guyana 1972, Jamaica 1976, Cuba 1979, Barbados 1981, Trinidad

1992, each one including an important literary symposium where writers and critics talked and debated, as well as the unforgettable combined shows of dancers, choirs, musicians of every persuasion and degree of sophistication. It is hard to put into words the sheer intoxication of Carifesta, a pan-Caribbean carnival where solidarity, even a feeling of belonging to one family, leaps language frontiers. It belongs to the creators, especially the least official and self-conscious, the village bands with home-made drums and bamboo saxophones, *ti-bois* and shak-shak — but the literary symposia add an earnest gloss, theorising the arts which are throbbing all night and spilling out of schools and halls into the streets. Brathwaite can be remembered radiating quiet joy at the abundant evidences of Afro-Caribbean cultural vitality. The flavour is caught by his friend Robin Dobru (Ravales) from Surinam, à propos a similar African event, in his poem 'The Festacman' :

> With a soul like a sponge
> I run around ...
> ... making the drum with Eddy Brathwaite
> ... being embraced in dashiki agbada kente kotomisi
> agisa ...
> rediscovering my name with Nicolas Guillén [22]

Brathwaite reported at length on the 1972 Guyana Carifesta for the *Barbados Advocate*. This initial gathering was particularly notable for encounters between the three (or is it five?) Guianas, and for increasing awareness among the islanders of the Amerindian foundation. By 1976 Brathwaite was centre stage, and gave a main paper on the final day of the literary sessions, 30th July, 'History of the Voice: The Development of Nation-Language in West Indian Poetry'[23]. A.J. Seymour was in the Chair and among those who spoke in a very vigorous discussion were Louise Bennett, Wole Soyinka, Roberto Retamar, young French West Indians defending *créole* and George Irish — in short it was a privileged pan-Caribbean exchange. Cuba, 1979, brought the poets conclusively out of the lecture-hall and into the arena to recite and consecrate collective values. Brathwaite took his place at the rostrum in Havana's gigantic covered stadium (with Louise Bennett, Depestre and Dobru) as an icon for the well-drilled bands of young pioneers, and a vast international crowd at the opening ceremony on 16th July. In 1981, at home in Barbados, he again took part in debates and readings, and again dramatised versions of his work were performed.

A fundamental analogy suggests itself between these gatherings and a favoured structure in Brathwaite's imagination: aggregation. The introduction to *Contradictory Omens* refers to a "melange/montage style", affirming that definition (of the creole system) can only derive from "a proliferation of images: a multiplication of complex probes: a cooperative effort from us all" (*Contradictory Omens*, 6). The bibliographer, enthusiastically compiling with the help of his wife ever lengthening lists of sources; the poet, delighting in puns, where the slash allows two or more meanings to coexist, the cumulative enrichment of key images (as explored for the pebble by Pam Mordecai for example[24]) which occurs in all the longer poems and indeed at the level of the whole oeuvre; these suggest confirmation by quantity, accumulation of evidences in preference to linear or dialectical progression.

Brathwaite's pan-Caribbean vision may be best seen in the celebration of affinities, pleasure in recognition, but it is not a superficial uncritical collecting. His values are heightened by awareness of a shared historical process, marked by alienation and loss. Glissant reads Brathwaite's concept of a "submarine unity" as evoking the drowned Africans weighted with cannon balls and cast overboard when a slave-ship was pursued, a tragic ballasting of the seas, haunting invisibly the psychic depths. He links it positively, however, to his own guiding idea, his "Poétique de la relation", a Caribbean identity moving on from (African) roots to rhizomes, a multitude of branching links which extend horizontally to interconnect the peoples of the Caribbean[25]. Organic like the bedrock of Brathwaite's *Mother Poem*, these links, like coral, slowly build foundations out of the sea.

* * *

In conclusion, then, we can stress these features of Brathwaite's pan-Caribbean consciousness: a grounding in a geological perception of a submerged cordillera with the islands as peaks, a buried unity slowly reaching the surface of full consciousness, analogous to his (and our) constantly increasing knowledge of the Caribbean and African past. We can highlight his sense of African religion as the key factor in the psychic resistance of the slaves, which in many cases also inspired the actual freedom struggles of the maroons. He draws lessons from Africa which cover every facet of social organization, family and village life, techniques of creativity, especially in the arts of performance, music and dance, oral poetry, and personal adornment. His criticism suggests a blueprint for the writer: accepting a role in and for his/her Caribbean community, creating in the languages most appealing to ordinary folk, valuing what is most intimately their creativity in religion, music and words. This programme is pursued in less detail in relation to the wider Caribbean, but the encouragement to write for the voice in Sranen Tongo or French Creoles[26] is undoubtedly there.

It is unlikely that Brathwaite would claim great originality for his perspective, however hotly he (and his admirers) defend his positions against any adversary. He is the first to honour elders and precursors. Rather he has welded into a whole — for the vocation as poet and as historian are largely fused — insights from many sources. The pan-Caribbean enthusiasm was established early (what West Indian intellectual does not profess it?) but its course looks somewhat haphazard, encounters more than a programme of research. Many areas remain in shadow, while Haiti and Cuba hold the limelight. *Savacou*'s project resulted in only three poems translated (Guillén) and rather few ground-breaking articles (Glissant, Simone Schwarz-Bart). Crucially one can query a certain selectivity of vision with regard both to Haiti and to Cuba.

What cannot be challenged is the inspirational quality of Brathwaite's perspective for those who worked in his ambit. He relished issuing a challenge, setting out an agenda which was never merely a search for African roots, but an approach to Caribbean realities — first a tally of what existed and then a will to create on deeply indigenous lines. Inevitably, the inner voices of his poetry remain those he has grown and lived with, but his vision unifies that Caribbean Sea:

> through tides and reversals
> of shell-clinking water,
>
> through time and the hopes
> that were drowned in the deep
> sleeping sound of the bay.
>
> 'Vèvè, *The Arrivants*, 263

Notes

1. Frantz Fanon, 'Aux Antilles, naissance d'une nation?', *El Moudjahid*, 15.1.58, and in *Pour la révolution africaine* (Paris: F. Maspéro, 1969), 87-94.
2. Appendix to the second edition of *The Black Jacobins* (New York:

Vintage Books, 1963)

3. After his summer of researches in Cuba, Haiti, Puerto Rico, Williams stresses that "I was in 1940 a West Indian who had more direct and closer contact, historically and actually, with the Caribbean area as a whole than any other". See *Inward Hunger* (London: André Deutsch, 1969), 68. John La Rose attended the lecture on 'Four Poets of the Greater Antilles' (Guillén, Roumain and Brierre of Haiti, Palés Matos) given by Williams in Port-of-Spain in 1952.
4. Anne Walmsley, *The Caribbean Artists Movement 1966-1972: A Literary & Cultural History* (London: New Beacon, 1992). I should like to thank Anne Walmsley for her generous help with documentation and suggestions.
5. Walmsley, *CAM*, 203.
6. G. Rohlehr, *Pathfinder* (Port-of-Spain: private publication, 1981), 269.
7. Cf. the invaluable *Bim* index compiled by Reinhard Sander. Apart from a special number (June 1950), the French Caribbean received very little attention. Translations were of rather minor figures: R. Dorcély, D. Thaly, J. Brierre, except for Jacques Roumain, whose plangent dirge 'Guinée' and 'When the Tom-Tom Beats' appeared in 1953. Translations were by the *Black Orpheus* contributor, Miriam Koshland, though Michael Dash attributes them to Brathwaite ('The French Connection', *Bim* no 66/67 (1983) 110). The scope of book reviews widened somewhat.
8. Kamau Brathwaite himself valuably highlights the difference in "the STRUCTURE: mine being in parts/fragments: but still clearly defined PARTS: while the Césaire is like a seamless garment — had to read it in one long breath as it were". He adds that there is a crucial divergence also in "how we see the sea", and urges readers to explore the parallax (apparent displacements due to differing points of observation) rather than hunt for echoes. (Personal communication, 15 June 1992.)
9. V.S. Naipaul, *The Middle Passage* (London: André Deutsch, 1962), 29.
10. See Chapter V of *Muntu,* Janheinz Jahn's attempt to synthesize African philosophical concepts, using a wealth of illustrations, including the poets of Négritude: a work very influential in its time (English translation, London: Faber, 1961).
11. Edouard Glissant, *Le discours antillais* (Paris: Du Seuil, 1981), 201, quoted in the selected essays translated by Michael Dash: *Caribbean Discourse* (Charlottesville: University of Virginia, 1989), 109.
12. 'Léon Damas, Poet of Négritude', text in CAM newsletters 9 and 11 (1969).
13. Brathwaite cites Damas among examples of 'The Literature of African Expression' and of 'Reconnection' in his essay on 'The African Presence in Caribbean Literature' (reprinted from *Daedalus* in *Bim*, no 66/67, 1983, 178 and 181).

14. Note preface to Doubleday Anchor edition of *Life in a Haitian Valley* given in full in ASAWI Bulletin No. 5 'The Contribution of M.J. Herskovits to Afro-American Studies' (1972).
15. Like most commentators who wish to distance themselves from the sensational accounts of 'voodoo' used to influence public opinion in the U.S. (and justify intervention in Haitian affairs), Brathwaite invariably uses the forms adopted by Herskovits, Courlander, *et al.* ie *vodoun* or *vodun*.
16. Often drawing inspiration from Marina Maxwell's (strongly pan-Caribbean) challenge to artists and critics to come into the *hounfor* (sacred vodoun enclosure). See 'Towards a Revolution in the Arts', *Savacou*, no 2 (1970), 19-32.
17. The complicity of the *houngan* with the dictatorship of François Duvalier was notorious. In his CAM lecture of 16 August 1969, Brathwaite touches very briefly on the view that vodoun might be an "opium of the masses" but uses his observations to stress positively the "social inter-communication" (transcript, 33-36).
18. See special number of *Caribbean Quarterly,* vol 21, no 1/2 (1975), for example J.A. George Irish, 'Notes on a Historic Visit', 74-84.
19. At U.W.I. G.R. Coulthard (*Race and Colour in Caribbean Literature*, London: O.U.P., 1962) had pioneered the comparative study of Caribbean literature, and built up a network of personal contacts with writers working in Spanish and French, from which the University Library benefited. In the next generation, staff were West Indian, and teaching and research focused very strongly on the Spanish Caribbean and Latin America. In London, CAM invited speakers like Jean Franco (1968) and Dennis Sardinha who lectured on Guillén (1972), with John La Rose in particular taking the lead in promoting knowledge of the Spanish and French-speaking authors (Carpentier and Glissant, as well as Guillén and Césaire).
20. See Joseph Pereira, 'The Influence of the Casa de las Américas on English Caribbean Literature', Mona Conference paper (1982), 15-16.
21. Note, however, a perceptive article in *Le Monde*, 27 August 1981, by Catherine Humblot.
22. *Bim*, no 61 (1977), 13-14, with a companion piece on Carifesta 1972: "with eyes / like sponges / i search through georgetown..."
23. Published London: New Beacon Books, 1984.
24. *Carib*, no 5 (1989), 60-78.
25. Glissant, like the current proponents of 'Créolité', has sought to move forward from Césaire's position: Négritude, but not only Négritude, in theorising Caribbean identity. He distinguishes his own position as less mystical than that of Brathwaite, and not so strongly conditioned by a tradition of poetry for performance (personal interview, 14 March 1992).
26. Brathwaite's work is regularly set on the syllabuses of the Université Antilles-Guyane, and he has visited Guadeloupe to read his poetry.

Anne Walmsley

A Sense of Community: Kamau Brathwaite and the Caribbean Artists Movement

On 1 December 1967 Edward (not yet Kamau) Brathwaite spoke at a public session of the Caribbean Artists Movement (CAM) at the West Indian Students' Centre in London. Andrew Salkey and John La Rose sat on either side of him. The three had founded CAM one year earlier, with fellow writers, critics and artists from the English-speaking Caribbean. Their hopes were that CAM would enable Caribbean writers and artists to become better acquainted with each other and each other's work, to explore a Caribbean regional aesthetic, and to make Caribbean arts accessible to a wide audience in Britain and the Caribbean. For Brathwaite at least, one of CAM's main objectives was to counteract what he saw as a tendency towards individualism amongst his fellow Caribbean writers: "It's each man for himself and to hell with the community".[1] Interviewed about CAM a year after its formal programme came to an end, he said: "I was working on the African concept of the community. I felt that it was important".[2] Brathwaite brought to CAM a sense of community from his then recent experience of Ghana, and from memories of his childhood in Barbados. In turn Brathwaite drew from CAM a sense of community which he consciously valued at the time, and which he seems to have valued increasingly in retrospect. Community as a concept, as an ideal, as a necessary condition for creative work is the recurrent theme in this brief account of Brathwaite's work with the Caribbean Artists Movement.

Brathwaite's public talk to CAM in December 1967 was titled 'West Indian Poetry: An Area of Experience'. He introduced it by reading 'Ananse' from *Islands*, which ends with:

> the many-eye'd maker,
> creator,
> dry stony world-maker, word-breaker
> creator...
> In the yard barks at the stranger.
>
> *The Arrivants*, 167

The theme of his talk was, said Brathwaite, that the god had become a stranger to the community, "that we are strangers in a sense to our own community".[3] He stressed the importance of understanding "the relationship between ourselves and... the elements of our folk culture", of focusing on the folk tradition of a specific community.[4] At the end of the talk Brathwaite read 'Grandfather', also from *Islands*, claiming that he himself had a clear idea where his own sense of community came from: the extended family system of his childhood. And he spoke of CAM as a community:

> This is only slowly coming to me since the formation of CAM, and John, I know feels the same way and Andrew here... and this is because of a reaction to this whole imposition of a culture onto another one, an anti-authoritarianism, a distrust of people who hold power and who like to use power... You've got to be able to break it down, to hand it over, to share it, and this is connected with a sense of community... and this is why CAM is structured in this strange way.[5]

Brathwaite's sense of a community grew with and sustained all his CAM work: as secretary, with his wife, Doris, from its start in December 1966 until their return to Jamaica in October 1968; as editor — at first, with Kenneth Ramchand, then alone — of the CAM journal, *Savacou*; through his continuing links with CAM (U.K.) culminating in the special issue of *Savacou*, Nos 9/10 (1974) with John La Rose and Andrew Salkey as guest editors. Brathwaite shared La Rose's belief that CAM's informal structure was "absolutely necessary for a community of artists and people interested in the arts, if they are to retain their independence and function effectively".[6] Salkey later commented, "It's an almost mirage-like structure... Our history has been full of authoritarians. But the work gets done."[7] "The work" got done, as all CAM members recognized, mainly thanks to the CAM secretaries. After the Brathwaites left Britain, La Rose and Salkey were joint (acting) secretaries, assisted by James Berry and Donald Hinds, until CAM's programme ended in mid 1972. CAM's work changed and diversified during the five years of its active life, as members returned to the Caribbean, and in response to the changing climate in Britain. It was, however, the CAM programme of events and activities which ran for three years from December 1966 which made CAM a movement of such significance and far-reaching influence: a programme of regular monthly public sessions at the Students' Centre and frequent private sessions in CAM members' homes, an annual conference, frequent art exhibitions, a newsletter. As Salkey put it, at the end of CAM's Second Conference: "Heartfelt thanks to Edward and Doris Brathwaite for their enormous work in CAM, for starting the damn thing and getting us moving".[8] Without Brathwaite CAM would undoubtedly never have achieved the vitality, strength and momentum of its two first years. It might indeed have gone no further than a small, exclusive group.

In October 1965 Brathwaite had been seconded for three years from the Department of History at the University of the West Indies, Mona, Jamaica campus in order to work for a doctorate at the University of Sussex. His work with CAM was carried out during these postgraduate years when he researched and wrote up his doctorate, subsequently published as *The Development of Creole Society in Jamaica 1770-1820*. He also completed for publication the three long poems *Rights of Passage*, *Masks* and *Islands*. In addition he was active as editor of a new series of secondary school history books, *The People Who Came*, and as a literary critic. Brathwaite brought to CAM all his training and expertise: as a scholar and historian, as a poet, critic and editor. His work for CAM built on all his experience and discoveries; of nine years' work in Ghana as an education officer and founder (and writer for) a children's theatre; of one year's work in St Lucia as Extra-Mural Tutor. He gave CAM unstintingly of his prodigious creative energy and organizing ability, despite the risk of damage to his academic studies and career. In turn CAM provided Brathwaite with the ground and climate which made possible his full flowering: an autonomous organization outside the constraints of academic or governmental institutions; a platform where his dual function as historian and poet was accepted, indeed welcomed; a responsive, creative audience; close reciprocating friendships; above all, a community of fellow artists and critics with whom to share and exchange dreams and visions, and with whom to go some way towards their realization.

I

When Brathwaite and John La Rose first met, in London in the autumn of 1966, they found they shared similar ideas of forming a group or organization of Caribbean writers. La Rose's main motivation seems to have been belief in the close interaction of creative people from a common background, exploring new directions in the arts. Brathwaite likewise was concerned that Caribbean writers and artists should know each other and each others' work. Arriving in London he was shocked to find them so scattered; as a writer himself, he recalls, "my idea was that I'd like to meet other people who were writing and so on, and why is it that we cannot get together?".[9] La Rose and Brathwaite agreed that Andrew Salkey would be essential in such a venture. A couple of months later, in December 1966, the three men invited fellow writers, artists and critics to a meeting at which it was agreed to form the association which soon became CAM.

This meeting was held at the Brathwaites' flat. Before it took place, Brathwaite had made approaches to people who would, he considered, be helpful to the organization as he conceived it. Letters to Bryan King, Chairman of the Board of Governors of the West Indian Students' Centre, and to Edward Lucie-Smith, fellow West Indian-born poet, reveal that Brathwaite was interested in forming an organization which would provide far more than a chance for West Indian writers and artists to meet each other. It would enable West Indian writers and artists to talk with British and Commonwealth writers and artists — particularly from Africa; it would not be confined to practising, established writers and artists but would be open to "students and others who feel they have something to say"; [10] it would not be confined to the work of English-speaking West Indians but would embrace the whole Caribbean region. Brathwaite already saw this as a public organization which could, he hoped, meet at the Students' Centre, and whose proceedings would be tape-recorded towards an archive, and could meanwhile be transcribed and included in a magazine "which would reflect the work of the group".[11] CAM eventually included all these aspects. Brathwaite initiated CAM as the public organization which it quickly became.

Just as Brathwaite initiated CAM as an open, public organization, so he took responsibility for arranging its programme of public sessions, held every month at the West Indian Students' Centre, and the two residential conferences, held at the University of Kent. Speakers suggested and initially contacted by members of the CAM committee were formally invited by letter by Brathwaite — with a careful brief; he also thanked them by letter afterwards — individually and appropriately. Brathwaite was involved too in arranging, and often in hosting, the less formal, private sessions open to CAM members only. Although it was Brathwaite who, at the start of CAM, pressed for public meetings, he never ceased to value the private ones where, as he wrote, "the *real* work goes on"[12] and where "interchange is much freer".[13] Often these followed a public session, allowing more talk between the speakers — for example, after the first symposium of West Indian artists. At certain points in CAM's history, small sessions seemed more apt than public sessions. In March 1968 Brathwaite wrote to Gordon Rohlehr: "I am proposing that we revert to the small group format. There is a great deal to talk about and think about; and I don't think we are achieving that in the public lectures".[14] The informal, unstructured meetings of the CAM 'committee' were other such small-group sessions, also initiated by Brathwaite during his period as Organizing Secretary — as he dubbed himself.

Brathwaite's early expressed aim of recording all sessions — public and private — was one for which he himself took overall responsibility. For most public sessions, Doris Brathwaite transported the tape recorder on her motorbike and operated it; for the conferences, Brathwaite liaised with Louis James over securing the recordings taped by the University of Kent's audio-visual unit. Brathwaite himself undertook much of the transcribing and editing and checking back with speakers. In a letter to C.L.R. James he wrote: "Here is the checked but not yet edited transcript of your Canterbury talk. There are one or two words, signalled by X, in the margin, that I'd like your help with... Enjoyed it all over again, listening to the tape".[15] Almost all the talks given at CAM public sessions and conferences in its two first years were thus reproduced, in whole or part, in CAM Newsletters. The Newsletters also contained listings of CAM and other Caribbean writers' and artists' activities: publications, exhibitions, film, plays, travels, awards, and so on. Brathwaite was responsible for rounding up this information. Even when, during his final summer, Louis James took over editorship of the CAM Newsletter, Brathwaite continued to handle CAM News; he was at the hub and knew most what was going on — and wanted it widely known.

The contacts made and the correspondence sustained by Brathwaite during his two-year secretaryship of CAM were many and varied. He approached British writers and editors such as Ted Hughes and Alan Ross, believing that they would be interested in CAM. He contacted young artists and writers, drawing them into CAM whenever possible. Brathwaite took relations with relevant institutions very seriously. His approaches to the West Indian Students' Centre were formal and correct. He unceasingly tried to interest and involve the West Indian High Commissioners in the work of CAM. When the wires became crossed — as with the Jamaican High Commission over its request to sponsor its own Jamaican members of CAM, or with the West India Committee and its proposed art exhibition at the House of Commons, Brathwaite took pains in carefully drafted letters to straighten matters out. His contacts and correspondence with British publishing houses were especially effective, leading to the attendance and participation of several editors in CAM public events, to increased use of West Indian artists for Caribbean book jackets and illustrations and, for example, to Faber asking Brathwaite — in November 1967 — for the names of young writers who should be considered for the first of its *Introduction* series concerned with poets.

Brathwaite's attempts to get British journalists to write about CAM met with little success. He himself took on the role of publicising and defining CAM's aims and achievements in Caribbean newspapers, in BBC and Central Office of Information interviews. When I offered to write an account of the First CAM Conference for *Bim*, Brathwaite encouraged and checked it. He was always determined that CAM should be known about both in the Caribbean and in Britain, and thus form a bridge between the exiles and those at home.

Brathwaite was not however CAM's Organizing Secretary simply in terms of such practicalities. His own active work and beliefs as poet, critic, editor and historian were a central force in the ethos and impetus of the movement.

II

CAM was launched in March 1967 when Brathwaite gave, at John La Rose's invitation, his first public reading of *Rights of Passage*, recently published by Oxford University Press. The reading was a landmark in every way. Not only was this the first published Caribbean poem to attempt epic length and scope, it was the first major poem to articulate the experience and condition of the West Indian immigrant in Britain. Also, it broke new ground for Caribbean poetry in rhythm and language. Brathwaite's own sustained solo reading, or rather performance, similarly launched poetry to be heard as well as read on the page. In every way, this reading signposted new directions for Caribbean poetry. Complete readings of *Masks* and *Islands* were given by Brathwaite to CAM audiences in subsequent years, and a selection from all three at the Second

Conference. The CAM audience thus was given access to Brathwaite's new poetry, and held it as exemplary. John La Rose cited it as an attempt to arrive at a synthesis between Standard English and 'dialect', in reply to a question from the audience at a CAM public session as to "whether you feel you radicals are not coming to the masses in the same way the calypso composers do".[16] Andrew Salkey described Brathwaite as having "engendered a revolution in Caribbean poetic diction" and "freed a number of people who have come under his influence".[17] Brathwaite's awards from the Poetry Society, his Argo records, his appearances in Poetry International all confirmed CAM's confidence in its Organizing Secretary's high standing as a poet.

Critical appreciation and recognition of what Brathwaite was attempting in *Rights of Passage* was welcomed, and checked, by the poet himself within CAM. When Gordon Rohlehr, speaking to CAM on 'Sparrow and the Language of Calypso' in April 1967 asserted, "It seems to me that there is in the spoken language of Trinidad a potential for rhythmic organization which our poets have not yet discovered, or if they have, have not yet exploited",[18] Brathwaite was quick to challenge such generalisations about "our poets", pointing out "the successful use of West Indian speech rhythms by Walcott, Lorrimer Alexander, Wordsworth McAndrew, Dennis Scott. And of course *Rights of Passage* is committed to this approach right down the line".[19] When Louis James spoke on 'Caribbean Poetry in English: Some Problems' at the First Conference, he posed what he saw as the limitations of 'dialect', and claimed to know of no poet other than Dennis Scott, in 'Uncle Time', who could extend experience by use of 'dialect'. Brathwaite cited his own poem 'The Dust' from *Rights of Passage* as "an attempt to express through concrete terms, a metaphysic". [20] In his talk on 'West Indian Poetry: An Area of Experience' — a conference follow-up session — Brathwaite expanded his concept of 'dialect' and explained its centrality in his poetry:

> By dialect we don't just mean taking off a word, a little syllable at the end of a word, but it is the thought process behind it. My poem 'Ananse' [from *Islands*], although it is not in dialect, the attempt to reincarnate the spider back into the original creative god that he was, is a form of dialect.[21]

Such demonstrations and defence of his own poetry were, however, only a small part of Brathwaite's parallel recognition of and encouragement for new directions in the work of fellow Caribbean writers and artists. Brathwaite, critic and editor, is alongside his poet self all the way. Instead of reading his work, as planned, in the early private session which followed Orlando Patterson's talk on 'Is There a West Indian Aesthetic?', Brathwaite spoke on correspondences between jazz and contemporary Caribbean culture, which he believed constituted the direction of a West Indian aesthetic — and he cited George Lamming and Sam Selvon as using the basic elements of a jazz aesthetic in their fiction. The first public session which followed his reading of *Rights of Passage* was entitled 'New Directions in West Indian Literature' and gave a platform on which Wilson Harris, Michael Anthony and Orlando Patterson spoke about such directions in their fiction, much of it breaking with colonial European models. Brathwaite was constantly looking in CAM for opportunities to discuss, and to formulate, appropriate critical criteria for Caribbean writers. When Diana Athill of the publishers Andre Deutsch told (by letter) a CAM symposium that "our first aim is publishing books which we think good", Brathwaite questioned her criterion for 'good', suggesting that it was influenced by a particular (European) tradition.[22] Speaking to CAM in August 1969, back in London after a year in Jamaica, he said: "We can move in the Caribbean towards an artistic alternative, a social alternative, to our so-far accepted Eurocentric kind of culture"; he urged "new aesthetic tools", a "revolution of consciousness".[23] In his final talk to CAM, in September 1971, he described the "new cultural signals in the Caribbean" — challenges to the dominant European culture in colonial society by "Caribbean peoples' constituent cultures: African, Indian, Amerindian, Chinese", and equally by such new forms of cultural expression as Derek Walcott's Theatre Workshop, Rex Nettleford's Jamaica National Dance Theatre Company, Marina Maxwell's Yard Theatre — and, in music, ska and "the reggae".[24]

Brathwaite's constant search for and encouragement of new directions of Caribbean creativity is evident during his secretaryship of CAM and as editor of *Savacou.* He gave the young, as yet unpublished Faustin Charles (on Kenneth Ramchand's recommendation) a chance to read, alongside John La Rose, at an early CAM private session; he made sure that at both conferences, young, unknown writers had a chance to read and speak. CAM's policy, as he explained it, was that:

> Everybody is not only equal in CAM but our attitude to everyone of you is the same... We're not going to say, "We're

> only going for the big names, we're only going for the validated people"... We're accepting everybody because it is the only way we can find out what is going on. How can we release our energy which we know is there unless we have a climate where everybody can feel free to get up and make a fool of themselves, if it comes to that?[25]

After chairing a CAM session which included particularly constructive discussion, Brathwaite thanked the audience "for expanding this thing into all sorts of interesting areas".[26] He expressed appreciation of the high level of audience participation at the Second Conference.

Brathwaite's practice of keeping his ear close to the ground for new, significant writers bore fruit most demonstrably in *Savacou*, when he included young Rastafarian poets such as Bongo Jerry and Ras Dizzy in Nos 3/4 (1970), commissioned Lucille Mair to edit an entire issue of women's writing, No 13 (1977), and, with *New Poets from Jamaica*, Nos 14/15 (1979/80) for the first time gave substantial space to 'performance poets' Michael Smith and Oku Onuora, and included more women than men as contributors.

III

CAM's writer-founders were interested in all the arts, and encouraged membership and activities from visual artists and theatre people in particular. Before handing over responsibility for the visual arts to Karl 'Jerry' Craig after CAM's first year, Brathwaite was very active in this area: pressing for a CAM art exhibition at the Students' Centre and inviting artists to take part in it, asking artists to speak at public and private sessions, arranging for visits by CAM members to artists' studios, including details of artists' work in press publicity. He urged, and made possible, more commissions by publishers to Caribbean artists, and himself asked Winston Branch to do the sleeve of his Argo records of *Rights of Passage*. At the artists' symposium at the Second Conference, he stated:

> Eventually on the arts side we want to have reproductions of paintings and drawings by West Indian artists, not just in England... We would hope to have a documentary slide representation of CAM artists.[27]

Brathwaite's interest in and encouragement for the performing arts — born in Ghana, nurtured in St Lucia — is evident in the

CAM symposium at the First Conference, when three successful professional actors and theatre directors — Bari Jonson and Lloyd Reckord of Jamaica, Horace James of Trinidad — performed and spoke. A far wider panel of theatre people took part in a CAM symposium on West Indian theatre a few months later. It was one of three follow-up sessions; Brathwaite wrote to Louis James with details of titles, participants and dates, adding: "Have already spoken about it to John and Andrew who okay it. Comments/ suggestions appreciated as soon as poss. as people to be written to and programme to go out".[28] Brathwaite invited Ram John Holder, in addition to taking part in the symposium, to put on his play *Eviction Blues* — performed at the Notting Hill Festival and the Commonwealth Institute — also at the Students' Centre, for CAM: "The important thing, though, is that CAM should be involved in this effort at this point. My dream is that all productions such as yours should at some time or other come into CAM. This is the only way we can get some meaningful discussion going".[29] Most of Brathwaite's 'News from the Caribbean' for the CAM Newsletter when he was in Jamaica for a couple of months early in 1968 is concerned with the state of West Indian theatre, which he described as "a community art". After returning to Jamaica for good in October 1968, he and Doris were much involved in, and regarded as CAM activity, Marina Maxwell's Yard Theatre. When the actor Bari Jonson returned to Jamaica in 1970 after twenty-five years in Britain, the first people he sought out were the Brathwaites.

From the start of CAM, its writer-founders also saw CAM as a means of enabling Caribbean artists working in different media to interrelate with each other. Brathwaite is on record as having encouraged and taken part in many such opportunities. At the private session which he arranged to follow the public symposium of West Indian artists in June 1967, they would, he wrote to Louis James, "be talking about Aubrey Williams's point about the use of 'relics' and 'memory' and I've asked Wilson Harris to come along for this. It will, I hope, be a useful interchange between writers and artists".[30] Brathwaite's own interchange as a poet is on record especially with Aubrey Williams and Ronald Moody. His response to Williams's paintings developed, through CAM, from beginner requests in Williams's studio early in 1967 to "build up and break down a painting... We want to know about your creative process",[31] to 'Timehri', the talk he gave at the opening of Williams's first show in Jamaica in March 1970, in which his insights and appreciation of a fellow CAM member's work were given eloquent expression.[32]

An exchange of letters with Ronald Moody in late 1967 gives early evidence of the mutual understanding between poet and sculptor. After attending a preview of the Portrait Sculptors Exhibition Brathwaite wrote to Moody that in his piece, 'Sheila Henry', "There are enormous subtleties inherent in it and in a setting where nearly all the other things were, as you put it, mirror images, 'Sheila' just stood out".[33] Moody replied:

> I am glad that I thought of asking Doris and yourself because I like your approach. The West Indian intellectuals, in their approach to painting and sculpture, seem to me either to be coloured by the prevailing fashion of what ought to be thought or written, or downright blindness, seldom from an inner necessity. One thing that struck me about your poetry is the burning inner necessity, which found the most suitable form for its expression.[34]

When Moody paid a rare return visit to Jamaica in 1972, Brathwaite wrote an informed and appreciative article about his work, and his CAM connection, for the *Jamaica Gleaner*.

IV

Brathwaite the historian's concern with recording, transcribing and publishing what was said at CAM sessions was paralleled by the care he took to preserve evidence of the history of the movement. Most of the contacts and arrangements which he made as Organizing Secretary were by letter; he kept not only people's letters to him, but dated carbon copies of his own, self-typed letters to them — in addition to every sort of document connected with CAM. His sense of history in the making was also evident in remarks at CAM sessions. At the end of the first public session he said: "We didn't expect such a wonderful crowd here this evening and I don't know what to do next";[35] at the end of the Orlando Patterson/John Hearne session, "Where else but in CAM... can you have an artist not only explaining in great depth what he feels, but also have a fellow writer fearlessly and honestly giving a contrary view?".[36] As chairman of the two sessions on the Havana Congress, Brathwaite prefaced the first, on 5 April, with reference to the assassination of Martin Luther King in Memphis, U.S.A.; the second, on 20 April, to Enoch Powell's 'rivers of blood' speech in Birmingham, U.K., pointing out the historical significance of both recent events.

Brathwaite's historical sense and training is evident in his talks to CAM, whether ostensibly on poetry, about African vestiges in Caribbean society, or about cultural signals in the contemporary Caribbean. His absorption in the material for and writing up of his thesis on *The Development of Creole Society* overflowed into all that he said in CAM, and contributed to his consistent 'social creole ideology'. "My expression of West Indian society is a very positive one" was how he opened his comments at the first public session, continuing, "I don't find that the indigenous forms which we have in the West Indies should be despised".[37] He pressed again and again for the need to look closely at these indigenous forms, to understand one's own tradition. In his first public talk to CAM, in December 1967, he urged embrace of "an entirely different West Indian tradition" from that of the dominant Great Tradition, imposed by colonialism — the folk-based Little Tradition. Artists and intellectuals, he believed, had an important role as go-betweens, as agents of integration between the Great and Little Traditions. Writers were already concerned with the folk — in material and language; sociologists apparently less so. In his second public talk to CAM, in August 1969, he pleaded for recognition of "an alternative, living tradition in the Caribbean", of "a folk continuum at the basis of Caribbean society":

> From this ground of beginning [folk culture], it seems to me it would be possible for us to nurture a concept of wholeness, of community and of continuity.[38]

In both talks he stressed the importance for Caribbean people of examining, of knowing about and of coming to terms with their past, because "the past and the present are continuous, no break".[39]

Invitations to speakers for CAM sessions indicate Brathwaite's belief in the importance of contributions by selected Caribbean historians. C.L.R. James was asked to give the final lecture in the first public series; Elsa Goveia to be keynote speaker at the First Conference; Gordon Lewis was invited, but unable, to take a comparable role at the Second. Amongst Brathwaite's papers is his handwritten copy of a passage from C.L.R. James's talk to CAM in July 1967, suggesting its echo in his own experience:

> We have no history in the past. We have nothing that we can look back to as our own. And therefore all the West Indians who come to Europe, one of the first things that they do is to get some historical conception and place the civilization

> in which they are in a historical framework.[40]

Brathwaite played part of the taped recording of Goveia's First Conference speech during his own talk to CAM in December 1967, stressing the need for certain choices in what he described as "this dichotomy situation". Goveia had said:

> Until we have made this choice we are not going to be in a position to be really creative as individuals because our energies are going to be absorbed by the terrible job of working from two completely different sets of premises... Until we make a decision about the way in which we want the future to be built it is not going to be possible to find enough creative energy in the West Indies to produce the new culture which we need.[41]

In Gordon Lewis's landmark book, *Main Currents in Caribbean Thought: The Historical Evolution of Caribbean Society in Its Ideological Aspects, 1492-1900*, Brathwaite is amongst the few historians from the English-speaking Caribbean to whom reference is made. Despite finding the evidence for Brathwaite's thesis in *Creole Society* "hardly persuasive", Lewis summarizes and supports Brathwaite's plea in *Caribbean Man in Space and Time* for a new historiography "rooted in the concept of process rather than structure, and having as its base the whole, total experience of the inner plantation".[42]

V

In the early months of organizing CAM, when Brathwaite was brimming with ideas for what it might achieve, when sessions at the Students' Centre attracted a large and varied crowd, and when all Brathwaite's approaches to individuals and institutions met with eager responses, he wrote to Rohlehr:

> There is so much we can do, it seems to me... I'm only sorry that I'm not really free to devote all my time and energy to this enterprise. It seems to me very much worth pursuing and doing as well as possible. If only I had some cash, man. Some money; enough to live on for a year; I'd do just that. But these are just dreams; dreams and visions.[43]

After CAM had been going for a year Brathwaite left its organization in the hands of a new secretary, Marina Maxwell, and asked individual members of the committee to be responsible for its various aspects: exhibitions, bookselling, the newsletter, literature, theatre and so on. But when he returned to London two months later he found the committee divided, without a secretary and no obvious successor. As he put it to Don Wilson — an early CAM member, now back in Jamaica:

> CAM is struggling to survive at the moment. Marina Maxwell who'd taken over as Sec will be back in J'ca soon after you get this letter. This leaves me the difficult choice of sacrificing the chance of doing the kind of thesis I should like to do (or doing the thesis at all) or continuing to run CAM until it's time for me to leave... We've only ourselves to blame. As long as the Faustian individual continues to dominate our way of thinking and behaving, we are going to get nowhere.[44]

When, at the Second Conference, a few months later, Student Centre activists repeatedly pressed CAM to hold events in Brixton and to "become spiritually part of the black community"[45] Brathwaite reaffirmed the loose structure of CAM. It was, he said, up to individual members to do such things if they wished; they constituted CAM, there was no CAM body to ask. While artists themselves were in control of CAM, they would avoid any direct commitment to "the black community". But as CAM became larger and took in more non-artists, it would change and take CAM out.

Then, back home at U.W.I., Brathwaite called a number of writers to a preliminary meeting to explore the setting up of a branch of CAM in Jamaica — as he and fellow CAM members in London had always imagined would happen. But, as he wrote afterwards to Salkey, "We just split apart on the personalities alone".[46] The meeting was also divided as to whether its meetings should be private or public, who should be members, whether CAM should be based on or off campus, if off campus, in the 'ghetto' or Red Hills. After the natural accord between Brathwaite and fellow CAM founder-members in London, Brathwaite felt unable to pursue a prospective CAM Jamaica with division on so many aspects. The potential membership seemed to Brathwaite incapable of creating a sense of community. He commented, many years later: "I realized that it would ruin the whole spirit of CAM if I attempted to work under those conditions".[47]

None of Brathwaite's other attempts to interest people elsewhere in the Caribbean to form a branch of CAM came to fruition. At the

Convention of Caribbean Writers in Guyana in February 1970 the Brathwaites, La Rose and Salkey held a special meeting at which they talked about CAM and urged the setting up a Caribbean CAM, but nothing resulted. The following year, at the first Carifesta, Brathwaite again put the case for a Caribbean CAM; as he recalls, "people were very keen. But then... the Carifesta Secretariat felt that they would be the best people to deal with it... We haven't heard of it since".[48] There is no record of Brathwaite making further attempts to re-form CAM.

CAM was of its place and time; it could not be recreated, just as it could not live beyond its time. Immediately after the First Conference, when expectations for CAM seemed limitless, John La Rose wrote to Brathwaite: "The vital spark of life and spontaneity, I have discovered, in my own life, is not long-lasting. Glowing embers remain and we mistake it for fire. I mention this only so that we would know what to expect".[49] But the vital spark lasted long enough, and was bright enough, to create bonds in the CAM community which continue to bear fruit. Brathwaite himself looks back on CAM as "the most important happy happening to Caribbean artists in the second demarche of the twentieth century and a friendship which, now that I think about it, has been the fundament from which not only me but an ever increasing number of us have rooted/greened our various achievements on".[50]

Notes

1. Letter from Edward Brathwaite to Don Wilson, 23 March 1968.
2. Paullette Perrier, 'Harmattan: Whose Ancestor am I?', *Journal of Black Poetry* Vol 1, No 17, Summer 1973, 22.
3. Transcript of recording of CAM session, 1 December 1967, 1.
4. ibid, 3.
5. ibid, 15.
6. Transcript of recording of CAM session, 1 April 1970, 8.
7. Adrian Mitchell, 'Adrian Mitchell talks to Jamaican novelist Andrew Salkey and Trinidadian poet John La Rose', *The Guardian*, 4 April 1972.
8. Transcript of recording of Round-Up, Second CAM Conference, 2 September 1968, 1.
9. Kamau Brathwaite interviewed by Anne Walmsley, 15 March 1986.
10. Letter from Edward Brathwaite to Bryan King, 30 November 1966.
11. Letter from Edward Brathwaite to Edward Lucie-Smith, 12 December 1966.
12. Letter from Edward Brathwaite to Elliott Parris, 16 July 1967.

13. Letter from Edward Brathwaite to Jon Stallworthy, 15 October 1967.
14. Letter from Edward Brathwaite to Gordon Rohlehr, 27 March 1968.
15. Letter from Edward Brathwaite to C.L.R. James, 29 November 1967.
16. Transcript of recording of CAM session, 3 May 1968, 32.
17. Transcript of recording of CAM session, 16 August 1969, 7.
18. Transcript of recording of CAM session, 7 April 1967, 13.
19. 'Gordon Rohlehr's "Sparrow and the Language of Calypso", CAM Comment', *Caribbean Quarterly* 14: 1&2, 1968, 91-2.
20. Transcript of recording of CAM session, 17 September 1967, 9.
21. Transcript of recording of CAM session, 1 December 1967, 14.
22. Transcript of recording of CAM session, 13 October 1967, 44.
23. Transcript of recording of CAM session, 15 August 1969, 39.
24. James Berry, 'Focus', *West Indian World*, 8 October 1971, 4.
25. Transcript of recording of CAM session, 1 December 1967, 16.
26. Transcript of recording of CAM session, 3 May 1968, 34.
27. Transcript of recording of CAM session, 1 September 1968, 33.
28. Letter from Edward Brathwaite to Louis James, 24 September 1967.
29. Letter from Edward Brathwaite to Ram John Holder, 22 October 1967.
30. Letter from Edward Brathwaite to Louis James, 11 June 1967.
31. Transcript of recording of CAM session, 23 June 1967, 62.
32. Edward Brathwaite, 'Timehri', *Savacou* 2, September 1970, 35-44.
33. Letter from Edward Brathwaite to Ronald Moody, 26 November 1967.
34. Letter from Ronald Moody to Edward Brathwaite, 1 December 1967.
35. Transcript of recording of CAM session, 10 March 1967, 31.
36. Transcript of recording of CAM session, 5 May 1967, 33.
37. Transcript of recording of CAM session, 10 March 1967, 25.
38. Transcript of recording of CAM session, 15 August 1969, 40.
39. ibid.
40. Transcript of recording of CAM session, 7 July 1967, 31.
41. Transcript of recording of CAM session, 16 September 1967, 14-15.
42. Gordon K. Lewis, *Main Currents in Caribbean Thought: The Historical Evolution of Caribbean Society in Its Ideological Aspects, 1492-1900* (Baltimore and London: Johns Hopkins University Press, 1983), 175.
43. Letter from Edward Brathwaite to Gordon Rohlehr, 11 March 1967.
44. Letter from Edward Brathwaite to Don Wilson, 23 March 1968.
45. Anne Walmsley, 'Notes on CAM's Second Conference', 8(A).
46. Letter from Edward Brathwaite to Andrew Salkey, 18 December 1968.
47. Kamau Brathwaite interviewed by Anne Walmsley, 15 March 1986, 6-7.
48. ibid.
49. Letter from John La Rose to Edward Brathwaite, 24 September 1967.
50. Kamau Brathwaite, 'John the Conqueror', *Foundations of a Movement: A Tribute to John La Rose on the Occasion of the 10th International Book Fair of Radical Black and Third World Books* (London: John La Rose Tribute Committee, 1991), 20.

Mervyn Morris

Overlapping Journeys: *The Arrivants*

Of the many useful and interesting discussions of *The Arrivants*[1] or of individual books in the trilogy, there are two I am anxious to recommend. Maureen Warner-Lewis' *Masks: Essays & Annotations*[2] and Gordon Rohlehr's *Pathfinder*[3] are of value not only for their critical judgements but also for the wealth of information they provide about the contexts of the poetry. Inter alia, Warner-Lewis guides us through West African detail, and Rohlehr elucidates many allusions to jazz and other manifestations of Africa-related New World culture. Anyone studying *The Arrivants* should make early contact with these two items, and will no doubt wish to explore the rest of the bibliography.

The present essay is introductory, offering a very brief outline of the trilogy, its origins, its shape, its main concerns, and a glance at some of its techniques.

In an autobiographical essay called 'Timehri'[4] Brathwaite describes himself as a Barbadian "from an urban village background, of parents with a "'middle-class' orientation" who made friends "with boys of stubbornly non-middle class origin". From Harrison College, "originally founded for children of the plantocracy and colonial civil servants and white professionals", Brathwaite won one of the prestigious Barbados scholarships "that traditionally took the ex-planters' sons 'home' to Oxbridge or London". It took him, "a potential Afro-Saxon", to Pembroke College, Cambridge, to read History. He wrote poems, most of them rejected by the Cambridge magazines. He felt neglected and misunderstood.[5]

> Then in 1953, George Lamming's *In the Castle of My Skin* appeared and everything was transformed. Here breathing to me from every pore of line and page, was the Barbados I had lived. The words, the rhythms, the cadences, the scenes, the people, their predicament. They all came back. They all were possible. All the more beautiful for having been published and praised by London, mother of metropolises.[6]

After graduation, he applied for jobs all over the place. "I was a West Indian, roofless[7] man of the world. I could go, belong, everywhere on the world-wide globe. I ended up in a village in Ghana.

It was my beginning". He began to feel connected to Africa.

> Slowly, slowly, ever so slowly; obscurely, slowly but surely, during the eight years that I lived there, I was coming to an awareness and understanding of community, of cultural wholeness, of the place of the individual within the tribe, in society. Slowly, slowly, ever so slowly, I came to a sense of identification of myself with these people, my living diviners. I came to connect my history with theirs, the bridge of my mind now linking Atlantic and ancestor, homeland and heartland. When I turned to leave, I was no longer a lonely individual talent; there was something wider, more subtle, more tentative: the self without ego, without I, without arrogance. And I came home to find that I had not really left. That it was still Africa; Africa in the Caribbean.[8]

Brathwaite returned to the Caribbean in 1962. "I had, at that moment of return," he writes, "completed the triangular trade of my historical origins. West Africa had given me a sense of place, of belonging; and that place and belonging, I knew, was the West Indies".[9]

Like many other publications by Brathwaite, *The Arrivants* draws attention to Caribbean continuities out of Africa, which a European overlay may sometimes obscure, and argues that the psychic wholeness of Caribbean black people requires fuller recognition of our African heritage. As Damian Grant wrote in an early review article:

> The theme, over the three books, might be summarized as the rediscovery of Africa; a rediscovery that has to be made by the twentieth-century Negro, a condition of his own proper freedom, selfhood and political independence. Brathwaite offers in fact to define and articulate the modern Negro consciousness, seen as a complication of past experience, present problems, and future possibilities.[10]

In response perhaps to talk about the trilogy's public mission, Brathwaite was emphatic in an interview: "This trilogy as a whole, is concerned first of all with *my* own experiences. I am trying to come to terms with being a West Indian who has travelled to Africa".[11] But he is trying also to present "the self without ego" and to express "an awareness and understanding of community, of cultural wholeness, of the place of the individual within the tribe". In *The Arrivants* he speaks through a series of personas or masks or, to put it differently, through a shifting persona who represents black experience in various manifestations. As Brathwaite notes, in *Rights of Passage* the persona, Tom, "undergoes a series of transformations — from ancestor to slave to prophet to Uncle Tom, and is finally translated into an image of the past out of which the future springs".[12] With reference to *Masks,* Warner-Lewis writes:

> The poet found that he could not get to the heart of his questionings unless he became other people and felt as they did at the crucial points of their existence: the slave, the ancestor, the king, the villager, the pioneer and clan-founder, and he himself, Brathwaite, the descendant and inheritor of all these. But the poet needs at times the detached mask of an onlooker, an outsider, the scholar with history at his fingertips.[13]

The Arrivants brings together "three long poems that... deal, in their different ways, with journeys".[14] "Time's walking river is long" (*The Arrivants*, 120). The order in which the books appeared is part of the point: the African book is the centre of the trilogy; and though the journeys never end, the poem leaves us in the Caribbean. The final book signs off with a series of present participles, whose suggestion of a continuing process is reinforced by the absence of punctuation after the final word:

> now waking
> making
>
> making
> with their
>
> rhythms some-
> thing torn
>
> and new[15]
>
> *The Arrivants*, 269-270

In *Rights of Passage* we meet personas of the New World Negro, the dislocated African, forever on the move and with little memory of ancestral Africa. "Where then is the nigger's / home?" "Will exile never // end?" (*The Arrivants*, 77). According to the author, "*Rights of Passage*... is about the black diaspora: the shattering journey out of Africa into New World plantation slavery, the song and dance of illusory emancipation, and the first recognition of identity. *Masks*... is the necessary and countervailing journey: ingathering of the multitudes: return of scattered psyches to the ancestral homeland: a movement from hurt to heart".[16] The epigraph to *Masks* is an Akan proverb: "Only the fool points at his origins with his left hand" [i.e. disrespectfully]. In the first half of the book, we travel through sections of African history and culture; in the second half, an African returns from the New World, in unavailing search of his buried navel string. Though the attempt at reconnection has been fraught with disappointment, contact with Africa has strengthened the persona. He will rise and stand on his feet. In *Islands* we are in the Caribbean, mostly, exploring Africa forgotten and retained; and, through a series of Afro-Caribbean figures, considering "the certainties/uncertainties of the Caribbean, taking up the theme of 'the gains and the losses', implicit in *Masks*".[17] As understanding deepens, there is movement towards correcting the cultural imbalance of the colonial heritage which has tended to privilege Europe. Near the end of the trilogy, in 'Vèvè', when the Word is invoked (*The Arrivants*, 266), Legba — "the Dahomean/Haitian god of the gateway"[18]— emerges from St John chapter one. "Christ will pray/ to Odomankoma // Nyame God / and Nyankopon" (*The Arrivants*, 267). As Rohlehr puts it, "Christ and Odomankoma are recognized as different names for the same concept of God as communicable immanent force in the universe and incarnate Word."[19]

Rights of Passage, Masks and *Islands* were republished together as *The Arrivants* in 1973. Reprints from 1978 at least have included a new and closely relevant epigraph.

> Well, muh ol' arrivance[20] ...is from
> Africa... That's muh ol' arrivants family. Muh
> gran'muddah an' muh gran' fadda. Well, they came
> out here as slavely... you unnerstan' ?
>
> Well, when them came now, I doan belongs to
> Africa, I belongs to Jamaica. I born here.
>
> Well, muh gran'parents, she teach me some of the
> African languages an' the rest I get it at the
> cotton-tree root... I take twenty-one days to get
> all the balance...
>
> So I just travel right up to hey, an' gradually
> come up, an' gradually come up, until I experience
> all about... the African set-up...
>
> Kumina Queen, Jamaica

The epigraph foregrounds African ancestry; and slavery as the reason African ancestors came to the Caribbean. It makes a point which is extensively explored in *Masks*: the speaker, a leader in an Africa-derived religious ritual, says plainly that she does not belong to Africa, she belongs to Jamaica, she was born here; and that she has been taught some African lore by her ancestors and has received some of it by intuition or by supernatural means ("at the cotton-tree root"). There is a direct connection with various concerns in the trilogy. The trauma of slavery is evoked in all three books. In *Masks* the African returning from the New World is forced to recognize that he no longer belongs in Africa. *Islands* examines manifestations of Africa in the New World, finding ancestral memory retained to some degree in religious ceremony ('Shepherd', 'Wake', 'Eating the Dead', 'Negus', 'Vèvè', for example) and the intuitive gropings of art (as in 'Jouvert' and 'Ogun').

Each book is divided into parts, each part into sections, some sections into numbered subsections. The transitions are often introduced by connectives (such as "and now", "but", "so", "for") which strengthen the appearance of continuity. Many sections seem to be poems complete in themselves, and some have indeed been published separately. But meaning in the trilogy is partly a function of placement, as passages extend or modify ideas introduced earlier and as their music plays against the movement of other passages. Acknowledging the influence of T.S. Eliot, Brathwaite has said: "The tone, the cadence and above all the organization of my long poems (and all three poems of my trilogy are long poems, not collections of poems) owe a great deal to him".[21]

Brathwaite also shares with Eliot a recurrent concern with memory and time. "And the wheel turns / and the future returns / wreathed in disguises"(*The Arrivants*, 168).[22] History repeats itself. As Mark McWatt has observed, "the reality one confronts in the poems, however clear or 'raw', is always coloured, as it were, by a sense of historical time, an overlay of reverberations from past events and personalities which cause in the reader a kind of mental or imaginative shift toward a historical perspective".[23]

For example, there is a sense in which the West Indian emigrants travelling to Europe in the 1950s replicate Columbus in the fifteenth century travelling in the other direction.

> What do they hope for
> what find there
> these New World mariners
> Columbus coursing kaffirs

What Cathay shores
for them are gleaming golden
what magic keys they carry to unlock
what gold endragoned doors?

2

Columbus from his after-
deck watched stars, absorbed in water,
melt in liquid amber drafting

through my summer air.
The Arrivants, 52

So too in *Masks* "the omowale/ex-african reverses the movement of the poem (ship to heartland rather than heartland to ship) and undertakes a journey of re/discovery of origins".[24] In the third part of *Masks*, at a moment centuries ago, the Africans captured for slavery reach the sea, where "voyages ended; / time stopped where its movement began;" (122) and at the beginning of Part IV (which follows) the persona recently arriving in West Africa is welcomed as a stranger: "you who have come / back a stranger / after three hundred years // welcome"(124).

Images merge cinematically, as again in 'Littoral'(170-173), near the beginning of *Islands*. In section one the blind fisherman (whose head is like a mask) is weaving a net, "his fingers knit as the dark rejoices / but he has his voices...". Section two presents one of those voices, a woman singer who "travels far back, explores / ruins". When the poem was published in 1960 the singer was Billie Holiday;[25] but in the immediate context of *Islands* she is an African ancestral memory, becomes Yaa Asantewa, "warrior and queen and keeper of the tribe". Between sections two and three we make another leap through time: from the blind fisherman on a Caribbean beach more or less now, into the hold of a slave-ship long ago.

He hopes
that light will break in the clearing
before her song ends...

3

But no light breaks under the decks
where the sails sing

The trilogy is held together partly by patterns of recurrent imagery. Journey, movement, time, river, sea; dust, sand, dryness, pebble, stone, rock, earth, soil, water, tendril, pistil, green, tree, hurricane; sun, moon, night, fire, sleep, awakening, dawn, morning, day, light, dark, womb, birth, blindness, sight; speech, shout, whisper, silence; drum, mask, dance, circle, music, song; gold, silver, black, red, whip, lash, iron, shackle, clink, clank, Uncle Tom; spider, fisherman — these are some of the images and some of the ways they cluster. They are of multiple significance, they inter-relate variously, they develop and change. So the spider, for example — Ananse, "the spider-hero of the Akans; earthly trickster, but once with the powers of the creator-gods"[26] — is both positive and negative, is used to suggest diminished memory of Africa ("Creation has burned to a spider", 164), is an agent of rebellion (heard by Tacky and L'Ouverture), is both untrustworthy and supremely creative ("stony world-maker, word-breaker, / creator", 167), and connects with the blind fisherman weaving "nets, embroideries" (170), the fisherman whose "fine webs fell softly" (263). The fisherman in turn shades into a mask: "his eyes stare out like an empty shell" (170): which reminds us of "his- / tory bleeds / behind my hollowed eyes" (148) and connects with many other references to masks, masking, role-playing, disguise.

Or take, for example, pebble, stone. "It will slay / giants // but never bear children" (196). Its potential in battle is acknowledged, but the emphasis here is on sterility. When "my island is a pebble" (196), when lightning strikes a "world of stone" (268) the main implications are negative. In 'Negus', on the other hand, "stone" is more positive, the instrument of existential rebellion: "fling me the stone / that will confound the void"(224).

There are references throughout to the drum, a central symbol of African culture. "God is dumb / until the drum / speaks" (97). "Drum" is the very first word of *The Arrivants,* and it is there at the end in 'Jouvert'. Wrenched from Africa, the New World blacks still remember the talking drum, "Atumpan talking and the harvest branch- / es" (13). The angry man in 'Folkways' feels "like a drum with a hole / in its belly" (31), an image later associated with Tom, in whose cabin there is "A rusted / bucket, hole kicked into its / bottom" (70, 248). The Rastafarian in 'Wings of a Dove' summons us to "beat dem drums / dem" (44). The poet-persona in the 'Prelude' of *Masks* invokes creative power: "Beat heaven / of the drum, beat" (91). Near the beginning of *Masks* we share in a ritual of creative preparation, 'The Making of the Drum' (94-97). The "quick drummer" (162) is part of the jazz scene in 'Jah'. Drums are crucial in 'Shepherd', helping towards possession: "the room rumbles / clouded with drums" (185), "the drum trembles" (186), "the drum speaks" (187); and when the Shepherd senses an ancestor, "can smell / his sweat / his musk of damp and slave // ships", the Shepherd himself becomes metaphorically a drum with which the ancestor communicates: "his heat hurts / me, my belly is tight / his hands hit // me into sound" and "Slowly / slowly / slowly / the dumb speaks" (188), the form of words suggesting — since "God is dumb / until the drum / speaks" (97) — that the drum and the Shepherd are divine instruments. Drums are important also in the voodoo ritual, "*Att / Att / Attibon/ / Attibon Legba / Attibon Legba / Ouvri bayi pou' moi / Ouvri bayi pou' moi...*" (224), open the gate for me. In 'Vèvè' the gods will arrive "welcomed by drumbeats" (265). There are also the drums of steel band music, the booming bass drum and the ping pong tenor pan as in "flowers bloom / their tom tom sun // heads raising / little steel pan // petals to the music's / doom // as the ping pong / dawn comes // riding / over shattered homes"(269).

Rhythmic patterns recur in various contexts. For example, the "It / it / it / it is not" (222) and "*Att / Att / Attibon // Attibon Legba...*" of 'Negus' (224) recall the beginning of 'Tano' (151), "dam / dam / damirifa / damirifa due...", each clearly suggesting drumbeats. But *damirifa due* is "an Akan cry of pity and sorrow meaning 'condolences'";[27] the soul of the returning African is gathered back into the ancestral fold. "Attibon Legba" moves in the opposite direction: it is an invocation to the gateway god, Legba, who facilitates access to other gods. The drumbeats return in 'Shepherd' ("Dumb / dumb / dumb", 185-187) but, through possession, there is reconnection with ancestors, and "Slowly / slowly / slowly / the dumb speaks" (188). Here "Slowly / slowly / slowly" — also recalled in 'Timehri' — reminds us of Osai Tutu, royal founder of the Ashanti Confederation, rising in ceremonial dignity (141).

The Arrivants is richly allusive, connecting a range of detail in the history and culture of various communities. Each volume has its prevailing tone, created partly by the diction, the rhythms of speech, and partly by allusions to music. We hear in *Rights of Passage* a New World soundtrack — worksong, Negro spritual, various styles of jazz, calypso, ska; in *Masks*, Akan drum rhythms, and jazz; in *Islands* — centred in the Caribbean — jazz again, and aural motifs of steel band, limbo dancing, Jamaican folksong, Haitian drums. Some of the music allusions[28] are to the words of songs — "just call my blue / black bloody spade / a spade" (29), for example, echoes "What did

I do / to be so black an' blue". Some are to the titles of tunes, such as 'New World A-Comin' (9) which alludes with irony to a Duke Ellington composition. There are musicians mentioned by name or nickname (such as Charlie Parker's, 'Bird'). Some of the allusions assume an intimate knowledge of the music.[29] Here, for example, is Brathwaite in response to an enquiry about the final pages (82-85) of *Rights of Passage*.

> I'd never be able to write "bird calls"...without having Parker in mind: especially since there is an LP of that name. So when I wrote it I heard that saxophone in addition to what I was really talking about: Noah's dove after the rain: which is again connected with Coltrane's greatest lyric 'After the Rain': which derives its beauty not only from itself, but also from its juxtaposition to his greatest storm, 'Impressions'.[30]

The music allusions are not just cultural background. They are often an important element of the meaning, as again, for example, in section two of 'Folkways' (33) which ends:

> rat tat tat
> on the flat-
> out whispering rails
> on the quick
> click
> boogie woogie
> hooeeee
> boogie woogie
> long long
> boogie woogie
> long long
> hooey long
> journey to town.

Pointing out "the connection between this passage and traditional railroad blues", Gordon Rohlehr has argued that Brathwaite is here "establishing the connection between Jazz and Journey; seeing jazz as yet another gift of the archetypal tribal experience in Africa, and its counterpart in the New World".[31]

Sometimes Brathwaite will more or less mimic the music or imitate rhythms as in that brilliant passage, or in "*Kon kon kon kon / Kun kun kun kun*" (98), or "Come-a look / come-a look / see wha' happen" (240), patterned on a Jamaican folksong. More often, however, there is a subtle tension between the speaking voice and the music reference, as in these lines which parody Caliban's drunken song (*The Tempest*, Act II, Scene ii) and also suggest the syncopation of road march music in Trinidad carnival:

Ban
Ban
Cal-
iban
like to play
pan
at the car-
nival;
pranc-
cing up to the lim-
bo silence
down
down
down
so the god won't drown
him
down
down
to the is-
land town
The Arrivants, 192

But Brathwaite does not insist that the speaking voice always be equal or dominant. He sometimes gives absolute priority to the music rhythm. In 'Wings of a Dove', for example, the emphatic rhythm is sometimes expressed in normal creole syntax, but at other moments normal syntax is ignored. "So beat dem drums / dem, spread // dem wings dem, / watch dem fly // dem" is normal speech; "soar dem / high dem" (44) is not.

This seems to be a choice he makes from time to time: to let the music rhythms take charge. When he prefers to, he convincingly represents speech. Indeed a major area of Brathwaite's achievement in *The Arrivants* is his flexible command of speech rhythms. His ear allows him to register various accents, including American and African:

See them zoot suits, man? Them black
Texan hats?
The Arrivants, 23

Akwaaba they smiled
meaning welcome

akwaaba they called
aye kooo

well have you walked
have you journeyed

welcome
The Arrivants, 124

He captures many West Indian voices, from standard English as in 'Mammon' (73-76) to Barbadian creole (he says "nation language")[32] in 'Cane' (225-229) and 'Tizzic' (260-261), Jamaican Revival preaching in 'The Stone Sermon' (254-256), Rastafarian speech in 'Wings of a Dove' (42-43). In section two of 'Francina' (215) standard English modulates into creole. In 'The Dust' (62-69), one of our finest poems in creole, he presents Barbadian women talking about their world and its worries, moving without strain into ultimate questions about the meaning of life.

An' then suddenly so
widdout rhyme
widdout reason

you crops start to die
you can't even see the sun in the sky;
an' suddenly so, without rhyme,

without reason, all you hope gone
ev'rything look like it comin' out wrong.
Why is that? What it mean?
(68-69)

'Rites' (197-203; a prose version had been published earlier[33]) is a West Indian classic, our quintessential cricket poem. It is clear from the cricket-loving tailor's lively monologue that the test match is, as Orlando Patterson has argued, "not so much a game as a collective ritual".[34] When things are going well for their side, spectators feel empowered. "All over de groun' fellers shakin' hands wid each other // as if was *they* wheelin' de willow / as if was *them* had the power" (200). When the batsman is doing well, a spectator brings a votive offering, as to a god — "a red fowl cock // goin quawk quawk quawk in 'e han'". A man who for twenty-five years has been "lickin' gloy / pun de Gover'ment stamps" (200-201) is transformed, noisily calling for blood. But when the game begins to favour the invading

English, there is silent consternation — "could'a hear de empire fart" (202) — then a babel of advice. The moral is drawn explicitly:

> when things goin' good, you cahn touch
> we, but leh murder start
> an' ol man, you cahn fine a man to hole up de side...
> *The Arrivants*, 203

The umpire/empire pun is characteristic of *The Arrivants*. Word-play abounds. "Miss- / issippi painfields" (51) is typical. The pun is arguably an aspect of the jazz technique, the literary analogue of the blue note (the flattened third or fifth or seventh), a note that makes you hear an adjacent semitone. In "Boss man lacks pride: / I am his hide // of darkness" (19) the Hyde is emphasized by the line break: I am his Hyde, his other self, the self of darkness. In "to hell / with Eu- / rope too" (29) we get: to hell with you, and with the rope as well. Sometimes the lineation visually reinforces meaning as in:

> the wise
> are di-
> vided
> *The Arrivants*, 130

or:

> O who now will help
> us, help-
> less, horse-
> less, leader-
> less, no
> hope, no
> Hawkins, no
> Cortez to come.
> *The Arrivants*, 10

Some early readers of *Rights of Passage* were disconcerted by the frequent division of words, by passages such as

> E-
> gypt
> in Af-
> rica
> Mesopo-
> tamia
> Mero-
> e
> *The Arrivants*, 35

especially as the division was often not aurally detectable in Brathwaite's own reading of the verse. Lineation is far less obtrusive in *Masks* and *Islands*. But *Rights of Passage*, Brathwaite has explained, was "a tale of deprivation, paradoxically balanced upon a sense of hope, of continuity and of unity: fragments that still held secrets of the whole. And this paradox came to be expressed in the poem in the counterpoint between the broken lines of the verse, and the shifting but basic rhythms of its impetus".[35]

The Arrivants is a major document of African reconnection. Brilliantly, it charts a set of overlapping psychic journeys to, from and within the New World and Africa, acknowledging achievement and some painful realities, examining self and community, past and present. The final lines of the trilogy celebrate awakening consciousness and the creative growth of the artist-persona and other Caribbean black people:

> hurts for-
>
> gotten, hearts
> no longer bound
>
> to black and bitter
> ashes in the ground
>
> now waking
> making
>
> making
> with their
>
> rhythms some-
> thing torn
>
> and new
>
> *The Arrivants*, 269-270

Notes

1. Pronounced ar-RIVE-ants. Edward Kamau Brathwaite, *The Arrivants* (London: Oxford University Press, 1973), comprised of *Rights of Passage* (1967), *Masks* (1968) and *Islands* (1969). For other works by Brathwaite and a selection of Brathwaite criticism, see the bibliography at the back of this book.

2. Maureen Warner-Lewis, *E. Kamau Brathwaite's Masks: Essays & Annotations* (Kingston: Institute of Caribbean Studies, 1992): a reissue of *Notes to Masks* (Benin City: Ethiope Publishing Corporation, 1977) with a revised version of 'Odomankoma 'Kyerema Se', an essay published in *Caribbean Quarterly* 19: 2, June 1973.
3. Gordon Rohlehr, *Pathfinder: Black Awakening in The Arrivants of Edward Kamau Brathwaite* (Trinidad: private publication, 1981).
4. Edward Brathwaite, 'Timehri', *Savacou* 2, September 1970, 35-44. For a slightly different version see Orde Coombs ed., *Is Massa Day Dead?* (New York: Doubleday/ Anchor Press, 1974), 29-44.
5. 'Timehri', *Savacou* 2, 36-37.
6. Ibid.
7. In *Is Massa Day Dead?* "rootless", 33. The word as in *Savacou* is much richer, playing against "rootlessness" earlier in the paragraph, and suggesting "unaccommodated man" and a Barbadian pronunciation of "ruthless".
8. Ibid., 38.
9. Rosalie Murphy & James Vinson eds., *Contemporary Poets of the English Language* (London: St James Press, 1970), 129.
10. Damian Grant, 'Emerging Image: the poetry of Edward Brathwaite', *Critical Quarterly* 12:2, Summer 1970, 186-187.
11. *The Poet Speaks* Record Ten, ed. Peter Orr (London: Argo, 1968).
12. Edward [Kamau] Brathwaite, Record Notes to *Rights of Passage* Record One (London: Argo, 1968).
13. Maureen Warner-Lewis, *Masks: Essays and Annotations,* 15.
14. Edward [Kamau] Brathwaite, Record Notes to *Islands* (London: Argo Records, 1973).
15. The concluding lines of *Rights of Passage* and *Masks* also emphasize process — each marks a stage in the psychic journey — but with a full stop at the end of the one, an ellipsis at the end of the other. Images of journey, dawn and music figure in the final pages of each book.
16. Edward [Kamau] Brathwaite. Recorded Notes to *Islands.*
17. Ibid.
18. *The Arrivants,* 273 (Glossary).
19. Rohlehr, *Pathfinder,* 314.
20. "Ol' arrivance" would be the same sound as "whole arrivants", meaning all my ancestors here (as well as my old ancestors or ancestry).
21. Rosalie Murphy & James Vinson eds., *Contemporary Poets of the English Language*, 129.
22. Cf. the opening lines of T.S. Eliot's *Burnt Norton*: "Time present and time past / Are both perhaps in time future, / And time future contained in time past."
23. Mark McWatt, in Daryl C. Dance ed., *Fifty Caribbean Writers* (Newport: Greenwood Press, 1986), 60.
24. Edward [Kamau] Brathwaite, Record Notes to *Masks* (London: Argo, 1972). The *omowale* is one who returns.
25. Rohlehr, *Pathfinder,* 192.
26. *The Arrivants,* 272 (Glossary).

27. Maureen Warner-Lewis, *Masks: Essays and Annotations*, 93-94.
28. See Gordon Rohlehr, *Pathfinder*, 333-340, Appendix One, 'Black/ Ground Music to *Rights of Passage*'.
29. "Knowing precisely what music is being alluded to, one can fruitfully explore the hidden network of allusions beneath the taut or casual surface of things", Rohlehr, *Pathfinder*, 333. In a passage at the beginning of *Masks* (90-91, "Gong-gongs / throw pebbles in the rout- / ed pools of silence..." etc), Jimmy Carnegie hears a John Coltrane solo. "Brathwaite," he writes, "has accomplished an almost impossible feat of 'transcription'." (J.A. Carnegie, 'The Face's Soul', review of *Masks*, *Public Opinion* (Kingston, Jamaica), August 2, 1968.
30. *Pathfinder*, 55.
31. Gordon Rohlehr, review article on *Islands*, *Caribbean Studies* 10:4, 178.
32. See Edward Kamau Brathwaite, *History of the Voice: The Development of Nation Language in Anglophone Caribbean Poetry* (London: New Beacon Books, 1984).
33. Edward [Kamau] Brathwaite, 'Cricket', in Andrew Salkey ed., *Caribbean Prose* (London: Evans Brothers, 1967), 61-67.
34. Orlando Patterson, 'The Ritual of Cricket', *Jamaica Journal* 3:1, March 1969.
35. Edward [Kamau] Brathwaite, Record Notes to *Rights of Passage* (London: Argo, 1968).

Nathaniel Mackey

Wringing the Word

Islands, the third book of Kamau Brathwaite's first trilogy *The Arrivants*, marks both an arrival and an embarkation. Following the diasporic panorama of *Rights of Passage* and the African focus of *Masks*, *Islands* initiates a return to the Caribbean, the undertaking of a groundedness long denied the "land- / less, harbour- / less spade" (*The Arrivants*, 34). The ground in question is literal (and, as the title of one of the book's poems reminds us, littoral), the Caribbean landscape and its characteristic features — shoreline, sand, coral and so forth. The grounding undertaken is figural, a poetic investment in the specifics of place, a linguistic embrace and embarkation which asks the West Indies: "where is your kingdom of the Word?" (*The Arrivants*, 222). Culture, the collective poesis which endows the habitation of a ground with meaning, is interrogated, meditated upon and contributed to by a thematization of the word which *Islands* inaugurates. Accompanying this thematization is a tendency toward linguistic play and experimentation, a foregrounding of language which becomes even more prominent in the trilogy which begins with *Mother Poem*. 'Chatter' rendered 'shatter', 'umpire' rendered 'empire' and the lines "children / summer- / saulting in the park" (*The Arrivants*, 190, 202, 181) are among the few instances in *Islands* of a practice which escalates quantumwise in the second trilogy. In this essay, looking at *Islands* and *Mother Poem* in particular, I will be discussing that escalation, the movement from landscape to wordscape, language thematized and acted upon.

The 'chatter/shatter' and 'umpire/empire' renderings are in fact a good place to begin. The former is one of many instances of an accent which falls on fragmentation from *Islands* on. Brathwaite writes in *Mother Poem* that "the child / is born to splinters // broken islands / broken homes," (*Mother Poem*, 108) echoing an insistence we find in *Islands*: not only "cracked note," "cracked mother," "cracked ground" and "broken tongue," but also "history... / ...stripped and torn" (*The Arrivants*, 162, 180, 187, 210, 216). Brathwaite grounds this insistence in the fragmentariness of insular topography, the islands' lack of the relative coherence possessed by larger land masses. As though the very ground, geography itself, underwrote and underscored such accent, he again and again, in the second trilogy, broods upon "this tilted cracked fragmentary landscape" (*Mother Poem*, 41) in writing which amounts to a fractured wordscape, poems typified by idiosyncratic line breaks and syllabications:

> but can you ever guess how i
> who have wracked
>
> you wrong
> long too to be black
>
> be
> come part of that hool that shrinks us all to stars
>
> how i
> with all these loco
>
> motives in me
> would like to straighten
>
> strangle eye/self out
>
> grow a beard wear dark glasses
> driving the pack straight far
>
> ward into indigo and vi
> olet and on into ice like a miss
>
> ile
>
> *Sun Poem*, 3-4

The 'chatter/shatter' rendering anticipates this later manner of speaking, both a broken mode and a breaking mode, as if to chatter were indeed to shatter. Broken speech, breaking speech, partakes of the ground, as announced in the invocation which concludes the next-to-last poem in *Islands*: "So on this ground, / write ... // on this ground / on this broken ground" (*The Arrivants*, 265-266). It fulfils the announcement of "some- / thing torn // and new" with which the book concludes (*The Arrivants*, 270).

The phrase "broken ground," as the lines "history ... / ... stripped and torn" indicate, has historical as well as topographic meaning, referring to social divisions and social conflicts which have plagued the Caribbean since the advent of European expansion in the late fifteenth century. The 'umpire/empire' rendering, as does much of

Brathwaite's linguistic play, underscores the centrality of slavery, the plantation system and colonialism to the history and the predicaments of the region. The verbal disruptions to which he resorts, together with his thematization of the word, address the cultural domination which accompanied and helped implement and sustain British imperialism. They not only address but also move to redress that domination. "I / must be given words to refashion futures / like a healer's hand," he writes in 'Negus'. And further on in the same poem:

> fling me the stone
> that will confound the void
> find me the rage
> and I will raze the colony
> fill me with words
> and I will blind your God.
> *The Arrivants,* 224

This aspiration gives a sense of prospect and promise to work which is otherwise a tally of deprivations. Broken speech, seeking to break new ground, brings a further sense of "broken ground" into play — the prospect and promise of a new beginning. (The fifth and final section of *Islands* is called 'Beginning'.) A sense of the emergence of an alternative cultural order, of being present at the inception of a new dispensation, pervades *Islands* and the second trilogy. Language, the cornerstone of cultural order, is accordingly prioritized. "My tongue is heavy with new language," the poet announces in the 'Rebellion' section of *Islands* (*The Arrivants,* 221).

Brathwaite's work both announces the emergence of a new language and acknowledges the impediments to its emergence, going so far as to advance impediment as a constituent of the language's newness. This is one of the most distinctive features of the writing which *Islands* announces and inaugurates. The sense of an initiation into new orders of speech is in part what Brathwaite's repeated references to pebbles imply, calling to mind the practice of speaking with pebbles in the mouth to improve pronunciation. One of the poems in *Islands* is called 'Pebbles' and in 'Eating the Dead' he writes: "I will return to the pebble" (*The Arrivants*, 196, 219). It is in this latter poem that he says his tongue is "heavy with new language," going on immediately, however, to add: "but I cannot give birth speech. // Pebbles surround me". The pebble is a multivalent figure whose meaning cuts more than one way. A figure for the resistances active in the encounter between conflicting orders of speech, the pebble simultaneously signifies promise and impediment. Even in the practice referred to above it functions antithetically, improving speech by impeding speech. Brathwaite's recourse to it carries even greater antithetic resonance, as he calls into question the very notion of proper speech, the elocutionary norm such improvement aspires to. In the Caribbean, of course, the notion of linguistic propriety is marked by colonialism and cultural domination, rooted in imposed, metropolitan models and canons which obstruct and delegitimate alternate modes of speech, the very modes Brathwaite is committed to advancing. The pebble signifies the diminishment and denigration of those alternate modes by a colonizing norm, by the biases intrinsic to imperial notions of propriety and improvement. It also signifies a resistance to so-called proper speech, a resistance which in Brathwaite's case is not, as in the conventional model of improvement, to be overcome, but rather encouraged, cultivated, carried farther. Hence the positive valence the figure carries as a symbol of linguistic and cultural self-determination. It comes to signify the vocalities and linguistic practices of Afro-Caribbean folk culture, tonalities and retentions Brathwaite tends especially to associate with women in a mothering role. "All that I have of her is voices," he writes of his grandmother in *Islands*:

> ...And in the night, I listened to her singing
> in a Vicks and Vapour Rub-like voice what you would call the blues
> *The Arrivants*, 240

Depth and resonance accrue to the figure by the time we get to *Sun Poem*:

> mothers were *loa* were stone crabs were fish traps of no
> they were pebbles of sound down the floor of a well
> *Sun Poem*, 77

The pebble is characterized in part by what it's up against, larger figures in stone which impede its emergence. In *Sun Poem*, Brathwaite coins a term to refer to one of the forms of material inscription whereby imperial authority sanctifies itself, statues monumentalizing the agents of colonial rule. As have other West Indian writers (Ismith Khan, for example, on the Woodford statue in *The Jumbie Bird*), he reflects critically upon the role of such statuary, its alienating impact upon the colonial subject. These monuments he calls "stammaments", a neologism which names a predicament while exemplifying the innovation which seeks to overcome it, the taking of linguistic liberties aimed at decolonizing the word:

> and yet there are those stammaments in stone
> that smile
>
> are fat or romanesque, athletic like good traffic
> cops
>
> piercing or blind to the world but never look
> ing like us
>
> *Sun Poem*, 62

Combining 'monument' and 'stammer', "stammament" says that such material inscriptions obstruct autochthonous culture, impede the emergence of postcolonial speech. It also says that postcolonial speech begins in a stammer, as in one of the poems in *Islands*, 'Negus':

> It
> it
> it
> it is not
>
> it
> it
> it
> it is not
>
> it is not
> it is not
> it is not enough
> it is not enough to be free
> of the red white and blue
> of the drag, of the dragon
>
> it is not
> it is not
> it is not enough
> it is not enough to be free
> of the whips, principalities and powers
> where is your kingdom of the Word?
>
> *The Arrivants*, 222

A further component of the coinage "stammament", the word 'stamen' we see suggestions of, implies that obstruction and the stutter it occasions are germinal, generative. Brathwaite, at the end of *Sun Poem*, speaks of "beating ... genesis // out of the stammering world" (*Sun Poem*, 97).

The difference between the pebble and the statue is not simply one of size. The statue is representational. It appropriates the solidity and the durability of stone to give a look of permanence, unalterability, to what is merely a regime. Size matters, however, in that the scale of monumental statuary not only magnifies and bestows grandeur but also suggests a coherence, a totalization, of which the smallness and the dispersion of pebbles imply the opposite. The statue is integrative, the pebble particulate. The statue is symbolic, the pebble semiotic. In accenting the pebble, Brathwaite counters the apparent solidity, impermeability and permanence of the social relations monumental statuary is meant to reinforce. His insistence upon the pebble is an insistence upon particles and provisionality, upon the gaps, fissures and volatility masked by monumental appearance. His "return to the pebble" primarily alerts us to the monumentality of language itself, the role played by notions of a stable, standard English in the maintenance of metropolitan norms. Returning to the smallest particles of language, syllables and letters, he assaults the apparent solidity and integrity of words, destabilizing them (showing them to be intrinsically unstable) by emphasizing the points at which they break, disassembling them and reassembling them in alternate spellings and neologistic coinages.

The second poem in *Islands*, 'Ananse', invokes its namesake trickster-creator as a "dry stony world-maker, word-breaker" (*The Arrivants*, 167). In *Mother Poem*, Brathwaite identifies the mother figure with Ananse, saying that "spiders make patterns in her mind" and having her say, "i is spiders weavin / away" (*Mother Poem*, 25, 99). Both are word-breakers: "me mudda // brek / de word" (*Mother Poem*, 59). Both are figures for an activity which increasingly takes place in Brathwaite's poems. Line breaks which occur in the midst of a word are the most persistent instance of such activity, occurring regularly throughout *The Arrivants* and continuing in more idiosyncratic fashion in the second trilogy. In *The Arrivants* and in *Mother Poem*, such breaks are hyphenated:

> spark eye
> crackle o' bone-
>
> juice an de whole sing-
> in forest on fire: whisp-

erin whips on de shiv-
erin stone o de kitch-

en where she turns
alone to the o-

ven burn-
in burn-

in world
without

world with-
out world

without
end

Mother Poem, 92-93

Beginning in *Sun Poem*, however, the hyphens are frequently dropped, making the breaks more emphatic, as in this passage from *X/Self*:

chad sinks

sa
hara wakes out slowly

the dry snake of the harm
attan the harmattan reaches into our wells into our smiles in

to our cook
ing pot oil in

to the water re
flecting our walls in

to the bone
of the mutton in

to our dry
gully eyes

X/Self, 32

Words are broken not only by line breaks but by punctuation marks inserted between syllables and even between letters within the same syllable. *Mother Poem* introduces a use of the slash which we see in *Sun Poem* and *X/Self* as well:

hear the pen/nies drop/in
lissen while they fall
ev/ry one for jee/sus
he shall have them all

drop/in drop/in drop/in drop/in
hear those pen/nies fall
ev/ry one for jee/sus
he shall have them all
Mother Poem, 11

Colons are also employed in this way. We find "i:ron" and "us:ed" in *Mother Poem* (45, 97), "us:ed" in *Sun Poem* as well (93), "immo-bil:e" in *X/Self* (31). *Sun Poem* introduces the use of spacing to break words:

we're going to a wonderful place
we're going to a won der ful place
over the hills and far away
we're going to a wonder full place
Sun Poem, 40

X/Self takes this farther, employing spacing and punctuation, a period, at the same time:

for if the laws be crook. ed
if pathways to the palace where/in
justice/es are not made strait

there will be
buildings rushing upwards on a scream of sand
X/Self, 20

These practices remind us, at the graphic level, of the divisibility and the alterability of words, their permeability to alternate arrangement, variability, change. The visibility these practices accord variation, their graphic departure from standard, presumably stable procedure, undermines monumental premises. Again, landscape and wordscape correspond, the permeability of words recalling that of the poet's native ground. "This poem," Brathwaite writes of *Mother Poem*, "is about porous limestone: my mother, Barbados"(*Mother Poem*, ix). The permeability of words, their susceptibility to alternate arrangement, is also made evident in the second trilogy by a recourse to anagrammatic rearrangement, a permutability which also leads to idiosyncratic spellings, puns and "sound-word" coinages. In *Mother Poem*, "mane" anagrammatically alters 'name' and 'mean', "nan" plays upon 'ann', "nam" upon 'man' and so forth (*Mother Poem*, 55, 74-75). Likewise, 'glided' is rendered "gilded" in *Sun Poem*, where we also find 'lion' and 'loin' played upon one another and the neologism "godderal" derived from 'doggerel' (*Sun Poem*, 13, 49), while in *X/Self* we see "for/nicalia" derived from 'california' and so on (*X/Self*, 88).

Rearrangements of the particles — the pebbles — of language advance phonic and semantic as well as orthographic alterations. In 'Ananse,' Brathwaite says that the spider, the "word-breaker," "squats on the tips // of our language," going on to speak of it spinning "webs of sound" and "revealing... shadows of meaning" (*The Arrivants*, 165-166). His recourse to punning, the suggestion of 'stairs' in the lines "he stumps up the stares / of our windows" (*The Arrivants*, 165), exemplifies the Ananseen tactic the poem announces. Already in 'Jah', the first poem in *Islands*, Brathwaite has referred to "bridges of sound" (*The Arrivants*, 162). He increasingly exploits these bridges, the "webs of sound" which connect a word to other words ('shatter' to 'chatter', 'empire' to 'umpire'), the echoes of other words and other meanings within a word. Words are reopened, broken open, their semantic integrity unsealed by "shadows of meaning" which are played upon and thereby shown to permeate "the Word".

Throughout the second trilogy, the meanings activated through word play do tend to be "shadowy," accentuating the negative, "dark," dysfunctional character of the status quo. Early in *Mother Poem*, in 'Bell', a warehouse is called a "wear- // house," underscoring the damage done to the speaker's husband, who worked in it:

> i never did know when he start comin home
> wid a wheeze: wid a cough: wid a stone in e chess
> so he cud hardly breed, c'dear
>
> when de duss dat e ketch in dat sun-
> dayless wear-
>
> house
> brek e up like a stick
>
> *Mother Poem*, 13

In 'Pig mornin', thirty-five cents become "dirty-five cents" (*Mother Poem*, 30). Likewise, a shamrock is called a "shame- / rock," weekly pay is called "weakly pay" and the ill effects of being unable to read and write are orthographically highlighted in 'Miss Own':

> for the shoe is a safe cottage to the illiterate peasant
> needing light, running water, the indestructible plastic of the soft ill
> lit/erate present
> *Mother Poem*, 35-36

Farther on in the book, the merchant/owner doesn't simply sit in the great house; we're told that he "shits in the great house" (*Mother Poem*, 54). Farther still, grass rather than growing is said to be "growling along the hillside," panes of glass are called "pains of glass," steps that go no farther are said to "go no father," daily bread is "dearly bread," a kingdom is a "king/doom" and so on (*Mother Poem*, 77-79, 83, 85). This tendency continues in *Sun Poem* and *X/Self*.

The phonic and semantic slippages Brathwaite cultivates resonate with reminders of injury and deprivation, wounds which run deep in the social fabric. These resonances are dissonances, reminders of discord, disharmony, disaster. In *Mother Poem*, he coins a term, "skeletone", which names and is an instance of this (*Mother Poem*, 17, 40). The term recalls his announcement in *Islands*: "I will sing songs of the skeleton" (*The Arrivants*, 219). His work, that is, will disinter the dead and recall the injustices they were done, resound with the ringing of bones, the "skeletonality" evoked in 'Cherries':

> she will bend forward with the hoe: *huh*
> and the gravel will answer her: *so*
>
> she will swing upward with the hoe: *huh*
> and the bones of the plantation will come ringing to meet her: *so*
> *Mother Poem*, 77-78

The ringing of bones redefines resonance, takes it in a direction contrary to expectation. It is a ringing which can only be imagined, a ringing which is difficult to imagine. Hearing the dull thud of bone as resonance epitomizes and offers an apt figure for Brathwaite's antithetic, oppositional poetics. Rooted in social disaffection and critique, "skeletonality" submits the ground to a qualitative audit, accenting the toll taken by the plantation past and its continuing repercussions.

In *Mother Poem*, bones ring in contrast and opposition to bells whose conventional resonance represents dominance and regimentation, the ruling order:

> quick step/chip step
> as punctual as cat'olic bells
> *Mother Poem*, 15

The bells are those of school as well as church, the teacher Chalkstick's bicycle bells (*Mother Poem*, 19, 22) and

> ... the sound of schoolbells
> squares: triangles: hookey hockey matches
>
> desks: gas chambers: forward march
> *Mother Poem*, 24

Brathwaite makes the intent of "skeletonality" clear very early: "bell that i will break and pour its sound in the vèvè" (*Mother Poem*, 8). His writing, emulating the symbolic chalk designs which are drawn on the ground as part of *vodoun* ritual, will alter sound to mark the African presence in the West Indies. Through the figures of bell and bone he offers a thematization of sound which is concomitant with his work's phonic dislocations. Bone is an alternate bell, an antithetic bell suggesting not only victimization but also revolt, a movement toward liberation ("let freedom ring"). The deployment of these figures in *Mother Poem* recalls a conflation of corpse and bell at one point in *Islands*, where the hanged body of Paul Bogle, leader of a nineteenth-century revolt, is called a "dead bell":

> chapel bells bringing freedom's
> dark clash, bayonet's clangour of iron
> on chain, Bogle's legs swinging steep from their steeple of pain,
> dead clapper, dead leader, dead bell,
> leaden tongue, the snapped neck
> slacker and slacker
> *The Arrivants*, 233

This "dead clapper, ... / leaden tongue" is an earlier version of "skeletone".

"Skeletonality" indicts and rebels against English, takes revenge on the language of empire, implicating English and its presumed norms in the subjugation of colonized people. Brathwaite, as have many colonial/postcolonial writers, critiques the role of the schools, disseminators of "the Word," in the maintenance of metropolitan dominance. In *Islands*, he writes:

> they go to school to the head-
> master's cries,
>
> read a black-
> board of words, angles,
> lies;
> they fall
>
> over their examinations.
> It is a fence that surrounds them.
> *The Arrivants*, 174-175

He also speaks of the "cottonfields of Oxford" (*The Arrivants*, 168). In *Mother Poem*, the equation of colonial/neo-colonial education with mystification and miseducation continues:

> how can there be a carved trail
> when schools teach their children blasphemies:
> the blasphemy that the word is law when spoken by an english
> engineer
> that our teaching must reflect these verities
> *Mother Poem*, 31

He speaks of "children locked up into their cell // blocks of school" (*Mother Poem*, 25). His calling a student "another black hostage / of verbs" (*Mother Poem*, 24) indicates the crucial, synecdochic relationship of language to the regimentation the schools impose. Liberties taken with language are thus acts of defiance. They curse and condemn the language from whose norms they diverge. Brathwaite writes of the mother figure in *Mother Poem*, the word-breaker: "she crumples words into curses" (*Mother Poem*, 47). He has already, on the same page, called her "black sycorax my mother," identifying the speaker in the poem with Shakespeare's anagrammatic invention, Caliban. Her "curses" thus recall Caliban's lines in *The Tempest*, spoken to Prospero: "You taught me language, and my profit on't / Is, I know how to curse".

Brathwaite notes in *X/Self* that "Caliban has become an anti-colonial/Third World symbol of cultural and linguistic revolt" (*X/Self*, 116).[1] An identification of the second trilogy's linguistic license with Caliban's "profit" is explicitly made in the notes to *Sun Poem*, where he dubs the coinages to which he increasingly resorts "calibanisms". The term "cavicle", for example, he defines as a "'calibanism' for clavicle; the cave between neck and collarbone" (*Sun Poem*, 100). Brathwaite has argued that language was the area in which enslaved Africans most successfully rebelled against their masters, refusing to speak as they were taught but instead using — and abusing — English in ways which made it their own. He makes this argument in *The Development of Creole Society in Jamaica 1770-1820*, in a chapter entitled 'The "Folk" Culture of the Slaves'. As his use of the Ananse figure makes clear, in his linguistic experimentation he takes his cue from West Indian folk culture, the vernacular recasting of English he calls nation-language. His ability to sound and see 'cave' in 'clavicle' to fashion "cavicle" recalls a nation-language term such as "likkle", which manages to sound a suggestion of 'lick' and 'trickle' one might otherwise not hear in the word 'little'. The troubling accent he brings to bear upon English, the shadows of sound and meaning he brings out in a word, emulates the qualitative audit to which 'down' seems to have been put to become 'dung' in folk pronunciation.

It is not surprising, then, that nation-language itself assumes a much more prominent, pervasive role in the second trilogy than in the first. In *The Arrivants*, nation-language tends to be isolated, reserved for individual poems such as 'The Dust', 'Rites' and 'Cane' (*The Arrivants*, 62-69, 197-203, 225-229), rather than dispersed and disseminated throughout the work as in *Mother Poem*, *Sun Poem* and *X/Self*. In the second trilogy, Brathwaite addresses the challenge he spoke of in an interview conducted by Stewart Brown in 1989: "I think the real challenge for the artist who knows his English and mediates between the two languages is to develop an English which increasingly reflects the nature of nation-language".[2] His "calibanisms" do this, inventing a third lexicon which is neither English nor nation-language in work which, while continuing to use English, makes greater use of nation-language, of its particular syntax and grammar as well as individual words. English is shown to be subject to alternate arrangement at the phrasal and sentence levels as well as at the lexical level. Nation-language grammar and syntax do with words and parts of speech what anagrammatic rearrangements do with letters:

> an to know that he hads was to walk down de noon
> down dat long windin day
> to we home
>
> *Mother Poem*, 15

Inspired by nation-language, Brathwaite increasingly takes grammatic and syntactic liberties with English, as when in *Sun Poem* he writes of the fishermen "walking out of the night down the street ahead of the sun and under the leaves of the seagrape and cordia trees whose flowers were fast fading stars in the touching them softly night" (*Sun Poem*, 25). The adjectival placement of "touching them softly" reorders accepted usage, 'the light which was touching them softly'.

In addition to nation-language, Brathwaite has taken Afro-Caribbean religious and musical practices as models of cultural self-definition, examples of Calibanic resistance and a creative response to social dislocation. In *Islands*, the poem 'Caliban' evokes two such practices, steel band music and limbo, thematizing "silence" as a limbo stick which must be gone under, a "long dark night" to be undergone. This thematization continues the emphasis put on non-speech in 'Shepherd', the poem which precedes it, a poem in which the African pantheon is "dumb," awaiting and eventually, through music, achieving "speech"(*The Arrivants*, 185-190). The second section of 'Caliban' ends:

> Ban
> Ban
> Cal-
> iban like to play
> pan at the Car-
> nival;
> dip-
> ping down
> and the black
> gods call-
> ing, back
> he falls
> through the water's
> cries
> down
> down
> down
> where the music hides
> him
> down
> down
> down
> where the si-
> lence lies.
>
> *The Arrivants*, 193

The third section ends:

> out of the dark
> and the dumb gods are raising me
>
> up
> up
> up
>
> and the music is saving me
>
> hot
> slow
> step
>
> on the burning ground.
> *The Arrivants*, 195

The play on dumbness, playing dumb and the double meaning of "the si- / lence lies" are tokens of a bifurcation between two types of telling, what is said and what is said through not being said. The dumb gods are not really dumb and to go down is to come back up. The silence lies in more ways than one.

Silence, as John Cage, Pierre Macherey and others have pointed out, is unacknowledged sound. The Calibanic gesture is one of sounding silence, plumbing sounds which would otherwise not be heard. Brathwaite's thematization of silence is part and parcel of his thematization of the word, for silence is meaning and sound suppressed by a linguistico-cultural regime calling itself "the Word". We find his recourse to the figure of silence accompanied by images of hyperaudition, another aspect of qualitative audit. These images report a heightened auditory perception of the natural environment, implicitly critiquing the constricted hearing regulated by "the Word," an order of relative silence in which "men make noises / louder than the sea's / voices" (*The Arrivants*, 205). These images project sounds and acts of hearing we would otherwise not imagine. In Islands, "clinks / of dew in the grass," "the polyp's thunder," "the boom / of the mango bursting its sweetness" and "the creak of forests" in a carved block of wood are all said to have been heard (*The Arrivants*, 178, 232-233, 243). In *Mother Poem*, grass is heard "growling" (77). In *Sun Poem*, we read of "a sun that he [Adam] heard in his ears" and are later told that "the sand always tinkled when he dived near the shore" (*Sun Poem*, 6, 25). When, in *Islands*, we read of waves "lap- // ping these shores with their silence" (*The

Arrivants, 238), having already been told of human sounds outshouting "the sea's / voices," we know that 'silence' is a relative term, referring to repressed articulacies whose mouthpiece the poet aims to become:

> and I see you, my wound-
> ed gift giver of sea
> spoken syllables: words salt on your lips
> on my lips
> *The Arrivants*, 238

Repressed articulacy is also emergent energy and anger, an apocalyptic return of the repressed whose harbinger silence becomes in the poem 'Anvil' "dark, defeated silence" become "a destroying silence" (*The Arrivants*, 249-250).

The sea, whose "lap- // ping ... silence" Brathwaite invokes, he calls "my mother / of water" (*The Arrivants*, 238). In the final poem in *Mother Poem*, 'Driftword', he returns to this conjunction of mother, sea and silence, writing of "her silent gutters of word-fall" and "the breaking of her flesh with foam" in the concluding lines of the book (*Mother Poem*, 117) — giving silence, as it were, the last word. Tobago-born Marlene Nourbese Philip writes of silence in ways which are relevant here. In the introduction to her book of poetry *She Tries Her Tongue, Her Silence Softly Breaks*, she writes of "the anguish that is English in colonial societies". She argues that the acquisition of English by Africans brought to the West Indies was as much deprivation as acquisition. To speak English was to acquiesce to the subordinate position — "the non-being of the African" — it meted out, to silence one's Africanity, self-image and experience:

> The paradox at the heart of the acquisition of this language is that the African learned both to speak and to be dumb at the same time, to give voice to the experience and i-mage, yet remain silent. That silence has had profound effect upon the English-speaking African Caribbean artist working in the medium of words.[3]

In a more recent work, *Looking for Livingstone: An Odyssey of Silence*, she gives silence a more positive, regenerative value, having the protagonist, identified only as The Traveller, reflect at one point: "in finding my own Silence I was finding my own power — of transformation". This reflection occurs following a conversation in which The Traveller is advised to weave "something new," composed of "word *and* silence":

> "...neither word alone, nor silence alone, but word and silence — weave, patch, sew together and remember it is *your* silence — all yours, untouched and uncorrupted. The word does not belong to you — it was owned and whored by others long, long before you set out on your travels — whore words." Then she laughed. "But to use your silence, you have to use the word."
> "Whore words?" I asked.
> "Yes, and there's the rub, my dear," she said, and gently drew me close and held me — "there's the rub — you need the word — whore words — to weave your silence."[4]

She is given this advice during her stay in the "land of needlewomen and weavers," the NEECLIS, a people whose name, like those of all the others with whom she stays during her travels, is an anagram of 'silence'.

As Philip's Traveller moves from the land of the ECNELIS to the land of the LENSECI and from there to that of the SCENILE and so forth, the anagrammatic play induces a sense less of movement than of stasis, a sense of being stuck within orthographic permutations whose parameters are all too clearly defined. The book's liberatory assertions notwithstanding, we sense the limits imposed by verbal discourse, a sense of limits which makes its thematization of silence all the more understandable and compelling. This brings to mind a comment on Samuel Beckett's work made by Ihab Hassan in *The Literature of Silence*:

> In a certain sense, all his works may be thought of as a parody of Ludwig Wittgenstein's notion that language is a set of games, akin to the arithmetic of primitive tribes. Beckett's parodies, which are full of self-spite, reveal a general tendency in anti-literature, one that Hugh Kenner describes brilliantly: "the dominant intellectual analogy of the present age is drawn not from biology, not from psychology (though these are sciences we are knowing about), but from general number theory". Art in a closed field thus becomes an absurd game of permutations, like Molloy sucking stones at the beach; and "the retreat from the word" — the phrase is George Steiner's — reduces language to pure ratio.[5]

Molloy sucking stones at the beach is not unrelated to Brathwaite's Caliban surrounded by pebbles — an absurdist kinship confirmed by a reference to the myth of Sisyphus, the founding myth of Albert

Camus's absurdism, on the back cover of Brathwaite's recent book of poetry, *Middle Passages:* "It marks a Sisyphean stage of Third World history in which things fall apart and everyone's achievements come tumbling back down upon their heads and into their hearts, like the great stone which King Sisyphus was condemned to keep heaving back up the same hill in hell".[6] The Sisyphean strain, however, is nothing new. It has been a feature of Brathwaite's work at least since *Rights of Passage*, whose opening poem, 'Prelude', exhorts, "Build now / the new / villages," and again, two pages later, "So build build / again the new / villages," only to announce at the end, "Flame burns the village down" (*The Arrivants*, 4-8). We find it again in the epigraph to *Islands* taken from James Baldwin's *Tell Me How Long the Train's Been Gone,* a passage in which a sense of long-awaited achievement is dispelled by the announcement "that it was all to be done again"(*The Arrivants*, 160).

It would be a mistake to read Brathwaite's work as a simple, triumphalist vindication of nation-language, a simple act of Calibanic restitution. The accent put upon silence at the end of *Mother Poem* — "so she lies / mutter of echoes, folded to silence" (*Mother Poem*, 114) — issues a caveat regarding linguistic projects, a warning which applies to both conformity and revolt. This recourse to metaphoric silence, to a thematization of silence, is the Sisyphean strain brought to bear upon language. It problematizes not only English but language in general, revealing that Brathwaite's Calibanic play is not a positivist pursuit of an ultimate adequation afforded by a new, presumably unproblematic language. The all but fiendish delight Brathwaite takes in the slippage to which words are prone raises doubts as to whether such erosion could ever be curtailed. Hence the parodic tendency in the work, a tendency which appears to have turned on the work itself when we get to a parody of Calibanic revolt such as the following:

and we marched upon the palace
declaring that the governor was black
and that his concubines would go abroad in naturelles or afro

wigs

we entered the holy carbolic echoing church
cool clean heel heil
and the madonna was made over in the image of my sister

hale mary full of grease

the lard is with thee
Mother Poem, 106-107

Likewise, the lisp with which Esse speaks in *Sun Poem* (73-83) further dislocates an English already dislocated by nation-language, as if to suggest that language, all language, is irremediable drift — a suggestion already made by the title of the final poem in *Mother Poem*, 'Driftword'.

Woven into Brathwaite's linguistic liberties is a wish for what lies beyond language and sound. This is one of the further implications of "skeletonality". The "bell that i will break and pour its sound in the vèvè" signals not only a breaking of sound but a breaking away from sound, breaking away into synaesthetic translation. In a note regarding this line, Brathwaite points out that in the Barbadian church "the bell is used as censer" (*Mother Poem*, 120). The bell, chiming "with a sound like breaking glass," is swung from side to side as though wafting scent — a synaesthetic swing into a silence of sorts, sound as incense. It is a swing which recalls the silent-synaesthetic trajectories in *Islands*, where "the eye screams" but is admitted to be "dumb," an anaesthetic-synaesthetic order of "the closed eye / broken eardrum" (*The Arrivants*, 186, 256, 211). Images of silence and sensory deprivation conspire with images of hyperaudition, suggesting an appetite for meaning and sensation large enough to squeeze the last drop of sound and sense from the world and from words. "Skeletonality," the bell whose chime we can't quite hear, like Wilson Harris's "Well of Silence,"[7] wrings the word.

Notes

1. For a discussion of such use of Caliban by West Indian and African writers, see Rob Nixon's 'Caribbean and African Appropriations of *The Tempest*' in *Politics and Poetic Value*, ed. Robert von Hallberg (Chicago: University of Chicago Press, 1987), 185-206.
2. Stewart Brown, 'Interview with Kamau Brathwaite', *Kyk-over-al* 40, December 1989, 85.
3. Marlene Nourbese Philip *She Tries Her Tongue, Her Silence Softly Breaks* (Charlottetown, Prince Edward Island: Ragweed Press, 1989), 16.
4. Marlene Nourbese Philip, *Looking for Livingstone: An Odyssey of Silence* (Stratford, Ontario: Mercury Press, 1991), 52-53.
5. Ihab Hassan, *The Literature of Silence: Henry Miller and Samuel Beckett*

(New York: Knopf, 1967), 9.

6. Kamau Brathwaite, *Middle Passages* (Newcastle-upon-Tyne: Bloodaxe Books, 1992), back cover.
7. Wilson Harris, *The Eye of the Scarecrow* (London: Faber and Faber, 1965), 95.

Stewart Brown

Sun Poem: The Rainbow Sign?

The Sun made patterns on the water that gave birth to children...[1]

In 'Timehri', an article he published in 1970, just after the three books which make up *The Arrivants* had appeared, Brathwaite asserted that

> The most significant feature of West Indian life and imagination since Emancipation has been its sense of rootlessness, of not belonging to the landscape; dissociation, in fact, of art from the act of living[2]

It was a condition of alienation evident at many levels of society but perhaps has its roots in the kinds of childhood memories Brathwaite describes in *Sun Poem*:

> not knowing the names of our flowers and trees
>
> scratchywist womans tongue hogplum stinkin toe
> we could only call our brothers robin hood
> or barnabas collins
> *Sun Poem*, 20

The task, and achievement, of the first generation of post colonial West Indian authors, he argued, had been to identify and analyse that fragmented consciousness. The task of the second generation, among whom he included himself, was to "transcend and heal it".

At the beginning of *Rights of Passage*, the first book of *The Arrivants* and so the start of Brathwaite's self conscious attempt at that healing, Tom, the distressed voice of the displaced African's travail through history, anticipates the sign that will mark the end of his search for stability, for home:

> the rainbow
> of Heaven:
> God's curved
> mourning
> calling
> 'Tom', *The Arrivants*, 14

Sun Poem, which is written in "the voices of the rainbow" is perhaps that sign. Certainly Tom's descendants, the voices of *Sun Poem*, have settled at — and for — what they must make home, the poem developing a focus on the history and culture of Barbados, Brathwaite's own home island, that was begun in *Mother Poem*. If *Mother Poem* tells the herstory of Barbados, the grand/mothering tradition as well as the idea of the island as a lover whose "glitter bays" have been prostituted by tourists and property speculators, *Sun Poem* claims the 'manscape'. Told through the voices of a rainbow which arcs the middle passage between the Caribbean and Africa, between the womb and the wake, *Sun Poem* is at once Brathwaite's most personal, autobiographical poem and yet also a poem that re-examines and amplifies those issues of regional/racial history/mythology that his earlier work had begun: the strands are inextricably intertwined.

The device of the healing rainbow, reconciling sun and sea, fire and water, is one that recurs throughout Brathwaite's work. As Gordon Rohlehr remarks in his essay elsewhere in this volume the rainbow is a symbol of both Christian lore — in the story of Noah — and of African mythologies that understand the rainbow in ways that are often very similar to that Genesis usage. Rohlehr (201) explores the Dogan beliefs that are suggested by Brathwaite's own fascination with the god Damballah, but there is also an Akan tradition which reinforces the notion of the rainbow as a symbol of healing. In Akan belief, baldly put, Nyame, the supreme God is associated with water and particularly with rain. The rainbow is perceived as a beneficence that comes with the end of a storm, it is a symbol of renewal and a sign of Nyame's continued care for the people.[3] In *Sun Poem* the rainbow is linked with the Akan concept of *sunsum* to structure the interweavings and juxtapositions of the various voices. Brathwaite has used the notion of *sunsum* — which he has adapted from Akan belief — before, most explicitly in *Masks*. *Sunsum* is a man's essential spirit, passed on from father to son, a vital linkage between the ancestors, the living and the yet unborn. It is both an inheritance and a duty. In his notes to *Sun Poem* Brathwaite defines *sunsum* as "the Akan word for soul, origin of spiritual life" (*Sun Poem*, 98), elsewhere he has called it "the spiritual blood" of a man, of a people.[4] The concept is appropriate, both to a consideration of Brathwaite's personal history — the almost-a-decade he spent in Ghana, working among the Akan people, effectively gave Brathwaite his direction both as historian and poet through his recognition of that *sunsum* connection between himself and the Akan/African culture — and more broadly to the history of a West Indian island which drew most of its people and much of its culture from West Africa. Add to that the puns — which Brathwaite has always enjoyed and made much creative (and sometimes profound) use of — on sun/son and sum/total in English, and the fact that *son* is also a Cuban/Caribbean folksong form, and we have a typically Brathwaitian creolization of a concept to suit his allusive/subversive purposes.

If such 'playing' with language is characteristic of Brathwaite's poetry, so is the recognition, implicit in every act of Calibanization, that this is a power-game the poet is playing. There is a *sunsum* linkage between the language of resistance the slaves evolved on the plantation and the development of that voice into a literary language validated by the Oxford University Press, most prestigious/canonical of all British publishing houses, who published Brathwaite's major works, including *Sun Poem*. This far into Brathwaite's career, the medium is at least part of the message. Other contributors to this book have analysed Brathwaite's linguistic strategies in great detail; enough to notice here that in *Sun Poem* Brathwaite's language — perhaps because the autobiographical element of the poem is so strong — develops an allusive and many layered intensity that sets it apart from the earlier work. In *Sun Poem* Brathwaite extends the metaphor of the rainbow to demonstrate the Bajan nation-language's literary/textual capacity to express the nuances of the whole rainbow of emotions, from the gurgling elation of discovery in 'YELLOW MINNIM' to the despair beyond words of 'INDIGONE'. There is also a definite Bajan inflection to the creole as he writes it in *Sun Poem* — whatever its emotional register. The flattened tones and extended vowel sounds and the characteristic clipping of words and phrases are suggested both by his orthography and the grammatical structure of his sentences. For example:

> but hole it! doan mine if it tickle de palm a you hann...
> *Sun Poem*, 23

or:

> i doan know why i is bodder wid you
> you is only a girl an cahn unnerstann what i sayin
> *Sun Poem*, 35

This is a voice very different from a Jamaican or Trinidadian creole speaker's. The dialogue in poems like 'The Dust' and 'Rites' in *The Arrivants* use versions of this voice but it is in *Mother Poem* and particularly *Sun Poem* that this inflection is most fully developed as the appropriate voice to 'control' the poem's unfolding.

This is the inner language of the most intimate, the personal — the most private — of experiences and emotions. It becomes, in *Sun Poem*, a language that can exclude those outside its particular cultural ambit— so it is not only the girl, in the quotation above — who "cahn unnerstann". For this is also the language of the "gutter", of a particular kind of stubborn (un)cowed male cultural resistance; at its most extreme it is the "noise" of what Brathwaite has called "fundamental" nation language.

The texture of the poem oscillates along the linguistic register between the intense and often oblique internal monologues of a boy, adam, (always lower case) trying to make some sense of his world, and a plainer, more 'public' consideration of the ways the island's struggling menfolk were either emasculated or elevated into rebels by the events of the island's history. Those two narrative strands are interwoven into an over-arching ritual of cyclical regeneration. *Sun Poem* is both a sonorous invocation of the Sacred, a praise song to the Sun that is both origin and end of those in/justices that is the history re-told throughout Brathwaite's work and at the same time a *grounding* of that story in the manscape of Barbados.

Sun Poem opens in that sacred mode in 'RED RISING', the first voice of the rainbow. Red, the colour of life/blood is also, in Akan tradition, symbolic of the sun, "the male element in society". 'RED RISING' recalls the first morning of creation:

> When the wheels of the sky were being fashioned
>
> When the sky first spoke in the voice of the rainbow
> *Sun Poem*, 2

which, 'poetically', is true of each red rising dawn, and establishes the cosmic *sunsum* logic of the poem as a whole. *Sun Poem* begins then, as a poem of generation, of "origen" — a word Brathwaite glosses as "the rainbow sense (literal, moral, mystical) of origin" (*Sun Poem*, 98) and of engendering.

So, in 'ORANGE ORIGEN', the second voice of the rainbow, the boy adam, whose growing into manhood the poem traces, is introduced. For much of the poem the reader sees adam in "fletches" of imagery viewed through the prism of the rainbow. The poem is vivid with light and colour and a sense of the importance of colour — not just predictably black and white but "a dull red love", "her skin against the gooseberry light", "the sudden green sun", "a silver shadow", etc. The awareness of colours is part of adam's adjustment to a new world when his family moves from the country of his early childhood to the relatively urban setting that will characterise his school years. It is also, through the sun-sum metaphor, a comment on the experience of displacement and discovery, the seeing afresh and anew of adam's first ancestors in the 'new world' of the Caribbean. The rainbow 'enables' the connection in imagination between the experience of the boy adam and in the historical memory of the poet, Brathwaite, whom adam becomes, to be "written in light"[5] as it were.

That rainbow/arc of life metaphor is continued and deepened in 'SON', the first part of which can be read is an intense praise-song for the birth of the poet's own son. The elation of this praise-song is tinged with an awareness of the inevitable end of life's rainbow, in the indigo "ice" of oblivion, a fate made bearable only by the *sunsum* continuity suggested in the list of forefathers and sons that precedes even the epigraph to the book:

James Edward 1844
Henry Lawson 1874
Edward Hilton 1908
Lawson Edward 1930
Michael Kwesi 1958

That the dates of the deaths of the earlier forefathers are not given is significant.

The texture of the poem alternates between intense, almost magic-realist passages and much more direct slices of adam's life as a boy growing up 'on' Brown's Beach,[6] but there is a lyricism, a tenderness about the writing that we hardly find in Brathwaite's work before:

when adam jumped he saw the akee tree and the tamarind tree

when the man-faced seeds and the coconut trees in the neighbours
yard and the shine on the galvanize roofs that looked on the bay

at browns beach and the man on the beach building pyramids and
the flash of the bat of the boys playing cricket and the girls playing
shrill in that part of the sea that ended with the *wish* on the shore

Sun Poem, 13

In the confrontation with Batto, the badjohn bully boy of Brown's Beach who "never had a mother like the land-boys had and he'd never even had to go to school..." but who had been to "dodds" — the borstal style institution "with high barbed wire and the cat-o-nine-tails far far away in the country" (*Sun Poem*, 15) adam can be seen as reliving in *sumsum* miniature the struggle against oppression and injustice that later in the poem Bussa, the leader of Barbados' most significant slave rebellion undertook. But Batto — like Bussa — is a rebel and there is both disapproval and admiration in adam's attitude towards him — a characteristically Bajan ambivalence the poem seems to suggest. For if the many passages of a remembered childhood are autobiographical they are also typical of a generation, a class and a community.

So, more or less the first half of the poem is taken up with incidents from adam's life, the flux of a Bajan boyhood: his continuing sense of wonder, his fantastical theories, his diving for sea-eggs, his dreams of becoming an 'infamous sailor'. Much of this is told through precisely heard dialogues like this one between adam and his sister:

> *you think* a-
> dam started
> *you think*
>
> *i cud dive from hey to de pilot?*
>   *to de pilot?*
>   *eyes opening out from her basin of blue*
>   *to de pilot*
>   *but it faaaaar* she said slowly
> travelling back homewards over the glistance
>   *you tink yu cud dive to de pilot?*
>   *Sun Poem*, 29

These dialogues are both wonderfully evocative of an innocent process of discovery and they begin to establish the character of adam, who is already trying out 'mannish' ideas, both in his reasoning and in his relationships with women, as the voice of his sister melds into the teasing "langridge" of esse, adam's first adolescent sweetheart, later in the poem.

But before that courtship begins adam must experience an important rite of passage in the guise of a Sunday-school outing — in buses with names like Breakneck Jane and Sunny Loo — over Hearse Hill to the rocky east coast of the island where the sea

was a giant of i:ron
a rasta of water with rumbelling muscles
and turrible turrible hair
Sun Poem, 42

That trip is described in 'THE CROSSING', which Brathwaite glosses in his notes as "the Middle Passage in reverse". The journey is from the Caribbean west coast sunset side of the island, now much developed by the tourist industry, where adam's family have settled, eastwards across the island to the Atlantic coast, nearest Caribbean landfall to Africa, indeed what Brathwaite has termed elsewhere "the farthest shore of Africa". That coast has always had a particular significance for Brathwaite, explored most pointedly in *Mother Poem*. In *Sun Poem* his discovery of "the ragged coasts where the sun came from" is a revelation to adam, and the journey to that 'Africa' (the "promised land" which is also, in the *sunsum* sense, the land of his fathers) is fraught with terrors. That "crossage", back toward the sunrise, opens a "sandy redge of memories", *sunsum*/sun-son visions that mark the end of childhood innocence and usher in 'NOOM', "the sound of noon, angelus of doom".

The central section of *Sun Poem*, 'NOOM' corresponds to the green of the rainbow. Green, in the Akan tradition, is associated with 'new life', and in *The Arrivants* is symbolic of growth and transition. Here 'NOOM' marks the end of innocence and a shift of tone into the public, political voice more reminiscent of *Rights of Passage*. In sharp, livid imagery spiked with Brathwaite's characteristic dark wit, we are shown another history of the island, that which has occurred since the arrival of Europeans 'fleeing from torture and sword' who, by dint of a convenient sleight of conscience, could justify the terrible Atlantic slave trade. And although, or because, it was the slaves' labour which made the plantations prosper, Africa and slavery were erased from the official memory, and all things associated with that past denigrated, from the language of "beach bus and gutter" to the gods of the Middle Passage whose apparent demise is chronicled in the powerful dream-prose (anticipating the *DreamStories*) of the second part of 'NOOM'. In the folk memory the African Loa — or spirit guide — emerged from the Atlantic, 'farthest shore', climbed to the highest part of the island, surveyed the condition of his displaced people and:

gazing full at the sun that was beating tormenting drums in his head he had raised his head in a shout so loud it had

entered the gullies and rocks and was heard in the hills and
howls of that place with a sound of wind in a cavern

it was noon

and his cry grew greater as the pain of the world grew black
for him and he staggered and fell slipped staggered and fell
down hackletons cliff
Sun Poem, 52

dead, into the sea. The denial of Africa is further represented in the transformation of the sun from deity, object of reverence and worship (to the extent that Akan society had/has a Sun King, avowed son of the Sun God) to, in the scientific/sanitized colonial ambience of twentieth century Barbados, a negative force that

...bores holes in leaf and paper
that destroys arches and the parchment of industry
it is a baas eyed gaoler keeping our people back
Sun Poem, 55

Such distortion and rejection of the past Brathwaite identifies as the cause of the alienation and rootlessness which *The Arrivants* chronicled.

However, the poem argues, the African spirit didn't die but rather went underground, becoming the race-memory of the folk, the stoicism of the exploited, and only surfaced in acts of defiance like Bussa's slave rebellion or "brave words (spoken) from pulpits". It became a dream, a rebellion of spirit symbolised in *Sun Poem* by Hannibal, the African ancestor whose daring achieved what the white world thought impossible. Hannibal is invoked as the 'BLUE LOA', whose submerged remembrance implicitly permeates the very coral of 'little England', but the blues is essentially a music of despair and in 'CLIPS' we are shown appropriate images — film clips — from the half-lives of the island's fathers: "the secular bourgeoisie family man of the property owning classes" with his financial worries and his sly peccadilloes; the hustlers, cool in

dread dark glasses rhygin hat
ites goatee beard jah voice and i-man gait
Sun Poem, 69

and between them the 'ordinary' men, those "mechanic clerk police/ men" whose lives inexorably shrank to a cycle of sweat and debt:

the houses we lived in
were rented, pay packet by freddies, food
cigarette bettin shop races de wife ina turn an me
monthly down puna cycle
Sun Poem, 70

The poem is both celebration and lamentation of their lives:

....heroes were in books
and few of our fathers were heroes
Sun Poem, 61

so the sons lacked models of either ambition or achievement. Even the public statues, the "stammaments", never looked "like us". But the poem would understand and honour the unsung accomplishments of Bajan men — carpenters, fishermen, teachers, civil servants — who literally made Barbados. Becoming what it demands, the poem includes a beautifully measured tribute to the 'invisible' enablers of the one class of Bajan warrior/heroes the society would acknowledge, men like Manny Martindale, Herman Griffiths, Wes Hall, Garfield Sobers, Joel Garner, Malcolm Marshall... but

there is still no memorial epigraph
to those thick-set quick-step groundsmen
who watered the crust of west indian cricket
Sun Poem, 62

Although adam reappears in 'RETURN OF THE SUN', old enough to be courting now and ambitious to engender his own son/sums, the poem is shading from blue to indigo and the darkness of old age. 'FLETCHES' is an affectionate, honouring, portrait of a father by his son, composed in "flashes of sunlight", those mysterious images that defy chronology or dating but often comprise the only link with that "place I didn't know a time I can't remember" which is childhood. And 'INDIGONE' is an anguished account of a family funeral

grand
father dead my father's further genitor
of futures past my borning ancestor

still burning in a room he'd left
and still lay in
Sun Poem, 92

But the inevitable and appropriate sadness of the occasion is redeemed, at least in memory, by the *sunsum* certainty of the poet and the poem. For out of the darkness of violet comes 'SON', the last voice of the rainbow, another startlingly vivid creation story which both recalls and anticipates that first 'RED RISING' where the dead man's:

> thrill-
> dren are coming up coming up coming up
> and the sun
>
> new.
>
> *Sun Poem*, 97

Sun Poem holds a pivotal position in Brathwaite's poetry — it arcs back to *Masks*, the central poem of *The Arrivants*, developing and reinforcing the connections between African mythology and Caribbean history, it lays the spiritual ground for *X/Self*, the final book of the second trilogy, which explores the possibilities for a protean Caribbean persona, born of the his-&-her/stories explored in *Mother Poem* and *Sun Poem*. Although he has written other poems, has moved towards a kind of prose in his diaries and dreamstories, Brathwaite has often spoken of his intention to write three interrelated trilogies which will together form a kind of grand Caribbean epic as his major creative enterprise. If we chart these books on a rainbow arch:

Sun Poem
Mother Poem *X/Self*
Islands *3:1*
Masks *3:2*
RoP *3:3*

then *Sun Poem*, his most self-knowing work, is the key stone, the "Noom" of Brathwaite's bow of creativity. The cyclical *sunsum* structure of the poem is essentially optimistic, healing, and *Sun Poem* can be read as a synthesis and focusing of all that had come before it in the way it interweaves the personal and the public, history and notions of home, the cosmic and the commonplace grist of Bajan life. But if *Sun Poem* represents the zenith of that rainbow arch, the height of optimism as it were, then it may also mark "the angelus of doom" in Brathwaite's work, announcing/anticipating darker explorations yet to come.

Notes

1. Pre-Columbian creation myth/sun poem, cited in Jacques Soustell, *The Art of Ancient Mexico* (London, Thames and Hudson, 1967).
2. 'Timehri', *Savacou* 2, 1970, 35.
3. I am indebted to Dr. Tom McKaskie, of the Centre of West African Studies, University of Birmingham, an authority on Akan mythology and Ashanti history, for this account.
4. Notes to *The Arrivants*, 275.
5. The phrase echoes Brathwaite's description of his method of composition on the word processor, "writing in light". See Stewart Brown, 'Interview with Edward Kamau Brathwaite', *Kyk-over-al* 40, December 89, 87.
6. In *Sun Poem* Brathwaite makes a distinction between the real "beach-boys" who lived there and the "land-boys" who only played on the beach. His sense of himself as being between the two cultures that distinction represents is explored in his essay 'Timehri', *Savacou* 2, 1970, 35-44.

Gordon Rohlehr

The Rehumanization of History: Regeneration of Spirit: Apocalypse and Revolution in Brathwaite's *The Arrivants* and *X/Self*

I
The Dehumanization of History

The Arrivants, particularly its central movement, *Masks*, is about the process where History is absorbed in Time's neuter and neutralizing continuum. Poems such as 'Chad' and 'Timbuctu' make this point with their respective focus on pre- and post-historical times, within the timeless context of the Sahara. Contemplating the ruins of the once great centre of learning and trade,Timbuctu, Brathwaite wonders what after all is the meaning of History, the accumulated bequest of human activity, in face of Marvellian "deserts of vast eternity".

Yet Brathwaite is centrally concerned with a History that he presents as dense, multi-layered, many-dimensioned and meaningful. He focuses both on its particularities and on the vast wide frame of human movement and making, within which particular moments of History are located. Human creative spirit saturates and energizes History, recalling and redeeming it from Time's neutralizing void. The constant impulse to make and move beyond, enables humankind to break a cyclic process of creation, destruction and reconstruction which could otherwise be seen as both implacable and pointless. *The Arrivants* and *X/Self* both explore the human impulse to make and move beyond, as well as to destroy and reconstruct.

If Time neutralizes human effort, thus existentially 'dehumanizing' History, humans in quite another sense are prime contributors to the dehumanization of their own activity. Brathwaite's focus on History as particular and willed human activity, has resulted in the prominence in his writing of concern with the question of human responsibility for the shape that History assumes. Thus, the central thrust of his writing has been less towards an illumination of Time as neutralizing agent, and more towards an appreciation of people as both the dehumanizers and rehumanizers of History.

This has involved exploration of the complementary aspects of the human Spirit: its destructive and creative impulses, and their strange interplay in the generation of History and civilization. In *The Arrivants*, Brathwaite's focus is on the interplay of African, Afro-American, Caribbean and Euro-American histories. There is, however, a widening of concern with Native American and Meso-American histories in *X/Self*, which is about Empire, its consequences and probable future, from Rome to the present time. *X/Self* makes it now possible to view *The Arrivants* as a major stage in the unfolding development of an idea concerning the unimmaculate conception of the New World.

Brathwaite locates the seed of origin in the disintegration of Rome and the outward encircling movement of the vulture of empire and conquest:

> rome burns
> and our slavery begins
>
> vultures wheel over kiev over kybir over ayub khan
> vultures wheel over the ganges over the crossed swords of shiva
>
> over the dead garden of mahatma gandhi
>
> vultures wheel over the styx over maggoire over the ice
> brick blocks of the alphs
>
> over the frozen body of el cid . of lidless legba l'ouverture
>
> ...
>
> they wheel high over the desert over tripoli and tunis over
> the head waters of the nile over
>
> chad over timbuctu over lagos over ile ife over ibadan and the
> fat markets of abomey
>
> 'Salt', *X/Self*, 8-9

The outward movement of the vulture, that is, of the destructive aspect of Spirit, touches the entire world. African slavery is simply one manifestation of the vulture, but it is one of the worst because slavery, the conversion of human being into capital, is a prime act in humanity's ceaseless dehumanization of History, lacerating both flesh and Spirit.

Slavery served as a catalyst in the propulsion of the material avarice of capitalism into societies which soon became enmeshed in systems of production and marketing they could not, and still cannot dream to control. Brathwaite describes the growth of capitalism in terms which suggest that once unleashed, it developed into an almost autonomous machine that even its inventors could not control. The poems in *X/Self* entitled 'Mont Blanc' and 'Nuum' *(X/Self,* 31-36) describe the emergence of this machine, the development of its technology, and its devastating impact on the rest of the world.

Brathwaite is even more explicit in a lecture entitled 'Metaphors of Underdevelopment: A Proem for Hernan Cortez', where he claims that Europe, still feeling disequilibrium after the collapse of the Roman Empire, stabilized itself by the evolution of a new world order, centred not on the mediaeval union of Church and State machines, but on money.

> and then money (MAMMON) became the centre of this shattered universe: markets, bourgs, bourse, traders, banks, bourgeoisie, taxes, tax-collectors, regulations, fines, prisons, leviathan, navigation, war, commerce, merchants, mercantilism; travel to new lands, explore, exploit, control: the shift of power outwards: spire, spear, arrow, bullet, cannonshot, ship, sail, horse, *the charge of the light brigade;* print, bible, heaven; the conquest of sky by sun-jet angel missile. no prayer, but purse, no custom anymore but customhouse and curse. marco polo overland to china; the portuguese by stepping stone to africa; columbus to san salvador; looking for power, for powder, gun/powder; converting the grain to gain, unholy grail.
>
> therefore: montezuma collapsed; chitzen itza defeated; geronimo doomed: saschatewa, mohica, esquimaux and whale worshippers are marked with the hex; timbuctu, kumasi, ile-ife, benin working its bronze, zimbabwe... hearing the future of the avalanche... disorder, horror of unburial, dischordant skeletones... caribs moving towards heroin and syphilis, cherokees moving towards the horse, the wesson rifle and the wagon chain: ibo and mago to barracoon and charnel ship; zulus towards soweto and the locomotive tank; masai beyond the elephant to the jumbo jet; caliban to new york, paris, london town.

Here then, is a comprehensive vision of the collision of Old and

New World histories as dehumanization to the point of recurrent genocide; a vision indeed, which presents many of the icons of progress in a negative light, as it grieves at the tragic interplay of human energy and the impulse to dominate, consume and destroy. It is in the face of this vision that Brathwaite measures the capacity of the human Spirit to rehumanize what it has dehumanized. In the process, he repeatedly explores interrelated concepts of Spirit, Apocalypse and Revolution.

II
Spirit

Brathwaite's idea of Spirit has been shaped from several sources: Christian, Hegelian, Akan and Dogon. Commenting on the imagery of *X/Self*, for example, he writes in 'Metaphors of Underdevelopment' that: "Mt Blanc is a symbol of materialism; while Kilimanjaro, its opposite, is a symbol of the spirit". Thus the materialism of expansionist Europe undermines first European, then African and New World spirituality. Here the vision is simple and dualistic: Materialism/Europe/Mt Blanc versus Spirit/Africa/Kilimanjaro.

On the other hand, Brathwaite's 'Hegelianism' leads him to a more complex and more optimistic vision of Spirit as being continuously and progressively emergent from the dialectical dance of opposites in history. Thus, far from being simply the opposite of matter, Spirit is dialectically related to matter, which it confronts and vitalizes. This sense of Spirit as active, rather than inertly passive under the assault of matter, is just as pervasive in Brathwaite's poetry as the simple opposition of triumphant materialism and helplessly inert spirituality.

The African notion of Spirit as immanent all-pervasive and perhaps more real than matter, leads Brathwaite to the concept of "Nam". "Nam" is described thus:

> DISGUISE OF MAN IS NAM: MAN BACKWARDS. Etymologically it is a root word (African and Oceanic and Amerindian and Indo-European) meaning root or core or spirit... seed if you like or soul: dry and reduced and irreducible and green: the utter inner self.[1]

"Nam", a term like may others recently of Brathwaite's own coinage, is generically related to 'Onyame', the Akan Creator God,

'Yam', sustaining staple food on both sides of the Atlantic, 'name' and Dogon 'Nummo', the original creative Word. "Nam" is a firstness of Spirit and a kernel-seed of Being which might be obscured or imprisoned but is, like Newtonian matter, susceptible to neither creation nor destruction. "Nam" is also the essential personhood inherent in every human being which, surviving man's direst efforts at its mutilation, is perpetually rediscoverable.

When, however, the human Spirit has been historically brutalized:

> broken by time, by neglect, the tough boots
> of Columbus, of pirate, the red boots of flame;
> cracked soles of Africa, broken by whip
>
> 'Coral', *The Arrivants*, 233

the process of recovering Nam becomes arduous. Several of Brathwaite's poems deal with the shattering of primal vision and Spirit. 'The Visibility Trigger' (*X/Self*, 48-50) a poem that comes close to the centre of *X/Self*, describes this shattering in terms of images of the broken circle and the riven despoliated tree. Circle is wholeness of psyche, integrity of aboriginal world-view; cyclic sense of time and work: sensibility in harmony with the rhythms of the land and the cosmos. With the intrusion of the European, circle becomes target to be shattered by missile. Custom, courtesy, communion, symbolized by the kola nut which the elders offer the interloper, are answered by gunfire as Brathwaite imaginatively reenters the moment of the 'fall', of the murdering of Spirit.

Desecration and diminishment of Spirit are taken a stage further as Europe and Africa together participate in the Slave Trade. Brathwaite reenters this moment both through the directly descriptive chorus of the newly enslaved which ends the 'New World A-Comin' sequence in *Rights of Passage*, and indirectly in 'Noom', the central sequence of *Sun Poem*, through fabricated myth. 'Noom' tells a story of the imprisonment and reduction of the Nummo. The word "noom" is a neologism which combines 'noon' with 'doom' and thus suggests its meaning: the negation of "Nam", name and Nummo, and the darkening of the sun.

'Noom' describes the arrival of the loa — that is African Spirit: God as energy, life-force — on the rugged Eastern coast of Barbados, a moment that signals their separation from Dogon and Dahomey. This arrival is recounted in terms of Good Friday imagery — darkness at noon, the despairing cry of the dying god — which links the Nummo with Christ and suggests that both of these sun gods and sons of God lost their shining charisma in the process of slavery and enchainment which degraded their arrival in the New World.

'Noom', however, is not only about the fatal separation of the life-Spirit from its ancestral source, but also about the shape which this same Spirit imposes on the new landscape as it endures a harsh process of indigenization. 'Noom' is a creation myth which purports to explain why the Atlantic coast of Barbados, the coast which faces Africa, is in its ruggedness so uncharacteristic of the island's topography. The shape that the imprisoned Spirit imposes on the landscape is informed by pain, rage and protest, a quality of both desperation and revolt. Since in both *Mother Poem* and *Sun Poem*, landscape is closely related to hidden dimensions of Spirit, Brathwaite is suggesting the subterranean existence of an African presence in an island that one normally regards as the most anglicized of the Caribbean.

Another image of the reduction of Spirit appears in 'Kingston in the Kingdom of this World' (*Third World Poems*, 53-56), originally also titled 'Good Friday 1975'. If 'Noom' explores the moment of arrival in the New World, 'Kingston in the Kingdom of this World' explores the contemporary moment: the state of the Spirit after centuries of enchainment. The protagonist of this poem is Voice, Word, the Word in prison. Insofar as he is in Kingston, we can safely conclude that he is Black and 'conscious'. But, as the title of the poem suggests, Kingston is a microcosm of the kingdom of this world: the oppressive nature of Kingston is, as in several of the sequences of *X/Self,* part of the universal enchainment of Spirit. The voice in the poem is thus that of "Nam", firstness of Spirit, now burdened down by the imprisoning structures of the kingdom of this world, now raging and reduced. The voice is also that of Christ soliloquising in prison, abandoned by his disciples and awaiting trial and the death-sentence. He recalls the Sermon on the Mount, one of the cardinal social statements of his ministry, which included both beatitude and denunciation and was crowned by the feeding of multitudes who abandoned him when he failed to leave them guidelines as to how they, without either toiling or spinning, might emerge arrayed better than Solomon in all his glory.

Now in prison, Christ remembers his career as activist for the Spirit, the great fisherman of souls.

> The fish swim in their shoals of silence
> our flung nets are high wet clouds, drifting

He and his disciples had hauled in souls under the high clouds with their promise of rain: netting them with a doctrine that devalued the power structure, placed natural freedom of Spirit above material production, and gave a sense of worth to the ordinary and essential; the salt of the earth. Now without their messiah, the souls (shoals) are once more adrift, and the rain of redemption is blown away, or does not fall.

But there are extra dimensions to Brathwaite's "Voice" that are not to be explained by reference to Christ's Sermon on the Mount. The Voice, for example, declares:

with this reed i make music
with this pen i remember the word
with these lips i can remember the beginning of the world

These declarations associate the imprisoned Voice first with a Pan-like natural music, then with the poet as representative of all makers with the word, and finally with the "Word" of St. John's gospel, which existed in the beginning, was with God and was God.

'Kingston in the Kingdom of this World' is constructed on a series of contrasts between what the Voice, 'Nam', represents, and what prison, either as Blakean "mind-forg'd manacles" or physical lock up means. These contrasting states of being are presented in terms of contrasting rhythms and flows of energy which affect length of line. The idea of the reduction of spirit is converged in truncated lines that contrast with the mighty energy-filled lines in which the Voice proclaims its true identity as Spirit, Word of God.

gospel was a great wind freedom of savannas
gospel was a great mouth telling thunder of heroes
gospel was a cool touch warm with the sunlight like

water in claypots, healing

The descriptions of gospel have as much to do with the verbal powers of the shaman, as with the conventional Christ figure. Thunder — a reference to Shango — great wind, freedom, savannas, contrast with the gentler qualities of soothing, healing and spiritual restoration. The Voice associates itself with flowers, water, flutes and language, in contrast with withered beauty, ecological pollution, attenuated grace and debased language. The core of the poem comes when the Voice contrasts the "Authority" that he was trying to establish or restore to the world, with the debased authority of his captors.

> my authority was sunlight: the man who arose from
> the dead called me saviour
> his eyes had known moons older than jupiters

The man who arose from the dead is Lazarus, so at this point the Voice is that of 'Christ', affirming his life-giving restorative function. But the next line: "his eyes had known moons older than jupiters" suggests the Dogon, with their phenomenal knowledge of astronomy, much of which informs their philosophy and world-view. This parallel between the Christ-figure and the Nummo is constant in the poem, and will later inform *Sun Poem* ('Noom') and *X-Self* ('Xango'). It exists because of the interlocking cross-cultural contexts out of which Brathwaite's work generally grows.

Often, though, various cultural contexts are presented in opposition to each other. This may be seen in 'Kingston in the Kingdom of this World' in the contrast between the primal authority of the Nummo/Christ and that of kingdom of this world.

> ...the white eye of interrogator's terror
> siren price fix the law of undarkness
> the dreadness of the avalanches of unjudgement

"Undarkness" is a Brathwaite coinage by which Europe is seen through African eyes "undark" in much the same way that the Eurocentric vision often speaks of the 'non-white' world. "Undarkness" also denies light or vision to the bearers of the 'word' into the heart of darkness. The "law of undarkness" is the negation of the 'law of darkness'; that is African legal, political, social, economic and philosophical structures. The "avalanches of unjudgement" are what Europe — here associated with the engulfing and death-bringing snows of Mont Blanc — unleashes on all those conquered peoples. *X-Self* shows how Europe transplanted its mediaeval systems of tort and torture; its renaissance traditions of inquisition and witchhunt, and its modern inventions of state terrorism and concentration camp.

Part of the pain of the Spirit's imprisonment is that the disciples have either misunderstood or forgotten or rejected the non-materialistic gospel of the Sermon on the Mount, and accommodated themselves to the material interests of the kingdom of this world. This cry will be heard again in 'Shaman' (*X-Self*) and 'Hex' (*Mother Poem*).

i would call out but my lost
children cannot unshackle their

shadows of silver

The chains are no longer of iron, but of silver, the metal of betrayal. It is as much the disciples' indifference to what the Spirit represents — word, gospel, freedom, the authority of sunlight and imagination — as the perverted authority of the system — imprisonment, torture, exploitation, atrocity — that condemns the Spirit to indefinite detention, and this strangled soliloquy, which has not yet become public outcry.

III
Apocalypse

Spirit may be imprisoned or beaten, but in Brathwaite it is never totally defeated or killed. It is always capable of regeneration and part of Brathwaite's value as both historian and poet has been his stress on the human capacity for renewal through the coming into consciousness of the subjugated mind. Slaves, he notes[2] remained 'invisible' faceless unpersons until they revolted. Revolt results from implosions within the psyche of the reduced person, triggered by a growing historic consciousness of the reasons for subjugation. 'Kingston in the Kingdom of this World' dramatises the awakening of this historic consciousness; and though the voice in that poem has not yet called out to either the system's commissars or the lost children, such consciousness illuminates the necessity for action as, inevitably, the interior brooding of the subjugated Spirit becomes public and political.

At this point, implosion exteriorizes itself in social upheaval and may under extreme circumstances become revolution. The process by which the reawakened Spirit attempts to transform the withholding structures of a dehumanizing history is what is meant in this essay by 'Apocalypse'. Apocalypse as a social and political idea has always involved two acts or processes: the violent destruction of an old world and the coming into being of a new one. Implied in these processes have been the ideas of reversal, judgement, rectification and purgation, and the emergence of a new and just authority. In reality, neither process occurs in the manner anticipated. The old order never quite disappears, nor does a truly new order emerge.

Vestiges of the old order permeate the new, to mock the dreams of idealists who may have sacrificed everything for change.

Nevertheless, the idea of Apocalypse permeates modern, and particularly New World literatures, and has been employed to describe the iconoclastic urge in 'modernist' art forms, which are constantly seeking the new and strange. Douglas Robinson in his *American Apocalypses* describes the apocalyptic idea as:

> definitively seeking to explore the unveiling of the future in the present, the encroachment of a radically new order into a historical situation that has disintegrated into chaos.[3]

Inserted between the present and the future, the apocalyptic moment illuminates, as Hiroshima has illuminated, both the world as it is and the world as it might be.

West Indian literature too, is saturated with the spirit of Apocalypse in the sense that it perceives itself as dealing with the end of Old World structures and the inchoate emergence of New World ones. The ideas of a reordering, a transcension or even the abolition of History is common to several West Indian writers — Harris, Walcott, Lamming, Denis Williams, Brathwaite, Césaire, Carpentier and Glissant. In each case, it involves the subversion of traditional structures be they aesthetic, mental or political: though in each case, foreknowledge of the likelihood of the persistence of old worlds in new, has bred misgiving, tragic irony or desperate hope.

Derek Walcott, for instance, is simultaneously attracted to and repelled by the political aspect of the apocalyptic idea. In *Dream on Monkey Mountain*, Makak, after agonies of self-discovery and self-renunciation both of which centre on the explosive emergence of his smothered dreams of justice and revenge, reluctantly beheads the White Goddess — who may be muse or demon — and retreats to "the green beginnings of the world". These "green beginnings" seem to be an idealized region of the mind that is free from both the dehumanizing of the past and the burden which the present bears of rehumanizing History through violent negation. The "green beginnings" are a womb-like state of 'amnesia' beyond or before History, an 'adamic' state in a New World of the mind.

Walcott's pastoral retreat from a solution within History is the result of a fear, similar to D.H. Lawrence's dread of the proletarian dream of an apocalyptic reversal of the social order. Lawrence notes the attractiveness to the nonconformist poor all over the world, of the denunciations in "Revelation" of the great, the rich and the powerful.

> Down among the uneducated people you will still find Revelation rampant... The huge denunciation of Kings and Rulers, and of the whore that sitteth upon the waters, is entirely sympathetic to a Tuesday evening congregation of colliers' wives, on a black winter night, in the great barn-like Pentecost chapel. And the capital letters of the name: MYSTERY, BABYLON THE GREAT, THE MOTHER OF HARLOTS AND ABOMINATIONS OF THE EARTH thrill the old colliers today as they thrilled the Scotch Puritan peasants and the more ferocious of the early Christians.[4]

"Revelation" is welcomed by "the never truly humble poor" as:

> a grandiose scheme for wiping out and annihilating everybody who wasn't of the elect, the chosen people, in short, and of climbing up himself right to the throne of God.

Lawrence views with horror the desire of the poor to control and restructure their own destiny, and in an otherwise fascinating study, comes close to granting moral legitimacy to the powerful simply because they are powerful, and of dreading democracy simply because it is a doctrine espoused by the "weak" and "pseudo-humble".

In the case of Walcott, the fear is the traditional neurosis of the old plantocracy: that popular revolt in the Caribbean will rapidly degenerate into racist revenge.[5] Walcott saw this tendency in the Black Power movement of the late sixties and early seventies, and expressed his fear of Black people in the Caribbean coming into historical consciousness. This fear is translated into sardonic dismissal of 'black consciousness' in *Another Life* and 'What the Twilight Says: an Overture', and grotesque comedy in the trial scene from *Dream on Monkey Mountain,* where Lestrade's attempt to place the white world on trial is presented as absurd.

Walcott's misgivings are, in fact, shared by other writers, though there are differences in how each writer signals a caution about revolutionary vision, process and change, as well as varying degrees of scepticism and hope. Brathwaite, for example, recognizes the ambiguity of the apocalyptic moment: its simultaneously death-bearing and life-enhancing quality. Like Walcott, he recognizes that revolutions conducted by the terminally ill in spirit degenerate, as in 'Springblade', where thwarted and emasculated Jamaican youth transfer aggression from the "system" to the "sisters". Brathwaite's vision of Black youth in Harlem or Brooklyn in the post Black Power period, is even more hopeless.

> i see my brothers high and nodding
> shadow boxing to the tune of needles
> angels of the fix
> bartering their sanity for trips
> around the skeleton
>
> i hear them screaming
> REVOLUTION
> as the world revolves round
> marcus malcolm mississippi memphis
>
> but there ain't no vein
> of revolution
> only the blues
> and coltrane's gospel pain
> 'Glass', *Black & Blues*, 25

These youths, like those of 'Springblade', are terminal people. They represent the dead-end of normal social relationships and sanctions. They are seen as:

> victim(s) of the cities' victory
> victim(s) of the cities' skin and trinkets
> wilderness of wind and shellac
> 'Caliban', *Black & Blues*, 30-31

Marginalized to a point where they are almost outside of historical process, they are oblivious to past struggle. Brathwaite asserts that before one can make the leap from this terminal situation towards the generation of renewed personhood, one must first achieve the very thing that Walcott seems to fear: historical consciousness. Where some thinkers expect spiritual transformation to be a result of revolution, Brathwaite believes that personal epiphany must precede communal.

Brathwaite is particularly concerned with the paradoxes and difficulties which attend the advent of revolutionary awareness; not the least of which is whether "time's long attack" on the psyches of the subjugated has not been too devastating for any revolution of the mutilated to reverse. As the omowale recognizes in *Masks*,

> the termites' dark teeth, three
>
> hundred years working,

have patiently ruined my art
'Sunsum', *The Arrivants*, 150

This is the central issue of both *The Arrivants* and *X/Self*: how to move from subjugation to rebellion: then, having rebelled, how to keep pure the ideals for which one rebelled. Like D.H. Lawrence, Brathwaite recognises that the flame of rebellion is alive in even the most apparently humble folk. Unlike Lawrence, he accepts this rebellion as necessary, and in both *The Arrivants* and *X/Self* envisages the eventual emergence of an Ogun/Shango persona; a spirit of fire, energy and iron resolve, in the breasts of the subjugated. Even Tom, that embodiment of the reduced Spirit, who has learnt to perceive History as nullification, also nurtures a dream of Noah's rainbow with its promise of apocalyptic fire in some remote 'next-time' ('Tom', *The Arrivants*, 13-14). Though as a necessary survival mechanism he keeps his "hate smothered down / to the bone / to suit the part / [he's] playing" ('Didn't He Ramble', *The Arrivants*, 22), his urge to negate the nullifying process of his History never dies. It, however, takes a long time and doesn't clearly happen until 'Negus' (*The Arrivants*, 222).

Part of the irony of Tom's situation lies in his sons' transferral of their inherited revolutionary impulse from the dehumanizing system to Tom himself, whose gestures of protest have been too weak and too broodingly introverted to be sympathetically understood as such. Doubly ironic is the fact that they have also inherited, and will later display, mechanisms of role-playing more damaging than their father's. Tom knows himself even though he evades open rebellion. Tom's sons attempt open rebellion but evade self-knowledge. *The Arrivants* works towards a reconciliation of the two: self-knowledge and rebellion, without whose co-incidence any revolution is meaningless.

Tom's dream of a resurrection, a rising up or uprising of his people, steadily surfaces from the depths where he has, through his mechanism of self-censorship, confined it. By 'Wings of a Dove' it has begun to burn very close to the surface of consciousness. Here the protagonist is Brother Man, the finished product of urban waste, whose very being seems invaded by the parasitism through which his labour has been the sustenance of bourg and metropole. Though Brother Man may appear to resemble the derelict youth of 'Glass', he becomes, as the poem proceeds, the transformed reborn Voice and bearer of omen. He moves from the pacifist ethic of old-time Rastafarianism to becoming the mouthpiece of apocalyptic upheaval. The particular nature of his awakening — through possession by voice of Biblical prophets — reflects an aspect of proletarian experience that involves an immersion in the apocalyptic texts as a theology of liberation, or at least retribution.

Brathwaite's Rastafarians resemble Lawrence's puritanical colliers in this respect, though, as we have noted, his attitude towards the proletariat entering their voice is quite different from Lawrence's anti-democratic disdain. Brathwaite makes Brother Man, at this nexus of self-affirmation and political definition, the history-filled and prophetic voice of a wider proletariat. His mistrust of white men, con men, brown men and white-black men is not irrational xenophobia, but accurate appraisal of an emerging class of new rulers, that is simultaneously aggressive in its greed of gain and defensive in its cultural rootlessness. This class is viewed by Brother Man as having only an aborted future, and as being an omen of disembodied possibility.

> na
> feet feel firm
>
> pun de firm stones: na
> good pickney born
> from de flesh
> o' dem bones
>
> 'Wings of a Dove', *The Arrivants*, 44

The release of Spirit, the journey towards "Nam" begun in 'Wings of a Dove' is the central theme of *Islands* which may be viewed as deepening phases of a descent into submerged areas of the Collective Unconscious, each of which is preceded and catalysed by a different ritual of possession. Thus the persona enters the vestibule of the inferno of History and Self through the gateway of Jazz ('Jah', *The Arrivants*, 162). He begins the movement out of limbo with the pukkumina vibrations of 'Shepherd' (*The Arrivants*, 185) immediately after which he begins to prophesy in the many and strangely-blended tongues of Jeremiah, Sartre and Ferlinghetti ('Caliban', *The Arrivants*, 19). Secondary manifestations of *loa* become fairly frequent from now on, as, for example, in 'Limbo' (*The Arrivants*, 193-195) and 'Rites' (*The Arrivants*, 200) with its brief intimation of Ogun-Shango. Voices of prophecy pervasively inform the poem's sound as, for example, in 'Wake' (*The Arrivants*, 210-213) where we shift in an accommodation of ancestors, from West African to Haitian prayers, psalms, the invocation to Legba, echoes of the

Gospels and Jeremiah's pessimistic tones as the society rejects or simply ignores its prophets.

The apparently calm voices of the women in 'Cane' soon gives way to the *loa* of fire and passionate resolve, preparing the reader for 'Ogun' which, in its movement from the flat surfaces of everyday activity towards possession is in fact a summary of the movement of the entire trilogy from tough weather-beaten surface shell to the kernel-core of Nam, the tree's green original centre of Being. Ogun is timid Tom and crippled Legba in the process of discovering their own submerged Spirit. He is carving a block of wood partially eaten away by termites into an image of himself, his "Nam". The inert "block of wood" conveys metaphorical connotations of stupidity, apathy, dullness and doltishness, and represents the process of reification which Tom has endured; his past deformity of image and benumbed beaten Spirit.

The act of creation involves a rediscovery and release of Spirit, which preceded the movement towards the "lost iron" of revolutionary consciousness. Rebirth of Spirit is clearly signalled in the beautiful lines:

> until his hands could feel
>
> how it had swelled and shivered breathing air
> its weathered green burning to rings of time
>
> its contoured grain still tuned to roots and water
> 'Ogun', *The Arrivants*, 243

'Spirit' is literally, or generically, breath. Thus its possession of, or re-emergence within the weather-beaten but enduring heart of matter, is portrayed as a deep inhalation of breath by the medium. This is in itself a point of interest, since normally we think of the Creator breathing life into inert matter. Here, however, it is the apparently inert medium that inhales the breath of Spirit; which is another way of saying that Tom has ceased to smother the spirit which has always been imprisoned within him. Liberated, Spirit does not forego matter, but energizes, rehumanizes it and inspires it for the tasks of resurrecting the terminal person and transforming human institutions in the material world of History.

Such transformation involves the destruction of the corrupt aspects of the old order. But what is the process by which the refiner's fire of Spirit, liberated, moves beyond its mission of destruction to become an agent of regeneration? In 'Leopard' (*The*

Arrivants, 244) Brathwaite underlines the urgency of this question for Caribbean and New World peoples transfixed in this apocalyptic moment between the proven morbidity of the old order and the unknown and at times unimaginable future, by drawing attention via metaphor to the patterns of violence, rapine and conquest in the pre-diasporan history of Africa. Employing the image of the caged leopard as a metaphor of the situation of the exploited and explosive so-called developing counties, he makes a plea for humane liberation:

> Give him a tree to leap from,
> liberator; in pity let him
> once more move with his soft
>
> spotted and untroubled splendour
> among the thrills and whispers
> of his glinting kingdom;
> or unlock him and now let him
>
> from his triggered branch
> and guillotining vantage
> in one fine final falling
> fall upon the quick fear-
>
> footed deer or peer-
> less antelope whose beauty,
> ravaged with his sharp brutality
> propitiates the ancient guilt
>
> each feels toward the other:
> the victim's wish to hurt,
> the hunter's not to;
> and by this sacrifice
>
> of strong to helpless Other,
> healed and aneled;
> both hurt and hunter
> by this fatal lunge made whole.

The leopard is Spirit as a potentially free and fearsome energy which resides within the liberator — that is, the person about to free himself through violent effort. Yet Brathwaite allows the liberator two alternatives, the first of which is to relocate the leopard in its original and primal kingdom, a world conceived of as one of light and wonder. There Spirit or "Nam" is triumphant, free and at home, in full harmony with environment. Such restitution of primal

Spirit would require on the part of the liberator, revolutionary man on the verge of releasing this caged and fearful aspect of himself, a quality of compassion. Compassion is necessary if the pure naked premoral energy of Spirit is to be contained for creativity; just as Energy in William Blake becomes anarchic without its outward circumference of Reason. Compassion, or "pity" as it is termed in 'Leopard', is the restraining circumference which Brathwaite suggests to a Caribbean and Third World in which revolutionary upheaval is a perennial possibility, and in some countries almost an annual reality.

Brathwaite, however, as if he recognizes the unlikelihood of anyone choosing the first option in a world where the old order that the liberator seeks to transform is manifestly uncompassionate, spends much more time articulating the second. Here, Energy/Spirit is not relocated in its natural habitat — there's no returning to the ancestral kingdom — but unleashed for its final encounter with the enemy. This final encounter is both political and psycho-sexual, and is envisioned through an image which works simultaneously on these two planes. Hence the released leopard stalking and killing its prey suggests an army of sansculottes, triggering and guillotining their way towards liberty and the cemetery, as well as a rapist/murderer violently possessing his victim in the delusion that he is, through sexual revenge, healing himself of past hurt.

It is, curiously, the psycho-sexual aspect of the image that is developed; so much so that the original leopard image becomes subsidiary to the idea of rape, and rape is the image through which the retributive revenge of the oppressed is commented upon. The uncompassionate liberator may become, like the rapist, an unleashed wild-cat fulfilling a feral need for blood, rather than an apostle of new consciousness. While he may envisage a "peerless beauty" at the end of revolt, he destroys it in the act of violent possession.

Yet, ironically, he never achieves full conquest of his prey, since beneath her forced submission lies "the victim's wish to hurt"; that strange link which makes victim and assailant, masochist and sadist and, the poem implies, liberator and oppressor, monstrous doubles of each other. Awakening, or rather, bringing to the surface "the victim's wish to hurt," he has simply created another victim who will in time re-enact, as he is now doing, the vengeful psychology of the victim. The victim, in the act of destroying the violator and eradicating the strain of violation, will create new victims. "Nam", reacting to violation, can choose only this negative method for its self-defense.

Nor has he satisfied the latent desire which lies at the root of his attack. That love, suggested in his latent wish not to hurt, is the creative and redeemable aspect of Spirit which, since Spirit is an indestructible kernel seed of Being, dwells even in the most violent of men. But love can in such circumstances manifest itself only negatively, by effecting a crumbling of the all-conquering Ego while the Ego is in the very act of revenge through which it had hoped to fulfil itself. This is possibly, the meaning of the lines:

> and by this sacrifice
>
> of strong to helpless other
> healed and aneled;
> both hurt and hunter
> by this fatal lunge made whole.

where the assailant's strength collapses and the helpless victim conquers in a reversal of roles. The "wholeness" which the Ego gains in an epiphany of such terror is totally an illusion. The reality is one of mutual destruction, the annihilation of both Self and Other, both victor and victim. The word "aneled", which means anointed for burial, makes this clear. The ultimate revolutionary choice is between compassion and catastrophe.

This remarkable poem deals simultaneously with the bitter climax of three parallel confrontations: that of colonizer and colonized, male and female, and the one that has always been taking place within the human psyche between Eros and Thanatos, the creative and destructive aspects of Spirit. It is amazing that Brathwaite should, as early as 1961 when 'Leopard' first appeared, have equated these three levels of confrontation — the political, gender and psycho-sexual levels — and seen their joint resolution as the ultimate task of civilization, as it wavers between the options of terminality and the rehumanization of History.

IV
X/Self

If 'Leopard' foretells the tragic failure of any uncompassionate revolution, it also views as unlikely the prospect of a compassionate one. As it moved from the hopeful renaissance years of the sixties with their "exploding dimensions of sound" and political activity,

Brathwaite's poetry had to come to terms with the assassination of the Black Power and Civil Rights movements in their Christian, Islamic and urban guerillist phases. This brought him face to face with what he'd always known: the problem of even imagining the possibility of a successful rebellion of the weak, the underdeveloped and the divided. How was one to maintain hope in the face of so much failure among Africans at home and abroad? What prospects existed for a just reordering of History? Could this happen without recrimination and revenge? Can the products of a dehumanized process, History, transcend that process? How does one encounter and transform a structure of power on terms other than those predicated by that structure of power?

These questions, latent in *The Arrivants*, resurface in *X/Self*, a more complex exploration of the theme of Empire than *The Arrivants*, which is also concerned with the cyclic establishment and disintegration of Empires — the Egyptian, Sudanese and West African as well as the British Empires. The first half of *X/Self* deals with the everchanging proportions of "Rome" after eight centuries of Christianity. The poem suggests the validity of the Pirenne thesis, that the vast movement of Germanic peoples into the Roman Empire caused not the disintegration, but the consolidation of structure based on the intermeshing of Church and State. *X/Self* is about this consolidation of "Rome" as structure, law, ideology, cosmology, long after "Rome" has ceased to exist as the administrative centre of an empire. "Rome" emerges as a metaphor, a paradigm of the convergence of forces into a massive and dominant polity; so that today, "Rome" is America.

Since the consolidation of "Rome" is based on the reduction of her colonies *X/Self* explores patterns of equilibrium and disequilibrium; growth and degeneration. It is particularly concerned with the forced transplantation of these patterns in the New World, and moves beyond the predominantly African/Afro-American/Afro-Caribbean parameters of *The Arrivants*. The range of voices is wider in *X/Self*. More Europeans are allowed to speak. Meso-America is accorded a central place. Strange juxtapositions of voices and historical personages occur, as Charlemagne addresses his 'brother' Henri Christophe; Caesar and Nixon reveal resemblances; Othello, Tennyson, Cortez and a host of other historical and fictional characters appear in strange contexts.

The New World sensibility, a product of widely contradictory and at times bizarre forces, becomes 'X/Self' — the unknown undiscovered Self. This unknown Self exists in a context of overwhelming demoralization, whose main elements have been the direct results of Empire. Driven by his experience of the Caribbean city ('Kingston in the Kingdom of this World'), Brathwaite throughout the second half of *X/Self* provides a sustained vision of hunger, violence, emaciation, waste and defeat.

Yet the New World sensibility is potentially rich, precisely because of the strange mixture of elements — the magic of both Prospero and Sycorax — that has gone into its making. *X/Self* is among other things a journey into a mind that has been formed through a wide experience of literature and history. This mind is poised, sophisticated and intelligent in its understanding of various worlds. It has range and depth; and is as intense in its lamentation as its satirical laughter. *X/Self* is Brathwaite's most eloquent testimony, that relentless vision of ruin can reside in close proximity to a spirit of hope and affirmation.

Our main concern with *X/Self* is with what it tells us about the idea of a rehumanization of history through the activation of regenerated Spirit in a process of destruction and renewal. The poem is a prolonged exploration of the apocalyptic idea. It is about systems of imperial organization constantly coming into and going out of existence. Its eventual focus is on the terrible birth of the New World at the price of the annihilation of the great civilizations of Aztec, Inca, Maya and Ashanti. It recognizes the apocalyptic principle as central to both the foundations and the continued transformation and renewal of New World civilizations.

'Dies Irie' which occurs after we have completed one-third of the journey through *X/Self*, is a deliberate invocation of the apocalyptic moment. It follows a contemplation of how the Europe of industrialism, ecological waste and economic and cultural imperialism has penetrated, polluted and destroyed Asia and Africa. Linking the Bhopal disaster with Nazi gas chambers, Nagasaki with Viet Nam and Auchwitz, *X/Self* is a passionate outcry against the miners, militia and bankers of Imperialism.

they burn
they eat the land

they vomit it up
they leave lakes of desolation

ochre choler water

that returns no benediction

plantations of dead plankton
'Nuum', *X/Self*, 34-35

Empire, as presented in *X/Self,* has always operated without moral sanction. Contemporary imperialism is, however, more devastating because it is more advanced technologically, and more ruthlessly oriented towards the accumulation of Capital. It pollutes, devours and kills for profit, converting Ashanti to ashanty towns ("ashanty towns arise and rust within their oxides"). Benin, famous for its bronzes, becomes a catafalque — a tomb. The "ikons" left by the miners of empire are ash, starvation, bewilderment.

It is in the face of this reality that *X/Self* invokes the *Dies Irae,* which, employing Dread talk, he converts to "Dies Irie", a much desired, highly gratifying day. Brathwaite, having achieved his first objective, that of locating contemporary structures and practices of Empire in their historical context, now suggests the future — the apocalyptic downfall of Empire; the day of the resurgence of suppressed Spirit. "Dies Irie" is a parody of the Roman Catholic *Dies Irae,* which is a solemn evocation of the ideas of Doomsday and Judgement. It is a moment that Verdi and Mozart have celebrated in their respective requiems. Brathwaite, however, nativizes the concept of the *Dies Irae* and in two versions of this poem (i.e. in *Third World Poems* and *X/Self*) the music is played by Satchmo and Nyabinghi respectively. 'Dies Irie', like Revelation, on which it is based, is dream, "prophesay," an intense fantasy of retribution, shared by all suppressed peoples. It first identifies the idea of Apocalypse as a profoundly religious — indeed both Christian and 'pagan' — one. It is one of the things that Christianity (both Catholic and Calvinist) shares with 'paganism'.

Day of sulphur dreadful day
when the world shall pass away
so the priests and shamans say.
'Dies Irie', *X/Self*, 37

Apocalypse is also a political idea and will result from the international upsurgence of hitherto suppressed peoples, who will force Mont Blanc (Europe/America/Empire) to recognize its atrocities. The Apocalypse is conceived of as a sort of universal Assizes in which the whole of History and Time will be judged; particularly that dehumanized aspect of History and civilization which has glorified war and trade, and forged the link between the military and the industrial, annexing science, technology and even the arts and religion to economically strategic war-mongering.

The poem identifies the prosecutor against Mont Blanc: Ho Chi Minh, Marti, Makandal, Fedon, Fatah, Sun Yat Sen, Nyabingeh, the Sadinistas, Cuba, the Zulu, Sioux, Seminole and Shaka. The list is long and multinational. A few of the crimes of Mont Blanc are identified — My Lai, Sharpeville, Wounded Knee, the doctrines of herrenvolk and fascism, Soweto massacre, Harlem.... The heroes of Mont Blanc are named: Verwoerd, Vorster, Pik van Botha and Malan of South Africa, and the merchants and statesmen of Mont Blanc who support them.

The cry in the poem is for Justice and vengeance; its point being that Justice in History has always been the justice of the powerful, who have generally kept from the centre of their assessment of self and civilization their woeful record of atrocity and genocide. The resurrection and judgement of the dead in 'Dies Irie' is a dreadful epiphany, a revelation of the hidden areas of History; a reconceptualization of words such as History, Civilization, Power and Justice. (It is, incidentally, this same dream of historic justice that is mocked by Walcott in the trial scene of *Dream on Monkey Mountain*, where Lestrade, the mulatto who has just discovered his Blackness, attempts to place the entire white world on trial.)[6]

Brathwaite is of course fully aware of the improbability of any just reordering of History ever occurring but clings to a notion that one day judgement will be pronounced. It is this wavering between a sense of improbability and a hope for justice that informs his revision of the earlier version of 'Dies Irae' in *Third World Poems.* Louis Armstrong is replaced by Nyabingeh as the angel of the last trumpet. Armstrong represents the improbability of the dream of Apocalypse, Nyabingeh the hope for judgement. Something is gained in the sense that Nyabingeh are associated with dread and the message: Death to black and white oppressors. They are therefore more appropriate dark angels of the Apocalypse than Louis Armstrong, whose weapons against oppression were joy, elation, affirmation, and a deliberate wearing of the masks of coon entertainer and Uncle Tom: what is termed in *Rights of Passage* his "boot black smile"; his "warm humility".

On the other hand, one rather likes the idea, as improbable and absurd as it may seem, of confronting all the dreadful death-dealing machinery of Mont Blanc with the supremely affirmative elation of a Satchmo riff. One also favours the prospect of world leaders and war mongers past and present chipping towards the mercy seat of the "mighty and majestic godhead" to the joyful strains of 'When the Saints Go Marching Home', to receive their "sentences of righteous rage".

One also regrets the omission from *X/Self* of the line "saviour of the broken herd" — a line of deep, sad bitterness. For the broken herd keep yearning for a saviour, but seem doomed, even to the very end of *X/Self,* to remain broken. By definition, the "broken herd" can have no saviour; for if they had a saviour, they would hardly be broken. As helpless, leaderless and heroless as they have been described in *Rights of Passage,* the broken herd have been broken because their saviour himself has been broken too; that is, their religions, philosophies, selves and souls have been historically devastated. *X/Self* is largely about this devastation. Brathwaite replaces "saviour of the broken herd" by "herder of the lost herero" which, while it hopefully suggests a patriarchal Maasai presence capable of bringing together all the scattered and lost tribes is not as true emotionally as "saviour of the broken herd" a line that contains the bitter ambiguity of the apocalyptic dream: which is that it is dreamt only by the most devastated, those least likely ever to be able to fulfil it.

Brathwaite's problem of envisioning an apocalyptic reversal in the New World is compounded by his contemplation of the Haitian Revolution in 'Cap', a poem of the early seventies based on his response to a mural in Port-au-Prince depicting the country's history "as a single, unfolding episode in montage" (*X/Self,* 122). The poem begins by identifying the Arawak presence at the very crest of the cape where Christophe's fortress/monument is built. Since the Arawaks are a supposedly vanquished and virtually exterminated people, their presence here in this time can only mean that the true original ancestral Spirit of the land has not died, and awaits its time to defeat the conquistador. This is part of the general argument of *X/Self*: that the Spirit of the past is never quite vanquished. Thus "Rome" persists in spirit, and is reincarnated in a new time and place, as are "Africa" and Aztec/Arawak/Maya. Mont Blanc and Kilimanjaro have their equivalent in the New World in any of the great Central American volcanic mountains: Popocatepetl, Illimani, Coropuna, Cotopaxi, all of which are invoked as residences of the sleeping Spirit of fire, secreted in the land and people (*X/Self,* 103).

The Spirit of the Caribbean past, as presented in 'Cap', whether it manifested itself in Carib, Arawak or African — Lamming's "Tribe Boys" — was a spirit of resistance. This Spirit manifested itself in several moments: the suicidal martyrdom of the Caribs at Sauteurs; the Africans who jumped overboard while crossing the middle passage; the suicide of the defeated Maroons in Brazil in

1696; the courage with which Toussaint's barefooted battalions confronted French cannon during the Haitian Revolution. It is that Spirit which awaits anyone who thinks of ascending the peak of Cap Haitien, where, we are told, Toussaint is a *zemi*. Toussaint is a *zemi* only because he represented, while alive, the purest Spirit of revolution. Affirming the same value as the Arawaks, Toussaint becomes a *zemi* or a *loa*, an ancestral spirit. One notes that the Petro cult in Haiti combines native Caribbean (ie. Arawak, Carib etc) and African (Dahomean, Yoruba etc) religions. Dead in body, Toussaint becomes in Spirit the embodiment of this mergence of ancestral energies. Like Ananse in *Islands*, he stares from the flesh of the stone. That is, he is a frozen, inert, but potentially active presence. Frozen in stone, he achieves, like the static lovers in Keats's Grecian Urn, a kind of eternal potentiality, which can be reincarnated in the flesh of the living.

Toussaint also represents a timeless condemnation of all who have betrayed the Spirit of the land; and these may include Henri Christophe who simultaneously seeking magnificence and fearing extinction, virtually re-enslaved his people in order to build his monument on the Cape. Yet Toussaint may also represent the pure but frozen and unattainable ideals of Revolution. Revolution itself is a never-ending, paradoxical process.

> The steel of the machete
> the knife of the god
> thongs of the whips
>
> drink water like trees
> africaines from the slave ships
> dance out of the riflemen's loins
>
> become dessalines dessalines

The first four lines here suggest that the implements of war, revolt, forced labour and castigation have, through the Revolution, become part of a process of redemption. The words "drink water like trees" are a token of hope that all this bitter history may be rehumanized to produce grace, growth and graciousness. On the other hand, the next three lines provide a rapid succession of images which begin with "africaines from the slave ships". This reminds us of the high proportion of African-born slaves in Haiti's pre-revolutionary years, and suggests that the capacity for revolt existed because African Spirit had not been successfully quenched. These enslaved Africans "dance out of the riflemen's loins" to "become dessalines dessalines". These dancers are free spirits, born out of revolt, conceived in war ("the riflemen's loins").

Dessalines becomes the incarnation of their spirit of inflexible, and total, revolt. The repetition of "dessalines dessalines" sounds like the chant of popular acclaim. But Dessalines, who after the Revolution proclaimed himself Emperor, began a campaign to exterminate all whites, and was himself assassinated in 1806. As part of the passing tableau of history, Dessalines raises the question of whether revolutionaries are doomed to become dictators and reproduce the repressive structures against which they once revolted. Brathwaite, who poses this question in *The Arrivants*, suggests, as we saw in our analysis of 'Leopard', that limits need to be placed on the spirit of revolt; that an excessive spirit of recrimination can lead to a vengeful blood bath, which defeats and negates the spirit of liberty in whose name revolt originally took place. Dessalines was the tragic result of this excessive spirit of recrimination, and he left Haiti a heritage of:

> the spangle of death from the hot
> of the trees

He named no successor, and his assassination plunged Haiti into further internecine violence, out of which emerged Henri Christophe, another of the great military leaders of the Revolution.

We thus see Christophe next on the mural. But he is called "christophe columbus", that is, he is associated with the European discoverer, intruder, conquistador presence, whose paradoxical journey towards conquest and genocide and the dark epiphany of a terrifying self-knowledge, is explored in 'Titan' (*X/Self*, 61-63). Christophe's journey up the mountain is, like Cortez's invasion of the pyramid-temple of Akbal, the Aztec death-god, a degraded *via dolorosa* revealing only the Shadow, the dark double:

> and christophe columbus climbs upto his mountain top
> with the face of his horse in the faith of his shadow
>
> he stumbles on priest on an ivory slave on a spaniard
> the places of pain become pig
> snouts the black becomes white becomes black becomes rain
>
> falling to plunder the roof
> of the world.
>
> 'Cap', *X/Self*, 53-54

It is Christophe's mountain because it is the place where he built his monument, his citadel. The mountain/citadel is a concretization of his ego. Autocracy always seeks to overpower the average citizen's mind by monstrously immense architecture — pyramids, basilicae, colosseums, palaces of sane and mad Sun Kings Louis or Ludwig, great walls of China or Zimbabwe or Macchu Picchu, citadels.

Christophe climbs the mountain "with the face of his horse in the faith of his shadow" because he is proceeding resolutely towards a gloomy unknown; perhaps towards death. There's also the psychological dimension of Shadow; that is, the Id, the hidden and frightening Other side of one's nature. Christophe's epiphany is a discovering of this hidden Other not only within his own nature, but within the Revolution itself. Winning power after the civil strife that followed Dessalines's assassination, Christophe hastily remade himself in the image of the oppressor — fortress, emperor, forced labour on the citadel, a return to monarchical ideals which the revolution had been fought to destroy. This rapid transformation of Christophe into his opposite and double and Other, becomes a paradigm of the process of change/unchange that has been Haiti's history since the Revolution: "the black becomes white becomes black...". The faces change, but the pattern and process remain the same.

The irony of the idea of rain plundering the roof of the citadel, to which Christophe's megalomaniacal notion of 'the world' has shrunken, is that Christophe has constructed his fortress so well and so inaccessibly, that he needs fear only the rain; only what is natural, God-given and redemptive. Christophe's nemesis is not the feared uprising of a suppressed people; not the feared attack from the defeated European nations — France, Spain and England — but the spirit of Toussaint, who is now a *zemi.*

> he stares from the stone, from the eye
> lids of flame at his fate

Toussaint's tragic fate is not to have died in the frozen European fastness of the Jura mountain, a literal prisoner of Mont Blanc; but to have fought and died to produce the travesty that Christophe has become. He becomes Christophe's judge, the cloud of doom which, like the Aztecs, Christophe has sought to escape by means of his monument, and Dessalines, by means of the sacrificial wastage of lives.

This contradictory sense of the necessity for Revolution and the constant betrayal of Revolution permeates Brathwaite's two trilogies and *Black & Blues*. It is there in many of the post-1970 poems, inspired by a contemplation of the city of Kingston, Jamaica. We earlier mentioned 'Springblade' as an example of this ambivalent vision. *X/Self* is actually structured on such ambivalence. The poem is based on the dualities of Africa/Europe, Black/White, Caliban/Prospero, Slave/Free, Colonized/Colonizer, New World/Old World, Kilamanjaro/Mont Blanc, Spirituality/Materialism, the primal/the technological, pastoral innocence/urban degradation, the adamic landscape/the ecological wasteland, the opulence of poverty/the poverty of opulence. But more important than these dualities is the fact that they are presented not as Manichean opposites, but as the yin and yang of intermeshing states and processes. Caliban replaces Prospero and reproduces Prospero's system. The Old World penetrates the New and perpetuates itself, until plastic and cellophane become almost everyone's future. Old and New World protagonists, Charlemagne and Christophe, Cortez and Moctezuma become *semblables*, doubles.

In the face of not only the duality but the dialectic of forces alive in the making of New World history, Brathwaite's presentation of the ideas of apocalyptic destruction and rebirth becomes almost like a never-ending debate, where the issue remains unresolved almost to the very end of *X/Self*. History as presented in *X/Self* reveals that although moments of apocalyptic upheaval do occur in which entire empires go out of existence or come into being, the patterns of Empire and conquest and validation seldom change. Charlemagne, the Frankish conqueror of Rome and much of Europe, far from promoting his own Germanic civilization and culture, accepts the deeply engrained doctrine of Graeco-Roman superiority, and proceeds to renew the Latin/Christian civilization of the Holy Roman Empire at the expense of his supposedly inferior and heathen Germanic one, whose shamans were prevented on pain of death from practising the old religion.[7]

In the New World, the Aztecs adopted and extended the hierarchical structures of the older Toltec civilizations they had conquered, and in time were able to pervert history in order to claim a legitimate line of succession from the founders of the old Toltec Empire. Henri Christophe, as mesmerized by the idea of France's superiority as "Charlemagnia" was by Rome's, helped establish Euro-centred values and tastes as post-Revolutionary norms, and was partly responsible for the destruction, perversion or stagnation of Afro-Haitian civilization in the Caribbean. His failure is presented as the paradigm of the later failures of Afro-Saxon regimes in the twentieth century Caribbean (*X/Self*, 55-60).

Neo-colonial politicians, white, brown or black, speak in the accents of an autocracy and cultural imperialism learned from Europe. A South African 'aparthate' voice justifying the destruction of African nations and customs, reveals a startling affinity with a neo-colonial Black elitist voice. Both have a vested interest in maintaining structures based on economic privilege for a small ruling oligarchy, and dehumanization of labour. Thus the South African voice declaring:

soon i will be asked to ask them to forget forgive
their savage homelands their dark & dung & kraal & bantustans

and
call me bucky massa yes yes good yes god yes gold

therefore no mud hut villages wearing those pygmy straw
hats you will see within the pages of the phantomb

no afro hair dos in our schools no dialect around the holy
house
and on these

premises

fades smoothly into the neo-colonialist voice justifying its betrayal of democratic ideals and maintenance of "the status crow".

in fact, in order to avoid drop-face and rising cost of expec-
tations

there will be no more promises before election time
in fact there will no longer be election time
X/Self, 58

Such abrupt reversals are common in New World politics with its proliferation of dictatorships, military governments, and failed radical regimes.

Post-independence Caribbean politicians have only had small success in altering the fundamental structures of plantation society: great house and shanty, citadel and dungle, townhouse and wilderness. Political cynicism and exaggerated authoritarianism are, indeed, little more than masks to cover a failure that is reflected in the rigid dualities of class:

> without a future
> all houses will be condominiums buses towns
> landscraped plantations planned like towns
>
> chapel courthouses main guards & supermarket prisons empty church
> yards ring a round with roses of barb wire...

That is one version of urban Jamaica. This is the other

> beyond that there is rab & wilderness & terrorists &
> cultural gorillas
>
> caliban

The ruling-class Jamaican voice echoes that of the white South African or North American

> we don't want catch no niggers out here no way neither nor any
> rasta man nor hippie.
> *X/Self*, 59

because in each case the gap between the ruling élite and the scarecrow poor is filled with dread that can and does result in murder from either party.

The phrase "landscraped plantations" tells us that the city as a wasteland of condominium clusters is the contemporary version of the old plantation, with the the top soil scraped away to produce an ecological desert, that is both metaphor and an illustration of the true wilderness: the spiritual desert that it contains. The fakedness, fragility and utter deadness of the world are portrayed in 'Twoom' (room-womb-tomb), where a bourgeois art show featuring a display of white plaster of paris cats is contrasted with brutal images of life and death outside the art gallery. The neo-colonial city offers one a choice of morgues, both of which are under the eternal surveillance of the vultures of Empire (*X/Self*, 88-91).

The youth, who should possess the energy to attempt a transformation of this dead *manscape* are either indifferent or cynical, having listened in the past to too many futile or dishonest politicians ('Mai Village' *X/Self*, 69). The rebels among them fail to create Revolution: "the people's liberation army surrendering to sodom & gommorah in their bvd's" ('Twoom', *X/Self*, 90). The image — taken from the collapse of the Grenada Revolution — is the nadir of

X/Self: the poem's Naipaulian moment of utter hopelessness and pathetic absurdity.

V
Maroonage; Revolution; Xango

It is however, the turning point, and is followed by Section IV of *X/Self*, where the options of maroonage, and full-fledged rebellion are repeatedly explored, as the poem attempts to outline an alternative to "Sodom and Gommorah". One such alternative that actually precedes 'Twoom' is examined in 'Nam'. First entitled 'Soweto', 'Nam' is about rebirth of Spirit (Nam): and though the landscape of rebirth is South Africa, the name "Nam" may also be Viet Nam, where the vulture suffered its most significant defeat in contemporary times. Since Brathwaite first wrote 'Soweto' in 1979 the reactions of sympathy, particularly from radical youth worldwide, have been astounding. They suggest that it may still be possible to modify, if not transform, political process; to humanize the vulture.

The first seven lines of the poem refer to the changing cinematic image of the African from the savage demonic hordes of Tarzan films or horror stories; from the "rolling moth ball eyes" made popular by minstrelsy and maintained by Satchmo; to the images of resistance and rebellion which have grown since Soweto school children, by-passing their beaten elders, began the Azanian Revolution. This awakening is described in the image of a mighty dust storm: "oceans rolling over the dry sand of the savanna" — and it brings new hope to the poet who as 'shaman' changes his lamentation at the people's indifference to his warning, ('Shaman', *X/Self*, 65-68) to a magical naming of the tribes, as if to evoke from their very names, energy, power and resolution.

> and we know somewhere there is real fire
> kasuto mokhati namibia azania shaka the zulu kenyatta the shatt
> erer the maasai wandering into the everlasting shadow of jah
>
> 'Nam', *X/Self*, 73

The revolution will be "hell and halleluia," retributive fire and a welcome song of praise that the passive youth of 'Mai Village' have finally come off the fence and entered into their voice.

> bellowing against bullhorn and kleghorn

bellowing against bargwart and the searchlights of dogs
bellowing against crick and the kick in the stomach

Now there is constant outcry, where before in 'Kingston in the Kingdom of this World' the protagonist had not yet given vent to his urge to cry out. The poem remarks at the suddenness with which Soweto became the world's most massive issue since Nazism and Viet Nam. The poem makes the linkage by alluding to the genocide perpetrated by Germans in Namibia decades before Hitler.

Soweto awakens in the protagonist hope for the rebirth of Ogun Shango, and evokes a sense of the holy, expressed in his dream of a land whose myths, symbols, shrines and gods have been restored. Soweto signals the beginning of the apocalyptic moment through its recovery of Voice.

soon

soon

soweto

we have waited so long for this signal
this howl of your silence
this heat of herero this hero
'Nam', *X/Self*, 78

The millenarian faith of the poem is suggested in the passage adapted from Revelation proclaiming the fulfilment of the prophecy.

and i beheld the beast strangled howling in its own chains
led by the fetlocks
and the opulence useless
and the guns shattered and silent.
'Nam', *X/Self*, 78

This "and i beheld" not only enhances the shamanistic element of the poem, but reverses the omen with which 'The Visibility Trigger' ends:

and i beheld the cotton tree
guardian of graves rise upward from its monument of grass crying
aloud in its vertical hull calling
for crashes of branches vibrations of leaves
'Nam', *X/Self*, 49

Whereas in 'The Visibility Trigger' the shaman or sleeper of the tribe is recalling a dream turned nightmare of the shattering of the tribe, in 'Nam' the shamanistic voice appropriates the prophecy of St. John the Divine to declare the arrival of the Apocalypse.

This is the same moment that Brother Man dreamed of in 'Wings of a Dove'. In *X/Self*, it assumes visible shape in a poem/icon that is part volcano, part mushroom cloud. Sound is added to icon and image in this statement of hope:

and we rise

mushroom

mau

kilimanjaro

silvers of eagles

tears

savannas

nzingas of rivers

umkaklabulus of mountains

and the unutterable metal of the volcanoes

rising

rising

rising

burning

'Nam', *X/Self*, 79

Human effort, as suggested by the allusions to the Mau Mau and the Congolese warrior Queen Nzinga, is combined with the detonations of earth and sky. The presence of Ogun Shango is heard and felt in the thunder-claps of "umklakubulus" — a beautifully onomatopoeic Zulu word — and in the rumbling line: "the unutterable metal of the volcano".

Rebirth of Spirit requires prayer, invocation, incantation: shamanistic approaches to Word and Voice. Entering one's voice and giving voice are therefore important functions in Brathwaite's poetry. *Rights of Passage*, indeed, begins with a statement of the major functions of the Voice when it proclaims the poet's aim of exploring the:

> ...taut
> surfaces of things
> I sing
> I shout
> I groan
> I dream
> about
>
> *The Arrivants*, 4

The deepest and most necessary of these functions of the Voice, is that of becoming the channel for internal and suppressed or censored energies. This is how Spirit and Will become renewed for the herculean task of transforming a history of "wreck/age". After 'Nam', the major thrust in *X/Self* is towards the awakening of the Voice. The poem becomes more incantatory, more shamanistic; even though the poet as shaman has clearly recognized himself as a Cassandra figure or a sad Jeremiah, ignored or rejected by an indifferent world ('Shaman', *X/Self*, 65-68). Invocation, requiring a mixture of faith in prayer and magic, and a belief in the possibility of recalling "lost pain lost iron" lost energies, does not however blind the poet's eye to the odds against which such energies will have to be deployed.

'Stone', for example, offers maroonage, the original guerrilla warfare of the Caribbean, as an historical phenomenon that may guide future struggles against Mont Blanc ('Stone', *X/Self*, 93-95). Maroonage here has an extended meaning in that it involves a turning inwards on self: a deliberate disentanglement from Mont Blanc's economy of imposed detritus of word, food and toxic waste, or blandishments of "dangerous... generosities wrapped up in cellophane and xmas paper" ('Shaman', *X/Self*, 67). Maroonage is suggested in spite of the poet's awareness that the great Maroon communities of the past have been defeated, or have had to compromise with the enemy. He is also aware of the virtual impossibility of disentangling from America's cultural and economic web; the allurement of metropolitan taste, style, fad and fashion; the driven need to find even the most menial employment abroad in a context of real starvation at home.

In spite of such awareness he advocates maroonage as an absolute necessity, and invokes the spirit of Nanny Nanahemmaa — Jamaican Maroon Queen Mother — who like Toussaint in 'Cap', has become a *loa* or *zemi*, because of the quality of her historic resistance to the plantation's militia.[8] Nanny is invoked as a Muse of fertility and the natural life and as a talisman against drought and dry rot of Spirit. Similarly, the spirit of the "runagate" (runaway and renegade) is invoked as counter to the city's devastation.

runagate
runagate
runagate

look how our villages are grown up tall
into this strangled city

tales of another leader lost

solares bolivare palanquin

washed away with the frogs and the river end the mud & accompong

runagate
runagate
runagate

'Stone', *X/Self*, 95

There is always this great sense of 'in spite of' informing the courage of the poem's affirmations. Here it is the rebellion of the Maroon, in spite of the disappearance of tribe and village, the emergence of "strangled city". The "strangled city" reference is to Martin Carter's poem of the fifties: 'Not Hands like Mine', which tells of the gradual extermination of the Caribs, and the urban ordeal of the post-Emancipation African. Maroonage is advocated in spite of these realities, and in face of the deaths of resistance leaders and the erosion of the Cockpit Country fastness.

'Ice/Nya' is a recapitulation of the main idea of *X/Self*, that is that the unchecked expansion of Mont Blanc will mean the ultimate reduction of Kilimanjaro. A future of void, desert and counter-revolutionary regression is predicted for those peoples who remain passive and silent while they are being destroyed. Foreseeing the possibility of such a future, the poet again assumes the role of warner, prophet and shaman of the Apocalypse; 'Sun Song' 'Citadel' and 'Xango' all seeking to define the relationship between the creative Spirit and the apocalyptic moment.

'Sun Song', one of the original 'Harmattan Poems' of 1970-71, begins with a beautiful evocation of the Caribbean dry season, which contains a paradox of flowering in the midst of desolation. Drought in this poem is a state of expectancy, rather than the despair and defeat of Brathwaite's urban poems. In 'Sun Song' the harmattan is fore-runner of the hurricane, an Ogun Shango *loa*. The poem, therefore, ends with a passionate invocation of the spirit of flame, as a refiner's fire necessary for the world's cleansing. The apocalyptic idea is accepted and the apocalyptic moment summoned as the only means of vindicating past affirmations and ensuring future rebirth.

The second section of 'Citadel' parallels the 'Vèvè' section of *Islands* beginning "so on this ground / write". The poem of the Apocalypse will contain the qualities of Ogun Shango: iron and fire; firmness of Spirit, energy and will. It will demand its libation of blood; that is, passion, sacrifice and pain, before it becomes "iron/metal speaking freely of the fire". To speak "freely of the fire" is to give full voice to the idea of revolt; to uncensor the inhibited *loa* of revolution within oneself. The poem of the Apocalypse is music played by the blacksmith/warrior *loa* Ogun Shango: "the fire/harp blaze howling hot and long lambent in the grip of god" ('Citadel', *X/Self*, 101). Such music contains the sound of hellfire and recrimination ("howling hot"); yet it is also the opposite: "long and lambent". The dictionary definition of "lambent" is "playing lightly on a surface without burning it"; or "shining with a soft clear light without fierce heat". The poem then, must embody the two sides of Apocalypse: destructive/recriminatory and creative/renascent.

The poem is also healing, magic, obeah, alchemical spell against maljo, the baleful eye of Mont Blanc with its immense genius in parasitism and experience at creating and projecting distorted stereotypes.

> so we make pots
> potients against the sound of lamentations
> against the maljo blowing from the devil's ridge

The image of pot, insofar as it relates to Haitian religion, projects the poem as a vessel, govi, container and home for the secret inner

Self — "the gros-bon-ange".[9] As a container of Spirit, the poem protects "nam" from Prospero's reductive magic. As "potient" (potent potion), it protects against lamentations and the cold death-wind of Mont Blanc.

The poem is finally Ananse's fragile web, spun not in the Great House but in the tenement yard, out of which has grown the truly indigenous aesthetic of the Caribbean:

> and from the tennament, this sipple spider space we hold
> we make this narrow thread of silver spin the long time of sand

The thread from which the poem is woven is time itself, Marvell's and Eliot's vast desert stretching before and after, which in Brathwaite's work permeates the structures of History.

The final poem of *X/Self* is 'Xango'. In 'Xango', the *loa* of thunder, associated with Ogun, X/Self finally discovers his "Nam". This discovery, hinted through omens earlier in the poem, is similar to Tom's recovery of his Ogun personality in *Islands*. Both of Brathwaite's trilogies move towards the emergence of the Ogun/Shango family of *loa*. 'Xango' invokes the entire family: Erzulie, wife or consort of Ogun, Damballah and Agwe, and Shango. The *Black & Blues* version of the poem carries an epigraph: "The god Shango was conceived in love and rises to destroy the world". Shango, then, is the movement from love towards Apocalypse, paralleling Christ whose mission of love, healing and redemption is followed by his second coming as judge, with a mission mainly of condemnation and destruction.

The poem begins with a welcoming of renewed Spirit: "*Hail* / there is new breath here". The first member of the Ogun/Shango family to appear is Erzulie; "erzulie with green wings / feathers sheen of sperm". Muse not only of beauty but of fertility, Erzulie is the "new breath" of Spirit, the freshness of journeying that Brathwaite feels in producing his first poems since *The Arrivants* ('Xango' belongs to the first wave of poetry after *Islands*). Hence Erzulie is first welcomed as a consort of Agwe, *loa* of the ocean and all journeying across water.

> there is a west wind
> sails open eyes the conch shell sings hallelujahs

She is also the Muse of Africa manifesting herself in new ways in his poetry. Hence:

i take you at last my love
my night my dream my horse my gold/en horn my Africa

The Muse of Africa here is a combination of desire, dream, imagination and music. Joyful possession of this Muse creates vision, language and *"riddim"*.

we word with salt this moisture vision
we make from vision
black and bone and riddim

The reference here is to the Dogon creation myths described by Griaule in his *Conversations with Ogotemmeli* in which the Nummo, Creator-spirits in the form of serpents, infuse matter with life-force, which assumes the form of water and the Word.

> The life-force of the earth is water. God moulded the earth with water. Blood too he made out of water. Even in a stone there is this force, for there is moisture in everything.[10]

The poet who is giving words and savour to a vision perceived as moisture, is a type of Nummo; a vessel for and conveyer of the creative word. In 'Citadel', he speaks of "the cup of my word", an image which portrays language as a vessel containing moisture.

The "huh", "hah", "hah" are explosions of breath connected not only with the primal sounds of the *loa*'s lovemaking, but also with the early stages of divine language.

> the earth had a language, the first language of this world and the most primitive of all time. Its syntax was elementary, its verbs few, and its vocabulary without elegance. The words were breathed sounds scarcely differentiated from one another, but nevertheless vehicles. Such as it was, this ill-defined speech sufficed for the great works of the beginning of all things.[11]

'Xango', then, is a creation myth in which is described both the conception of Xango and his emergence as the Muse of *X/Self*. The boy Xango is distinguished by a number of icons: a gourd tree, "knotted snakes and coffle wires", "water courses, valleys, clotted blood", bamboo clumps, the rainbow and bougainvillaea petals. These icons identify him as an Afro-Caribbean Muse. The gourd tree which also appears in 'The Making of the Drum' bears the calabash whose dry rattling sound, by supplementing the detonations of the drum, is crucial to sustaining the energy and fervour of time's dancers (*The Arrivants*, 97). Herskovits notes that Erzulie, Xango's mother in this poem, is wife of Petro deity Simbi d'l'eau who "inhabits the mango and calabash trees".[12] Griaule writes that among the Dogon the calabash "is a symbol of the woman and of the sun, who is female".[13] The gourd icon, then, associates Xango with energy, rhythm and fervour, fertility and creativity, the female principle.

It also locates him within the Damballah/Ogun/Erzulie family of *loa*. Simbi d'l'eau is, like Damballah, symbolized as a snake, and is patron of fresh water and springs.[14] Xango's association with snakes confirms his relationship to Damballah or Simbi d'l'eau as a *loa* of fertility. The rainbow and river images also suggest Damballah. It should, however, be noted that Xango, like the Ogun of *The Arrivants*, bears the marks of New World plantation slavery: the chains of the slave coffles, and the clotted blood which in Brathwaite is a recurrent image of withered heritage, the dried-up or drying bloodline.

The impact of his emergence as Muse in Brathwaite's work is one of vitalization:

these tendrils knitted to the cold
un
pearl and wail
the earth on which he steps breaks furl
in rain
bow
tears

'Xango', *X/Self*, 108

The image of tendrils is suggested by earlier images of snakes and water courses. "Unpearl" is really 'unpurl', unravel, and follows from both "knotted" and "knitted". The word is related to the various images of uncurling and unfurling which one saw in *The Arrivants*, and like them, suggests awakening, unwinding, a "freeing up" of the poetry. "Pearl" is connected in earlier Brathwaite with images of crystal, jewels. It suggests processes of slow concentrated hardening and relates to the poetry of "hardness" and "imagism" which Brathwaite recognizes as the polar opposite of the shamanistic poetry of the Voice that he had begun to write during the sixties. The "unpearling" of the line, then, is its disintegration, its relaxation, its "deconcentration", its opening up under the impact of the

Voice. "Wail" may suggest "lament," though here it refers to the characteristic singing style of both Afro-American and Afro-Caribbean religious groups, and by analogy to the whole aesthetic of the Voice. Thus, taken as a whole, the passage celebrates the poet's entry into his Voice ("wail") and into the life and warmth of his African heritage after years of intricate entanglement ("tendrils") with the frigid death of Europe ("knitted to the cold").

The rainbow, apart from associating Xango with Damballah, is also the track along which Nummo travelled from sky to earth and is termed "the Nummo's track" by the Dogon.[15] It is connected with the life-force, the constant interplay between heaven and earth, sun and water.

> The rays of light and heat draw the water up, and also cause it to descend again in the form of rain. That is all to the good. The movement created by this coming and going is a good thing. By means of the rays the Nummo draws out, and gives back the life force. This movement indeed makes life.[16]

Apart from this, the rainbow in the Old Testament mythology signifies the Covenant between God and Noah that the world will never again be destroyed by water: only by fire. It is this Covenant, appropriated by Afro-Americans in one of their gospel songs, that James Baldwin recalls in his illuminating collection of essay/testimonies, *The Fire Next Time.* Brathwaite's Uncle Tom prays earnestly to "see the rainbow / of Heaven / God's curved / mourning / calling" (*The Arrivants*, 14).

The rainbow, then, is a perfect icon for Xango, signifying both his life-bearing and his destructive capacities. It spans the space between two Apocalypses — the past destruction by water in which the ancestral survivor was Noah, mythological father of Blacks and Whites, Ham, Shem and Japhet — and the future promised annihilation by fire. The rainbow is also the central symbol of *Sun Poem*, whose changes are linked with the colours of the spectrum.

Xango is also associated with bamboo clumps and flowers; natural vegetable life and "the tiger clue": an incongruous mixture of icons. The bamboo clumps connect him with Haitian *loa* of the Ogun family, Ogun Banandjo, Ogun Badagri and Ogun Batala — *loa* associated with travel, prophecy, connaissance, esoteric knowledge and healing. These *loa* live in bamboo clumps.[17] Xango, as *loa* of all that is natural and rooted, manifests himself in a correspondingly vital language when he possesses the poet as houngan or shaman.

his syllables
taste of wood of cedar lignum vitae phlox

these gutterals
are his mon general mon frère

Lignum vitae, wood or tree of life, indicates Xango's identity as a *loa* of beginning while "gutterals" (gutter plus gutturals), the primal elementary sounds of the Nummo, are associated with the poor Black people of the diaspora who have maintained ecstatic Orisha reverence in the Caribbean and Americas. Brathwaite's poetry is an attempt to employ the philosophy of these people as the basis of new complex metaphors. Such complexity arises naturally out of the liminal nature of the New World experience, which is by force of History, transcultural and many-veined.

Xango's association with the tiger icon could imply two things. The tiger may be a Blakean symbol of form transfused by fierce and fiery divine energy. Blake's poem 'Tyger' employs images of the forge, flame, anvil and blacksmith, which, translated into a Yoruba or Dahomean context would all apply to Ogun Shango who is among other things a blacksmith. The tiger may also be an Aztec telluric force, connected with the disappearance of a "sun", or order of time and history, and "the appearance of a new sun or tiger".[18]

X/Self is very much concerned with the re-emergence of the Spirit of Meso-American civilizations, and the Xango archetype embraces that rebirth as well. The association of Erzulie with the hummingbird, was the first signal in the poem of the return of Quetzalcoatl.

As Xango grows to manhood, he is revealed as an apocalyptic force and hailed by the poet as the militant energy that he bears within himself. The salutation"mon general mon frère" is an obvious echo of Baudelaire's "mon semblable mon frère", or T.S. Eliot's adaptation of Baudelaire's line in *The Waste Land.* Brathwaite perceives Xango as double ("semblable"), that often fearsome Other that is a hidden or censored part of Self. Emerging from the tomb of his past, the boulder of a burdensome and distorted history rolled away, Xango is a bell-ringer for liberty, announcing loudly to the awakening people the message of their freedom.

his childhood of a stone
is rolled away he rings from rebells of the bone his liberated day

The phrase "rebells of the bone" suggests both the bone-deep engrainment of rebellion in the Caribbean person, and the fact that such rebellion grows out of the very skeletonization of peoples by Mont Blanc.

The rest of the poem imagines the impact of reborn Xango on the present order. As the awakened force of 'native' America he reverses the advance of conquistador and capitalist, restoring herds of stampeding bison and stopping the flow of Coca Cola. This is perhaps, more pre-historic than post-historic Xango.

> the bison plunge into the thunders river
> hammering the red trail blazing west to chattanooga
>
> ....
>
> ....
> jp morgan is dead
> coca cola is drowned
>
> the statue of liberty's never been born

But history has happened, and the Statue of Liberty is as much a reality as the genocide of Native Americans. *X/Self,* indeed, has argued that the elevation of the former is intimately related to the extermination of the latter. Mont Blanc grows at the expense of Kilimanjaro: the technological feeds on the primal; the factory and mine replace the forest; lake becomes desert. Central to Mont Blanc's process, *X/Self* has argued, has been a genocide so pervasive that it has become normal, and is treated as peripheral in Mont Blanc's histories and efforts at self-assessment.

The dream of reversion to "the green beginnings of this world"[19] is, as Brathwaite is fully aware, an impossible one. His focus, therefore, is on the present condition of the New World person who, if he has in his music retained a vibrant oral tradition, may in his life be equally the product of a whoral one. He has embraced and absorbed so many contradictory influences, "book and bribe / bomb / blast and the wrecked village", "computer conjur man", abortion, pollution, police brutality and jazz, that he's become X/Self, an unknown quantity. A blend of ancestral and ultra-modern elements, computer and conjury, places him a little outside of the predictions of Prospero's arithmetic. The quality of his hurt, the strength of his survival, the enduring vitality of his creative force as seen in his ever-vibrant music, make him a time bomb.

Brathwaite views whatever explosions may come as both necessary and justifiable preludes to renewal.

for there is green at the root of his bullet
michaelangelo working away at the roof of his murderous rocket

Michaelangelo's heroic feat in painting the ceiling of the Sistine Chapel (1508-1512) was one of the great moments of the Italian Renaissance. Working for four years while lying on his back, Michaelangelo painted the story of the Creation of the World, the Creation of Adam and Eve, the Fall, and the Deluge — the full Judeo-Christian creation myth. At first glance it seems outrageous to compare this fact with that of a contemporary Xango-like freedom fighter creating his "murderous rocket" of liberation. Brathwaite, however, has argued in *X/Self* and some of his later essays that the magnificent achievements of Rome have been won at the price of great destruction in Europe and beyond. The Renaissance was happening at the same time as witch hunts and the Inquisition; the Church, with its history of bloody Crusades and intolerance, has been founded on the Abattoir.

Michaelangelo, then, embodies the central paradox of History: that of phenomenal creativity growing out of equally phenomenal destructiveness, grace juxtaposed to or issuing from the heart of atrocity. Xango, who seeks to bring into being a new world order, is equally a renaissance presence, and will embody the same paradox. It is also possible that Brathwaite has in mind not only Michaelangelo's depiction of Creation, but his rendering of The Last Judgement including the *Dies Irae,* in the same Sistine Chapel, twenty-three years later. Together, these two great themes distinguish Michaelangelo as an artist concerned with the beginning and ending of Time, and an appropriate Old World person to remember at the end of *X/Self,* a work that has explored the relationship between creation and destruction in the evolution of both a New World order and a new world-order.

Yet he is, ultimately, more concerned with the life-enhancing than the death bringing qualities of Xango.

greet
him
he speaks near

you

hear
him
he teaches

face
and youth
and how to use your seed and soul and lissom

touch
him
he will heal

you

word
and balm
and water

flow

embrace
him
he will shatter outwards to your light and calm and history

your thunder has come home

'Xango', *X/Self*, 111

Xango here is endowed with the healing properties of both Ogun Batala and Christ, while the association of "word" with "water" reaffirms his affinity with the Nummo.

The apocalyptic aspect of Xango is, however, not forgotten. Xango explodes when he is embraced. His explosion will have a profoundly disturbing effect on vision ("light") composure and History. The Apocalypse will make necessary the revisioning of concepts, values and human civilization itself. The last line, "your thunder has come home" tones down the original line "your *terror* has come home"[20] but still manages to convey the idea of karmic retribution falling on the head of the historically guilty. Such retribution, however, is not presented as an end in itself, but as the prelude to the reordering and rehumanization of History.

Xango, who is both the dead-end of a history of brutalization and the green beginning of a new order, is an omen of what could happen if all the devastated peoples of the world were to revolt and return to its monstrous source all the terror which has historically been visited upon them. His emergence is a warning to Mont Blanc about the urgent need to transform the frozen structures and processes of Empire in a world where more and more 'developing' nations have begun "speaking freely of the fire". His emergence also signals Brathwaite's belief in humanity's capacity to resist the inhuman conquistador principle, which in *X/Self* has been symbolized by the vulture or condor perpetually on the wing. Xango is a resurrection symbol; man's retrieval and recreation of his sense of the sacred and humane, if even at the price of violence.

The faith to believe that such rebirth remains perennially possible, has been difficult to sustain in *X/Self*, where at one point the poet/shaman declares:

> i just can't get/up stand up stand/up for i rights bob
> marley in this ya ghetto too much live i now in this wild evil
> world of axles wrecked gear boxes scatter/pillar levers
>
> the huge red silent pain of dead. fish dead. car screams
> their lobster sponges dried out breathe
> ing rasp & rust and rasspan angles banggalang & booming babylon
> 'Shaman', *X/Self*, 67

It does, however, endure this world in which it is beleaguered and beaten down by rusting machinery, the city's cacophony and overwhelming discord and dereliction. Against the archetype of reduced scarecrow man, cripple and mimic man, Brathwaite places that of Xango, the unshackled human Spirit and emancipated divinity of man, whose resurrection he views as the poet's eternal responsibility.

Wilson Harris, in his seminal essay, 'The Question of Form and Realism in the West Indian Artist',[21] observes that although artists may begin with a vision of the reduced person, they must:

> move that diminished creature through [their] work in a manner that is disturbing, so disturbing that vitality and power are realized as a very strong possibility.

Brathwaite, despite his consistent focus on images of human dereliction, shares in this aesthetics of hope, vitality and redemption, which may turn out to be the most valuable gift that the New World can offer the Old.

Notes

1. Brathwaite, E., 'Caribbean Culture: Two Paradigms', in Jurgen Martini ed., *Missile and Capsule* (Bremen, 1983), 36-37.
2. Brathwaite, E., *The Development of Creole Society* (Oxford: Clarendon Press, 1971).
3. Robinson, D., *American Apocalypses* (Baltimore & London: The John Hopkins University Press, 1985), xii.
4. Lawrence, D.H., ed. Mara Kalnis, *Apocalypse and the Writing on Revelation* (Cambridge: Cambridge University Press, 1980), 62.
5. Walcott, D., 'What the Twilight Says' in *Dream on Monkey Mountain & Other Plays* (New York: Farrar, Straus & Giroux), 1970, 2-40; 'The Muse of History' in Coombs, O. ed., *Is Massa Day Dead?* (New York: Doubleday, Anchor, 1974), 1-27.
6. Walcott D., *Dream on Monkey Mountain & Other Plays* (New York: Farrar, Straus and Giroux, 1970), 310-320.
7. Southern, R.W., *Western Society and the Church in the Middle Ages* (London: Penguin Books, 1970), 174.
8. Brathwaite, E., *Wars of Respect* (Kingston: Agency for Public Information [API], 1977).
9. Deren, M., *Divine Horsemen: Voodoo Gods of Haiti* (London: Thames & Hudson Ltd., 1970), 30 [first published 1953].
10. Griaule, M., *Conversations with Ogotemmeli: An introduction to Dogon Religious Ideas* (London: OUP, 1965).
11. ibid, 20.
12. Herskovits, M., *Life in a Haitian Valley* (New York: Doubleday, Anchor, 1971), 320.
13. Griaule, M., *Conversations with Ogotemameli*, 105.
14. Courlander, H., *The Drum and The Hoe: Life and Lore of the Haitian People* (Berkeley, Los Angeles, London: University of California Press 1960), 327.
15. Griaule, M., *Conversations with Ogotemameli*, 108.
16. Griaule. M., *Conversations with Ogotemameli*, 107.
17. Herskovits, *Life in a Haitian Valley*, 321.
18. Harris, W., 'Guyana Prize Address', in *Kyk-Over-Al* 30, June 1988, 29.
19. Walcott, D., 'Dream on Monkey Mountain', *Dream on Monkey Mountain and Other Plays*, 326.
20. Brathwaite, E., 'Shango', Massachusetts Review, 1974.
21. Harris, W., 'The Question of Form and Realism in the West Indian Artist', *Tradition, The Writer & Society* (London: New Beacon, 1967), 15.

Elaine Savory

Returning To Sycorax/ Prospero's Response: Kamau Brathwaite's Word Journey

> What is even more important, as we develop this business of emergent language in the Caribbean, is the actual rhythm and the syllables, the very *software*, in a way, of the language.
>
> *History of the Voice,* 9 [my italics]

Dear *mamma*

i writin yu dis letter/ *wha*?
guess what! pun a computer o/kay?
like i jine de mercantilists?

well not quite!...

if yu cyaan beat prospero
whistle
'Letter Sycorax', *Middle Passages,* 76-77[1]

> ...I look forward to getting publishers, because I'm finding it increasingly difficult, with the kind of work I'm developing, to find publishers who are consonant with it, who are really sympathetic.
>
> Mackey, 'Interview with Edward Kamau Brathwaite', 1992, 58

The Book and the Market

No-one who knows the work of Kamau Brathwaite can miss the fact of the immense contribution he has made over the past several decades to the recognition of linguistic creativity in the Caribbean and its contribution to decolonization and rehabilitation of a culture's collective self-confidence. Brathwaite is poet, essayist, cultural theorist and critic and historian. The fact of grammar makes the listing inevitable, but in fact all these roles combine and shift in every Brathwaite text, and that in itself has been an important part of the radical challenge which Brathwaite has made to the assumptions about genre divisions in English, divisions imposed on the Caribbean during colonialism and therefore derived from the imperial phase of British dominant culture.[2] At the centre of Brathwaite's achievement, however, lies the development of his conception of the word and its production and dissemination. This development has consistently tried to subvert the controls which international English, by its structure, tones, accents and dominant cultural assumptions, places on the "xpression"[3] of peoples of African descent, especially in the Caribbean. Most recently, he has begun to create with the help of computer software a poetic rhetoric which attempts to outwit the restraints of the book, the written text, by drawing on the resources of visual arts, (especially the "video" poems, for example in *Middle Passages* [1992] and *Shar* [1990]). In this, Brathwaite once again demonstrates his desire to discover a way to make English sing with the "xperience" of Caribbean people, for most of whom African cultural survivals and recreations are the core of both ancestral inheritances and contemporary sense of community. But it should also be said that recently Brathwaite has gone much further than before in combining poetry and prose, the intellectual essay, cultural critiques and historical vision, in what I would like to call a "pan-generic textuality", and to connect primarily to African traditions[4] of combining art forms and tones of expression rather than to anything postmodern in Euro-America.

What I propose to do here is to discuss first of all the most important aspects of Brathwaite's perception of the word, and to show what repercussions this has had for his relations with publishers. In making this kind of connection, I am of course placing Brathwaite's work squarely in the frame of cultural politics. No writer who wishes to see work turned into published text and disseminated beyond his/her immediate community can hope to escape the effects of what is clinically termed "market forces", (the word "force(s)" being most significant here, i.e. that which compels or attempts to compel a person to accept what might be most unacceptable, in the name of unrestrained economic pragmatisms). What is interesting about the publishing history of Brathwaite's work is that whereas at every stage (fortunately), there has been at least one publisher willing to take a risk, from time to time the work has been held up or rejected and the reason given or implied seems always connected to the prevailing expectations of the predominantly Western marketplace for the book.[5] This might seem inevitable, except that since Brathwaite's quality of work and major importance was established after the appearance of *The Arrivants* trilogy (by the late sixties), so that publishers might have assumed that there was an audience interested in his development as a writer.

If poets, (and I mention poets especially because their work is the least regarded by market forces, which has the effect, very often, far from giving them more space, of silencing them, especially when their work becomes radically unexpected),[6] if poets pursue the goal of decolonization or of preservation of a sense of a particular cultural community, especially in the so-called Third World, then they run an increased risk of becoming un/"market"/able. By breaking up the word in the way that Brathwaite so often does, we can see (visualize, conceptualize) more of the meaning from our point of view — being able to contain the writing within the limits which appease market forces becomes more and more difficult when the poetry seeks to liberate words themselves from oppressions, both economic and intellectual. For the poet who would have society changed, words are the only possible beginning: oppressions and liberations alike begin from conceptions and ideas expressed in language.

Returning to Sycorax: the word journey

Shakespeare's play *The Tempest*[7] has long provided, in the relation between Prospero and Caliban, an image of the parameters of colonial/colonized, especially with reference to language. Although Brathwaite's rereading of this relation has come fairly recently, I will discuss it here as an informing structure before looking at the history of his conceptualizing of the word. The fact, of course, that Brathwaite assumes knowledge of that relationship as a general cultural possession of his readership/audience tells us something unsurprising about our present cultural position. We know, I think, that though Shakespeare is an extraordinarily good writer and dramatist, our common knowledge of his plays owes more to political than to literary histories: had Shakespeare been merely the greatest writer to emerge from a little island off the shores of Europe with no history of empire and a language of limited world currency, our collective knowledge of him might only be what could be discovered and passed on by curious scholars willing to do more than usual investigative work[8]. However, not wishing to assume that we all know the details of Prospero's relation with Caliban and Brathwaite's gloss on it, I will briefly outline it here and it will serve as a conceptual frame for what follows.

Shakespeare's Prospero is a powerful lord of words, books and magical powers who has established himself on an island and displaced the cultural space and the imaginative freedom of its original inhabitants. Admittedly, like many of the Europeans who colonized the Americas, he has been rejected at home and forced to seek another place to live, but he nevertheless usurps the space of those who lived in the island before him, most obviously Caliban. Although Caliban protests that he has shared his knowledge of the island with Prospero and thus helped him survive there, Prospero confines him after accusing him of attempting to seduce his (Prospero's) daughter Miranda. Moreover, Prospero perceives Caliban as barely human, as the offspring of the witch Sycorax and a devil. But Caliban has learned Prospero's language, and knows "...my profit on't / Is, I know how to curse" (1964: 55). In Caribbean discourse, Prospero has long been seen as the enslaving white colonist of Euro-America, and Caliban as the African slave. Brathwaite has recently taken the story further and begun to explore the possibilities for Caliban in returning home, linguistically and therefore spiritually, to his mother, Sycorax, the true possessor of the island. As Brathwaite points out, there is more freedom for Caliban in turning to his mother's language, than in using his energy to curse Prospero in Prospero's own tongue. Using Prospero's language only marks Caliban as a futile revolutionary and confirms Prospero's power, and in any case, Caliban is a "gateway to an alternative which Prospero has recognized but censored out of Shakespeare's consciousness" (Mackey 1992: 46).[9]

In the recently published poem, 'Letter Sycorax', Brathwaite's poetic persona, presumably the Caliban who is now setting out to reconnect himself with his mother's world of words, playfully recounts his relationship with the computer:

seh about muse.
in computer &

mouse &
learn.

in prospero ling.
uage &

ting

Middle Passages, 82

The difference lies in the direction this Caliban chooses, for what he does is not "fe dem", but "fe we", and in a deliciously witty moment, he moves on from Shakespeare into our age to declare (as he did also in 'X/Self's Xth Letters from the Thirteen Provinces'):

> for nat one a we shd response if prospero get curse
> wid im own
> curser
>
> *Middle Passages*, 83

Brathwaite's concern with the wording of the Caribbean has expanded from the beginning of his writing up to the present and taken a number of different directions. But there is a clearly observable connection which runs right through all of the work. We can isolate briefly, (for the sake of limited space here) several interrelated concepts related to the word which are particularly important and which could be said to be *ancestrally* important in the recent development of his writing. It ought to be said here that Brathwaite is a poet first, with all that means in the context of the matrices[10] of African and Caribbean cultures which value both words and the makers of words, so that his essays, whether cultural, critical or historical, are often organised around images,[11] thus permitting meaning to be layered in several directions at once, something not easy to do in the language of Western academe. His conception of the substructures of words, their multiple meanings when segmented into syllables and played upon tonally, also yields some of the most fascinating of his intellectual and cultural theories (see especially *Contradictory Omens*, 1974)[12].

Nommo

In an essay, 'The African presence in Caribbean literature' (1970-73), Brathwaite explored the concept of *Nommo* in relation to Caribbean culture. This was a concept which Janheinz Jahn presented in relation to the continent in his *Muntu: the New African Culture* (1958) as:

> ...the life force, which produces all life, which influences "things" in the shape of the *word*.
>
> "The Nommo", says Ogotommeli, "is water and heat". The vital force that carries the word issues from the mouth in a water vapour which is both water and word. Thus Nommo is water and the glow of fire and seed and word in one. Nommo, the life force, is the fluid as such, a unity of

> spiritual-physical fluidity, giving life to everything, penetrating everything, causing everything...
>
> Ogotommeli says: "The word is for all in this world; it must be exchanged, so that it goes and comes, for it is good to give and be receive the forces of life".[13]

Brathwaite writes of the same concept:

> The word (*nommo* or name) is held to contain secret, [sic] power... People feel that a name is so important that a change in his name could transform a person's life. In traditional society, in fact, people often try to hide their names. That is why a Nigerian, for example, has so many names. Not only is it difficult to remember them, it is difficult to know which is the name that the man regards or identifies as his *nam.*
>
> *Roots,* 236-7

Thus how a word is constructed, or reconstructed, or sounded is vital to the connection it can make to those who still hear with an ear understanding the life force which words are to certain human communities (it used to be all, but after industrialism and post-modernism I am not sure I can still say so). Words then, for Brathwaite, are absolutely vital carriers of living experience, cultural ancestry and spiritual survival which make their own peace with the exigencies of material needs and how these are assessed and pursued. A community which is alive has its own "xperience" of words.

Nation Language

> The hurricane does not roar in pentameters
>
> *History of the Voice*, 10

In the crucial essay *History of the Voice* (1979/81; 1984), which is in many ways, like the essay *Contradictory Omens,* a pivot or turning point in his work,[14] Brathwaite traces the presiding rhythmical influences in European and Caribbean poetry. After rightly pointing out that before Chaucer, English poetry had alternative rhythms to the pentameter, rhythms which can speak to Caribbean writers now, and that its sovereignty has extended even to the United States and proved hard for poets to discard, Brathwaite goes on to explore the implications of his concern that poetic rhythm ought to approximate the "natural experience", the "environmental experience". In the Caribbean, the natural world does not announce itself in the measured tones of pentameter rhythm. Moreover, nation language,

Brathwaite's inspired term for the language(s) of the people, that complex and rich continuum from deepest Creole to accented but accessible international English, "largely ignores the pentameter" (*History of the Voice*, 13). Nation language is creative linguistic revisioning:

> English it may be in terms of some of its lexical features. But in its contours, its rhythm and timbre, its sound explosions, it is not English... Nation language... may be in English: but often it is in an English which is like a howl, or a shout or a machine-gun or the wind or a wave. It is also like the blues. And sometimes it is English and African together.
>
> *History of the Voice*, 13

Brathwaite had earlier explored the resonance of literary versions of jazz forms and their relevance to West Indian fiction (1967/8), as well as cultural diversity in the Caribbean, in *Contradictory Omens*, where he also attempted to find an intellectual "xpression" of his own[15], but it was in *History of the Voice* that he was very explicitly concerned to demonstrate that the presentation of the word, the emphasis of the word's sound and rhythm, in fact, provided the crucial element in striking out against Prospero's controls and turned the English word into something closer to the explicitly musical nature of words in African languages.

The idea of the natural world as essentially formative of image and line was an implicit element in Brathwaite's arguments from early on in his work as, for example, when he began his essay 'The African Presence in Caribbean Literature' with a poetic description of the way in which the West African desert wind of the beginning of the Western year, drifts across the Atlantic to cause the drought experienced by the Caribbean some months later. So, he went on, the slaves came from Africa and brought their own rhythms of life and culture to the Caribbean. The image of the hurricane, then, is another mode of linking Africa and the Caribbean, for hurricanes are born off the African coast, of winds and temperatures which originate on the continent itself. The poetic equivalent of the hurricane, then, would be the rhythmic reflection of human response to African experience as transmuted into Caribbean life. Similarly, this image is echoed in much of Brathwaite's work since, most thoroughly in *Shar/Hurricane Poem*, in which not only the shape of the words but their size and formation on the page indicate the sound they bring[16], the "noise", as Brathwaite put it in *History of the Voice:*

> Now I'd like to describe for you some of the characteristics of our nation language. First of all, it is from, as I've said, an oral tradition. The poetry, the culture itself, exists not in a dictionary but in the tradition of the spoken word. It is based as much on sound as it is on song. That is to say the noise that it makes is part of the meaning, and if you ignore the noise (or what you would think of as noise, shall I say) then you lose part of the meaning. Which is, again, why I have to have a tape recorder for this presentation. I want you to have a sound of it, rather than the sight of it.
>
> *History of the Voice*, 17

Brathwaite realizes that the concept of wording which is Eurocentric, i.e. dominant, scribal, textual Euro-American culture, the confining of the word to the page, cannot pass as relevant to the living experience of Caribbean (predominantly African-sourced) community. The clear goal of Brathwaite's use of language is to ensure the continuity and inspiration of the African community in the so-called New World, a community which can, if freed from the residual resentments of a long passage through deprivation and inhuman treatment, engender perhaps not only rehabilitation of its own injured members but those of other groups. This is a demanding agenda, and one which Brathwaite's texts recognize has no simple advancement: in the landscape of assassinated leaders, remaining prejudice and economic handicap and the spurious power of bucking the system through the chimera of drug-related rebellions, much which had been done, it seems, must be done again. This is xpressed in both the new poems in *Middle Passages* and the intensely moving and disturbing description in *Trench Town Rock* of Brathwaite's personal agonies in Jamaica, of not only barbarities visited on children and arbitrary murders, but his own experience of violation, dispossession and threat so intense that he describes it as a form of death[17]. In this context, in which the black community seems to be lacerating itself rather than healing from the wounds of the past, there is an urgency about keeping the faith that words can matter enough to redeem, renew and purify when they pass through the consciousness of a community-directed poet.

If we then can take the concept of the hurricane blowing in something other than Prospero's notion of the rhythm of words as denoting the centrality of the relation between the word and the living which gives rise to verbal exchange, and thus acknowledge the difference between ex/ and x/perience and ex/ and x/pression, then we are on the way to perceiving how importantly Brathwaite has continually challenged Prospero, even by 1979/80. But at that time, the ideas he spoke of were often expressed relatively conventionally, as this essay is written conventionally: so many lines a page, so many words a line, written from left to right, in international English grammar, with footnotes and recognizable conventions drawn from the prescriptions of the Western academy and therefore culturally specific, but taught as if universal. When he abandoned that format, as in *Contradictory Omens*, he received a number of obtuse responses from academics and publishing houses alike, who seemed to miss the whole point — that the hurricane was beginning to blow through the edges of Prospero's tidy world of Western academic conventions.

Coming Home

Since 1979, Brathwaite's forms have caught up with the implications of his ideas, and thus constitute a radical philosophical departure from conventional (colonially influenced) West Indian thinking. First of all there is the issue of, as Edouard Glissant terms it, "Caribbean Discourse", which for Brathwaite just as for Glissant, is a communal and oral language or languages, markedly difficult to situate in the form of the book, for the book brings all kinds of other and often dangerous cultural associations with it:

> When the experience of reading, then access to "knowledge", is *granted* to a fraction of a community with an oral tradition (and this is done by an elitist system of education), the resulting dislocation is limited in its effect. One part of this elite is "wild" about its brand new knowledge; the rest of the community retains for some time, and alongside this delirium, its sanity.
>
> If this "learning" spreads, without being related to an autonomous process of acquiring appropriate techniques, the disequilibrium of the élite becomes the norm that itself becomes "widespread", through which the entire subjugated community consents passively to surrender itself, its potential development, its real culture.
>
> And if such an operation is conducted against a community whose oral language bears the secret, unlikely, and elusive stamp of the written one (this is the case, as we shall see, with the Creole language in Martinique), dispossession is likely to be terminal. A close scrutiny of this dispossession is one way of fighting against collective self-destruction.[18]

Brathwaite's self-set task then, has been to on the one hand, reinforce a sense of collective self in Caribbean communities through the realization of both Caribbean forms of expression, especially at a time when African cultural survivals in the Caribbean were not only not generally recognized but also actively suppressed or marginalized, and on the other hand, to work towards some way of fusing orality and the book. Increasingly, since the late seventies, Brathwaite's poetry has expressed in its forms the breaking down of the word as Western icon and the reworking of it as African-Caribbean "xperience". As Brathwaite puts it in a recent interview, when asked about the fragmentation which has recently characterised some of his word-play:

> I think the coherence now would come more in the effect of the poem, you know. In fact, to be able to write a poem which is built up on fragmented slivers but still has an overall archetype of coherence — something that, like the form within music, that you might break it down into movements within the overall form, but that the overall form is very confident and certain.[19]

What informs these remarks is the problem which Brathwaite recognised in *History of the Voice*, i.e. the difficulty of capturing the essentially oral and performance nature of *nation language* on the published page. But by imaging the computer now as a medium which can help Caliban turn back towards his mother, Sycorax, by liberating him from some of the strictures of the written conventions of the English language text, Brathwaite has stepped into a space in which orality, the book and the screen combine to project an immediate sense of cultural identity and linguistic freedom.[20]

There are of course costs to this, as is too often the case for those who place themselves at the dangerous borderlands of cultural hegemonies. For, in effect, Brathwaite is striking out into a new territory, made of both influences of African, European and predominantly Caribbean cultures, but expressed as much through the computer's ability to draw sounds on the page as it is through the voice in a reading. This is an immensely important experiment, and crosses cultural borders in new and exciting ways. The computer makes the book speak, in this sense, and moreover, makes the space between words very much more obvious than they are even in a reading. This bridges the gap between the world of orality and the world of reading. Yet we are still reading, and it is still a book. Therefore, the condition of a book's creation is still dependent on the publisher and the marketplace.

Prospero's Response

> The first thing is that I look forward to getting publishers, because I'm finding it increasingly difficult, with the kind of work I'm developing, to find publishers who are consonant with it, who are really sympathetic. My feeling is that it's always an act of terror nowadays to deliver anything to a publisher, because you get, you know, these kinds of remarkable rejection slips of letters that, you know, the work is either inaccessible, though it ain't even Joyce or Derrida, or it don't have — like my present publishers in England have sent back these things about "We haven't got a public for this, for this kind of thing. There is no market for it, no interest in this kind of thing and" — best of all — "why don't you write a different book?"
>
> Mackey, 'An Interview with Kamau Brathwaite', 58

> The first thing is that I look forward to getting publishers because I'm finding it difficult, with the kind of work I'm developing, to find publishers who are consonant with it, who are really sympathetic. My feeling is that it's almost *an act of terror* nowadays to deliver anything to a publisher because you get, as you know, these kinds of remarkable rejection slips of letters that assume — or behave — like *you is an idiot* — or — you know— dem — yu kno (w) — dat — you know — the work is either inaccessible or it ain't Joyce or Derrida or who/what ever is the buzzword/ buzzthing/ bugname/ bugsyidea right then... you have to lissen to the outrage of what amounts to *why don't you write not what you've writ — but — why don't you write a different book?* — bwoy — navigate you present charts into coherent chaptures or captures — *surely dem muss know what dem sayin, what demn doin to you!* So that unless some Columbus or David Livingstone or Andre Breton comes along a whole swathe of Black/Third World/ Caribbean and dare I say world xpression/xperience is wiped out... and what I sayin here applies not only to my (white) metropolitan publishers who after all at least published some of me... But I'm thinking of our Black and Third world and Caribbean publishers — *don't ask what I can do for you — but what you can do for your culture* or something like that... the few of them...but I th/ink we could do — try — to do better...
>
> Unpubl. Ms: *Middle Passages: The Hambone Interview*, 142, 144

These two passages reflect the distance between a published interview and the creative improvisation on it which Brathwaite has recently completed and which is included in the *Middle Passages* manuscript. The former, though part of an interview which pleased Brathwaite very much, in that Nathaniel Mackey sensitively gave him a great deal of time and space in which to explore his concerns[21], is much less effective as an account of the frustrations of being silenced by publishers than the latter, and this is because the latter is informed by nation language. The manuscript *Middle Passages* is characterised not only by nation language but by the video effects of which we have spoken already here, and it is therefore a very effective extension of the poems which came out in *Middle Passages* (Bloodaxe 1992). Yet Bloodaxe quickly declined the "prose" work *Middle Passages*, which Brathwaite offered them on the day they published the poetry with the same title, giving as their reason that the "prose" did not constitute a book[22]. Indeed, in a sense other than they meant, they were right, in that Brathwaite had created again a challenge to the Western idea of the book through his video style of changing font style and sizes, his use of computer windows in the text, as well as his interpretation of the forms of the journal or diary, journalistic reportage, letter, autobiographical fragment, interview and poem. Whatever reasons the publishing house had for rejecting the manuscript, the effect is to cause a division of time and thus space between the poems and the prose which is not Brathwaite's wish, nor expresses the spirit of his pangeneric writing at this time.[23]

I would like to take the Prospero/Caliban story a little bit further. It may seem that since Brathwaite has published two trilogies of poetry volumes and ten volumes of poetry besides, as well as two volumes of plays and eleven volumes of historical, critical and/or cultural essays, that to complain about publication outlets might seem unnecessary. After all, two new volumes of work have recently appeared, one *Zea Mexican Diary* and the other a collection of stories, *DreamStories,* both new departures for Brathwaite, and in both cases the metropolitan publishers have agreed to reproduce the video style.[24]

But if we look at the history of Brathwaite's publications we see that a problematic trend has been present for some time, and is only now beginning to be resolved by the acceptance of the most recent work by presses with large distribution. The first two trilogies and *Other Exiles* were published by Oxford University Press[25] and therefore disseminated widely, and by an impressive Western publishing house name, something which ought not to be a factor in whether a book gets read or not, but in our culture of material signs and signals and over-crowded timetables, functions often as a significant filter. Of the remaining twenty-two titles, eight appeared via publishers who have access to large distribution (this might be stretching a point in the case of the two texts published by the London-based, excellent New Beacon Press, a Caribbean and African-centred bookstore/press which is enormously important to those in the field/culture but may not be able to extend distribution much further), eleven in Jamaica, two in Cuba and one in Mysore, India (this last may indeed have access to large distribution but within one enormous country where Caribbean interpretations of post-colonial issues may be of limited interest as yet).[26] Furthermore, the chronological profile shows that of the titles published in the Caribbean, nine appeared in the seventies, two in the eighties and two in the nineties. Of the thirteen Caribbean published titles, seven were published by the imprint of Savacou, with which Brathwaite has been centrally associated.[27] But Savacou, whilst having produced extremely important work, has a limited distribution network. What this publishing history means, briefly, is that as Brathwaite's work become increasingly experimental, ("video"), and as his forms increasingly followed the theoretical developments expressed in his essays since *History of the Voice*, publication from presses with large distributions and high visibility in the most prominent Western academies became increasingly problematic until the recent acceptance of *Zea Mexican Diary* and *DreamStories*.[28]

There are some aspects of this which I would like to discuss in more detail. The last volume of the first trilogy, *X/Self,* was published by Oxford University Press in 1987 and contained 'X/Self's Xth Letters from the Thirteen Provinces', which is an early version of 'Letter Sycorax'. The latter appears in the recently published *Middle Passages* (Bloodaxe, 1992). The OUP version is not as visually interesting as the later one, which can be attributed to Brathwaite's development of the later style in the years between 1987 and the early 1990s. But it is significant that the relationship with OUP seems to have ceased as the poetry became more fully conversant with the implications of Brathwaite's theories about the nature of the word since the middle seventies.[29]

What is happening here? I don't want to make any assumptions about the reasons for individual publishing decisions beyond my general view that they are increasingly subject, in recessionary times, to assumptions about the commercial implications of content and to publishers' views about the receptivity of a given audience to the work. But I'd like to play/fully (seriously) explore the Prospero story again another way. So far, we have seen the extension of Brathwaite's reimagining of Shakespeare's play to include Sycorax, the ancestral female principle who represents the possibility of really breaking his power, since she is anyway his predecessor as maker of magical changes and ruler of the island. He has also created a new character not present in *The Tempest*, Sister Stark, (the kartsted sister, dark star, also the ARK "from which we begin the second journey"),[30] who is Caliban's sister. Seeing Sycorax and Sister Stark as important shows Brathwaite's central symbolism of cultural politics moving from male-orientated to female orientated images of decolonization.

Yet while we speak of Caliban's potential liberation from Prospero, we have to recognize that while Prospero shrewdly regards the enclosure of Caliban's linguistic facilities as a useful strategy for containing Caliban's rebellion, he is not going to facilitate their dissemination to the widest possible audience, especially if this demands a rethinking of conventions of the book which have served Prospero's power well in the past. Interestingly, when Brathwaite comments that Prospero censored Caliban's possibilities out of Shakespeare's mind, and also suggests that Shakespeare spent a missing two years of his life in the Bahamas, where he became conscious of the circumstances of slavery and imperialism,[31] he is suggesting that the entrenched power which confines the oppressed and limits their creativity can even direct the unusually aware writer's hand. Prospero is a very resourceful magician indeed.

But I do not see those publishers who are reluctant as Prospero himself. To make the point about the role and nature of publishers with the power to help a writer of Brathwaite's stature but a failure of will, we ought to look again at Ariel.[32] Ariel, in Shakespeare's play, falls short of the necessary courage to make a creative challenge to Prospero's power. Prospero ought to be somewhat conscious of his need for Ariel, the able worker of transitions, most charming androgynous sprite. But Prospero has the power to torment Ariel with pains should s/he disobey Prospero's orders. Ariel is clearly creative and imaginative, the very kind of spirit you would expect to have a mind to rebel against controlling forces, or at least to wish to reorder things in his world. He/she does neither, though s/he did resist Sycorax, who therefore confined him/her in a cloven pine. Mere threats of similar punishments are enough to keep her/him willing to serve Prospero, who has nevertheless broken his promise to free Ariel after one year of service (he does do so at the end of the play). Perhaps, if any publisher who has hesitated about the marketability of Brathwaite's work should read this, s/he might consider whether fear of the twelve years of confinement in a "knotty oak", Prospero's (economic) revenge should they disobey, could be a part of the decision-making. For Ariel to be a solution, he/she has to be able to talk honestly and frankly and of her/his own volition to Caliban, and thus reconsider Sycorax's anger, and perhaps there lies a tale worth telling.

I want to end by returning to the beginning. One of the most important roles which Brathwaite serves for all of us is to begin to liberate us from the ignorance and the inhibited vision by which we understand the world, a vision which has marginalized or ignored Africa (as well as other cultures oppressed under Prospero's Western rule). But he does this not by elaborate argument, but by the magic of setting our minds free to roam over images and re-vision concepts and words we have always known and only partially understood. He gives us, in fact, a mode of framing highly emotional and political issues, of exploring complex intellectual ideas and ambivalences, by living with metaphor as a poet does. Through Brathwaite we return to the world of poetry as central, as source of all knowledge, as it was (and is) in most of the African world, was and is in a substantial part of the so-called Third World, and used to be in Europe and the now industrialised world.

Thus my discourse here of Prospero, Sycorax, Stark, Ariel and Caliban shows the influence of Brathwaite's imagination setting my own to work, and privileges poetic symbol — but not a private or obscure symbolism. The strength of Brathwaite's work is that he has always tended to take well known images and ideas and reshape them, thus opening up his world of rich association to the widest possible audience. It is therefore characteristic that he should have chosen Prospero and Caliban as a frame for one direction of his discourse, for the story of *The Tempest* is well known, even when the play might not be. It is also appropriate that we begin to image serious cultural discourse as working just as rigorously when utilizing the resource of Sycorax's imagination as when utilizing that of Prospero, or the range of popular and intellectual discourses all deriving their central imagery from so-called Western clusters of frames of perception. Much lip service is paid to multi-culturalism, but the fact is that it is cannot be realized through either of the two presently prevailing strategies: the continued dominance of discourses deriving from Western intellectual history and the discussion of so-called Third World or Minority cultural sources still contained within Western referential signposts. Both these strategies continue to privilege Prospero, the first explicitly, the second implicitly, and in the shape of postmodern discourses, even strike a blow against the centrality and power of the word itself.

Brathwaite, then, as I have tried to show in this paper, increasingly draws on his poetic technique as a conceptualizing frame shaping important cultural discourse, and in so doing shows how the traditions of African-centred aesthetic and vision of the centrality of the word can become more than revitalized and continued, but also vitally applicable to the lives and imaginations of people of all cultural origins. Through both understanding and respecting Brathwaite's work, we can see afresh the dangers of our present cultural situation, dangers which we see manifest on our television screens and in our newspapers each day without having the resources to interpret them in a creative framework, i.e. one which permits the possibility of transformations and the dissolution of oppressive power structures. I hope I have managed to adequately make the point that the role of poet as Brathwaite practices it becomes much like the old role of the poet in preindustrial societies: combining wordcraft, faith in the word as the cornerstone of human life and brilliant revisioning of the world in an attempt to cleanse and heal the community for whom the poet works. This is especially expressed in Brathwaite's desire that the "ego be decolonized into community"[32] i.e. that we stop using our intellectual and creative gifts to aggrandize individual careers, and contribute them collectively to the redemption of our world.

Thus we can read his development of the Prospero/Caliban story as a cultural parable, and in the tradition of his early work, such as *The Arrivants*, he thus liberates the mind to consider inherited knowledges another way, neither entirely from the past nor entirely from the present. For example, in his most recent imaging of the computer as Sycorax, he in one stroke eradicates the sense we have of the computer as a rather worrying handmaiden of "Western" technological and economic power and transforms it into the most ancient symbol of the magician, assuming another role and guise to those who are gifted with the empathy to listen. Sycorax, then, is the muse in the computer, for Brathwaite the transformative medium by which Caliban finally is reunited with his cultural source. We hear her, in the context of Brathwaite's powerful mythology, for the first time in four hundred years, and her voice is, as we might expect, both strong and extraordinarily unconventional by the standards of the cultural norms we have been accustomed to learning in the kingdoms of Prospero's word.

It is not a matter of abandoning Prospero for Sycorax but learning to hear both of them at the same time; eventually hoping that they may speak to one another freely and begin to resolve their differences (both being powerful makers of transformative images which are the core of very different world visions and therefore of cultural distinctions). The difficulty at the moment, however, is that Prospero, having had the upper hand for a long time, more often than not simply doesn't hear the echoes of Sycorax, and has a lot of ways of doing this. In the process, much as he may not yet realize this, he has lost a good deal of ground as a magician, however, for there is much he does not know and even his capacity to persuade with words has weakened, whereas Sycorax, from her hidden cave, has watched and listened to him for all this time and knows his secrets pretty well. It is obvious that if he does not prepare himself to begin to grow again mentally, he will continue to deceive himself that he has all the answers, and thus to rotate slowly in his own orbit, until Sycorax's return to the world is forced to be one of violent confrontation.

Much more constructive would be the beginning of a true self-liberation on the part of Prospero himself (as opposed to a tolerance of moments of Sycorax's world as contained margins of his own, often, in the context of academe, forced into an implicitly subordinate position in relation to the great names of European philosophical traditions). Who better to help him in this difficult journey, through which Prospero himself will have to begin to learn new languages and to respect world views divergent with his own, than Ariel, his trusted servant? As Brathwaite says, language is not only verbs and sentences "but the whole business of the structures that are built to control the colonial, to control the slave, to control the underclasses of the western world, to control the mind" (Mackey, 'An Interview with Kamau Brathwaite', 47). Ariel's helping hand to Caliban makes a great deal of a difference, as Caliban searches for his "own coral, his own roots" (Mackey, 'An Interview', 47). Brathwaite has of course made his own statement on the subject of publishing difficulties:

> So, as we go on exploring the Caribbean experience... Poems and prose things, ideas, things like a book called *Missile and Capsule,* which tries to look at Caribbean history in terms of

> those two icons. People in the United Kingdom are not interested, I'm told, in ideas of that kind. I don't know why, but I suspect it's because the ideas come from Caliban.
>
> Mackey, 'An Interview with Kamau Brathwaite', 58

Notes

1. This poem is an extension and revision of 'X/Self's Xth Letters from the Thirteen Provinces' and a comparison of the two poems is fruitful. Brathwaite sometimes overlaps elements of one volume with another — see for example the relation of poems in the trilogy *The Arrivants* to those in *Jah Music*. This is in fact one of the major ways in which he works, building constantly on a version of a work and rewriting it, often making it longer, ("building up building up building up from the original" he calls it, in a letter to myself, 1 November 1992).
2. I think we are by now familiar with the idea that genres arise out of particular socio-political and cultural conditions: the argument that the novel came into being because of the rise of the middle-class in Europe in the eighteenth century is a well known one, (see Ian Watt, *The Rise of the Novel* (Harmondsworth: Penguin, 1963). Similarly, we begin to understand that the era of video and extensive television has created an acute sense of the visual in young people now, and this has a strong influence on all the arts. Europe sectionalised artistic genres, but in African cultures, poetry, prose, secular and sacred forms overlapped and could be combined easily. The fusing of poetry and prose, by no means confined to Brathwaite but also practiced by younger poets of African-Caribbean ancestry such as Marlene Nourbese Philip and Claire Harris, signifies a refusal to be bounded by divisions which seem alien to Afro-centric aesthetics.
3. Recently, there has been much discussion in the United States as to the significance and provenance of 'X' as a cultural sign for black identity/ experience because of the soon to be released film of Malcolm X's life made by Spike Lee, (see, for example, 'Who Owns "X"?' *New York Times*, Sunday 8 November 1992, 9:2) and varied signification within African cultures in the United States and the Caribbean makes Brathwaite's interpretation of it particularly effective in speaking for and to a whole people as well as indicating sometimes an individual situation or moment. Brathwaite's work refutes the division between high art and popular art because he utilizes so many popular forms and through them speaks generally, whilst making considerable intellectual and aesthetic demands on the reader/audience. The use of the italic X is another graphic sign of difference, if it is conveyed in the published form, of course.
4. By this I mean first of all the African cultural refusal to separate for

example secular and non-secular activity, and the ways in which language and music and the visual elements of masking and symbolic gesture and movement constitute interrelated discourses in African ceremony and public life.

5. Brathwaite accounts for the earliest stages of his relations with publishers thus: "They hit me down before I cd even get started w/ the rejection of the novella *The Boy & the Sea* written while still at Cambridge 1953-5, because it did not conform to the stereotype of Caribb prose fiction they had already established" (letter to Elaine Savory, 1 November 1992).
6. I use the word "unexpected" here because even radical forms can become conventional once we are used to them. The most challenging experience for a reader/critic/publisher is to be able to detect a new voice in a text, whether by an unknown writer or an established one.
7. Believed to be the last play written by Shakespeare and dated sometime during the fall and winter of 1610-11.
8. I am not of course suggesting that it isn't important to know Shakespeare's work, nor that there are not many people outside England who genuinely enjoy and admire it, but that it is an accident of history, (and in relation to the Caribbean, colonial, imperial history) that any of the plays survived to become central to English literary traditions, and of colonial and imperial history that they then were exported so widely.
9. Brathwaite makes it clear in this discussion that he does not see Caliban as a binary opposite of Prospero, but as another pathway.
10. I mean by this those creative sources which build on the past, particularly on the strong spiritual traditions which incorporated art and which have often become politically important as defences against oppression in recent times, especially in the Caribbean and the United States. In the Caribbean, we could speak specifically of the power of words in the Shango cults, pocomania, voudon, and Rastafarian rituals, and the power of the preacher in the African-American church who so easily moves into the position of leader in political terms partly because of the all-inclusive vision of the role of religion in African-centred cultures.
11. He has particularly emphasized certain images as important in his work: the missile, the capsule, Prospero and Caliban, the hurricane and jazz are some of these.
12. In this essay, Brathwaite also xpresses his ideas by means of dislocating sentences in the manner of a poet's line ordering: " When/ wherever culture/ groups meet/ confront each other..." (1974: 62).
13. Jahn, Janheinz, *Muntu: The New African Culture* (London: Faber, 1961), 124.
14. By turning point, I mean that Brathwaite's essays have often gathered up the implications of relations between form and content in a previous phase of poetry and then crystallised them so that the next poetic phase goes further in demonstrating or pursuing them. Thus

Contradictory Omens stands between the *The Arrivants* and the second trilogy, and *History of the Voice* between *Mother Poem* and the increasingly more unexpected *Sun Poem* and *X/Self*. See also Gordon Rohlehr's argument about the linkage of Brathwaite's essays and poetry in his extensive study of *The Arrivants* (the period up to the late sixties) in *Black Awakening* (1981).

15. In the essay, 'Jazz and the West Indian Novel' (1967/8), now included in *Roots* (1986), Brathwaite begins to set out theoretically what he was feeling his way through in the poems in *The Arrivants* which so strikingly demonstrate the role of jazz as New World mediator of African rhythms and cultural perspectives. But the essay followed norms of Western academic discourses in the sense of how it set about presenting the ideas. In *Contradictory Omens,* Brathwaite was much more committed to exploring the limits of the academic essay form as a mode of xpression. He ran into resistance to this both at the conference at Johns Hopkins University where he presented the essay as a paper first, and with publishers, so that he ended up publishing it under the Savacou imprint to protect it from interference. See the introduction to *Contradictory Omens* (1974), where he talks of the Caribbean environment needing its own aesthetic, and being the only delegate to a conference "dripping with the tropical sun", (*Contradictory Omens*, 5). He was moving towards a realization of the difficulties of persuading either African or North American "establishments" of the need for a different Caribbean mode of shaping ideas. See also the final statement, poetic in form, "the unity is submarine", (*Contradictory Omens*, 64), absolutely appropriate but in itself a challenge to the academic conventions of the essay.
16. The words in this poem convey by their increasing size the threat and the sheer energy of the hurricane. It comes to signify a kind of destructive, nearly fatal cleaning out of old orders. The title, *Shar,* derives from Sharon, the name of Brathwaite's niece who died of lymphoma on July 28 1990. Hurricane Gilbert hit Jamaica on 12 September 1988 and substantially damaged Brathwaite's home and invaluable library. Brathwaite wrote the poem in 1988 and revised it after Sharon's death. Also in 1990, Brathwaite lost his father. The poem is both a fulfilment of the statements Brathwaite had been making about the way hurricanes manifest in a poem and an intense cry of pain and movement towards healing.
17. At the day-long conference celebrating his work, on 24 October 1992 at Eugenio Maria de Hostos Community College, C.U.N.Y., New York, Brathwaite read a new piece in which he declared himself to have been assassinated in Jamaica. He pointed out that the conference was held on the second anniversary of the attack on him at his home in Marley Manor in Kingston, and he has conceptualized the conference as a kind of resurrection, a "tidalectic xperience". *Trench Town Rock,* published in *Hambone* 10, is an almost unbearably intense and vivid account of the attack and the circumstances in Jamaica at the time,

utilizing the video style, computer "windows" in the text, prose, poetry, drama and newspaper reports.

18. Glissant, Edouard, *Caribbean Discourse* (Charlottsville: University Press of Virginia, 1989), 11-12.
19. Mackey, Nathaniel, 'An Interview with Kamau Brathwaite', *Hambone* 9, Winter 1991, 45-59, 48. See also page 12 of this book for a full reprint of the interview.
20. At the Hostos Conference, Brathwaite spoke of Sycorax as the muse in the computer, and said that sometimes he cannot get the computer to function properly if he is not in the right frame to receive Sycorax's messages. This is more than a playful and imagistic way of accounting for the way in which the computer has become the ally of Brathwaite's poetic challenge to Prospero's world. It is a challenge to presently prevalent Western secular modes of intellectual apprehension of the world because it offers a spiritual explanation for the occurrence of poetic inspiration — something which is profoundly associated with the role of the poet in traditional African cultures.
21. In the oral presentation of an earlier draft of this paper, I mistakenly criticized the Hambone interview for its lack of nation language, having misunderstood Brathwaite's explanation of the genesis of the *Middle Passages* manuscript which includes a nation language version of the interview but which followed not preceded it. It was good to sort out the details with Brathwaite and thus discover more evidence of my basic concern (the coming into print of Brathwaite's most recent challenges to Western conceptions of genre and poetic form). I am most grateful to Brathwaite for his willingness to share manuscript material and to talk through the stages of his recent writing with me.
22. Brathwaite comments (letter to Elaine Savory, 1 November 1992) that OUP used the same language previously when returning the manuscript of the Sir Winston Scott Memorial Lecture Brathwaite gave in January 1988 at the Central Bank in Bridgetown, Barbados. I was there at that lecture and it was very important, and ought by now to have been in print so that those of us who are following Brathwaite's journey can see it fully accounted for, rather than be continually negotiating around gaps and hiatuses not created by the writer.
23. Brathwaite comments on the question of divisions between genres that he first notes this division when Merle Hodge's *Crick Crack Monkey* (London : 1970) was accepted by Andre Deutsch but her essay, 'Damas', was turned down. There is no more interesting connection than that between the different voices of a writer, in different moods and occupying different generic spaces, all of which connect in the writer's imagination at some level. This is another kind of connection from the "pan-generic" writing of which I also speak in this paper.
24. The *Zea Mexican Diary* is published by the University of Wisconsin and Longman published *DreamStories* in 1994.

25. Brathwaite says that *Rites of Passage*, the first volume of *The Arrivants* "was sent to OUP without my knowing by Hugh Dunphy of the Bolivar Bookstore (Kingston) who at the time was the OUP rep in Ja, and I will perhaps never know how he got hold of one of the several stencil copies of it I had run off w/ the xpectation that that wd have to be the xtent of my publication... (letter to Elaine Savory, 1 November 1992).
26. Publishers with large distribution: *Third World Poems* (Longman, 1983); *Middle Passages* (Bloodaxe, 1992); *Four Plays for Primary Schools* (Longman, 1964); *Odale's Choice* (Evans, 1967); *The People Who Came* (Longman, 1968-72; 90-92); *Folk Culture of the Slaves in Jamaica* (New Beacon, 1970); *The Development of Creole Society in Jamaica* (Clarendon Press, 1971); *History of the Voice: The Development of Nation Language in Anglophone Caribbean Poetry* (New Beacon, 1984); texts published in Jamaica: *Days and Nights* (Caldwell, 1975); *Soweto* (Savacou, 1979); *Word Making Man* (Savacou, 1979); *Jah Music* (Savacou, 1986); *Sappho Sakyi's Meditations* (Savacou 1990); *Shar/Hurricane Poem* (Savacou 1990); *Contradictory Omens* (Savacou 1974); *Our Ancestral Heritage* (Carifesta 1976); *Wars of Respect* (API, 1977); *Barbados Poetry* (Savacou 1979); *Jamaica Poetry: A Checklist 1686-1978* (Jamaica Library Service 1979); texts published in Cuba: *Black and Blues* (Casa de las Americas 1976); *Roots: Essays in Caribbean Literature* (Casa de las Americas 1986); *The Colonial Encounter* (University of Mysore, India 1984).
27. Brathwaite had worked with the Caribbean Artists Movement in London and later in Jamaica began to think of a similar grouping there. This did not really come about, but out of this period was born the first issues of *Savacou*, the journal, and subsequently the publishing imprint, which was active in the 1970s and 1980s and has published, apart from Brathwaite's work, poems by A.L. Hendriks, Anthony Bland, Anthony McNeill, Beverly E. Brown, Bob Stewart, Jean Goulbourne and Roberto Retamar.
28. At this time, Brathwaite has some major works in progress or held up in the press, including his study of *White Power in Jamaica: the interdynamics of slave control* and what he describes as the full versions of *Love Axe/1* and *Missile and Capsule.*
29. Brathwaite's account of the relationship hopes that it may continue, but for the moment nothing is forthcoming except the hope that the two trilogies OUP have already published stay in print, and also *Other Exiles*.
30. Brathwaite, letter to Elaine Savory, 1 November 1992. Brathwaite has spoken of Sister Stark several times publicly at literary gatherings, seminars etc, (building up, building up), and clearly her voice is imminent in his work. He has also spoken of her presence in the work of the Barbadian/America writer Paule Marshall, (specificially *Daughters*, 1991).
31. Again, this half-play/ful suggestion is a way of recuperating Shake-

spearian insight into the world in which Caliban exists, for Brathwaite acknowledges that the imagination which created both Caliban and Prospero knew a great deal beyond the limits of much of his expansionist culture as it was xperienced in the Caribbean.

32. Michael Dash, in his article 'Ariel's Discourse: French Caribbean Writing After the Storm', (*Journal of West Indian Literature* 1:1, October 1986, 49-58), considers the images of Ariel in the writings of Aime Césaire and Edouard Glissant. Dash discusses the image of Ariel as transcendent in work by both writers, offering a grounded vision of connectedness to the land and an escape from the oppositional extremes of Prospero/Caliban. Though we've seen the Prospero/Caliban/Ariel imagery in the work of George Lamming, Aime Césaire and Fernandez Retanar, and most recently, in a woman-centred interpretation by Marlene Nourbese Philip, I am concerned here only with Brathwaite's interpretations. Those who wish to trace the provenance of these may wish to seek out a paper Brathwaite gave to the New York Academy of Sciences Conference on Slavery and the New World Plantations (1977) called 'Caliban, Ariel and Unprospero in the conflict of creolization'.
33. Brathwaite, at Hostos Community College, 24 October 1992.

Kamau Brathwaite

Metaphors of Underdevelopment: A Proem for Hernan Cortez

Look at his hands
cactus cracked, pricked,
worn smooth by the hoe
limestone soil's colour;
he has lost three fingers
of his left hand falling
asleep at the mill;
the black crushing grin
of the iron tooth'd ratchets
grinding the farley hill cane
have eaten him lame
and no one is to blame

the crunched bone was juicy
to the iron, there was no difference
between his knuckle joints
and ratoon shoots: the soil
receives the liquor with cool flutes;
three fingers are not even worth
a stick of cane; the blood
mix does not show, the star-
gaze crystal sugar shines
no brighter for the cripple blow

and nothing more to show
for thirty years' spine-
curving labour in clear
rain, glass-eyed, coming off the sea,
fattening up the mud
in the valleys, cours-
ing down hillsides, causing the toil of the deep
well-laid roots, gripping soil,
to come steadily loose, junction and joint
between shoot and its flower to be made nonsense of

> and the shame, the shame, the shame-
> lessness of it all, the name-
> less days in the burnt cane-
> fields without love; crack of its
> loud trash, spinn-
> ing ashes; wrack of salt odour that will
> not free his throat; the cutlass fall-
> ing, fall-
> ing, fall-
> ing: sweat, grit between fingers, chigga
> hatching its sweet nest of pain in his toe,
> and now this and now this
>
> an old man, prickled
> to sleep by the weather, his labour,
> losing his hands...

I

as far as i'm concerned, this is not simply a bajan labourer, he is a person caught in the centre of an explosion — a catastrophe — a cultural catastrophe — which this region was / is the matrix (axle) of. and all those broken fingers, the ratchets ... all those images there are not only the images of contemporary exploitative technology, but are engines of a much wider cycle of destiny ... i mean, how is it that we have these people who work thirty years, who become crippled by their labour, who retain their integrity, but who are still ignored by the society ... we see them all the time ...

so what i'm going to talk about is this labourer in my context. and this context is one of culture and by culture i mean the texture and life-style of peoples ... culture seen as dialectic of motion. history as achievement/failure, flux & equilibrium; as catastrophe; or rather, as equilibrium *and* catastrophe.

in this context we must try to understand the new world of the caribbean — the new world *and* the caribbean — what explosions occurred to create the symbolic fragments of continents that we now call islands and inhabit: what destroyed the myth or fact or dream of el dorado, lost atlantis, prospero's drowned island, ponce de leon's fountain of youth ... these are all images that curl around our imagination and cling: the notion of some infinitely gentle, infinitely suffering thing ...

what caused the death of the amerindians, the holocaust of slavery, the birth of tom and caliban?

II

now, in terms of my own culture-view, it all began with the collapse of the pillars of hercules and the fall of the roman empire...

III

this imperial achievement had created an equilibirum of *materia* and spirit, of metropole and province, of law and chaos; and this entity which we call ROME made possible therefore, within the world that it in a sense had created, a definition of values: *judex, index, lex*

with the decline and fall of rome, flux appeared: movements of magic into the metropole; custom replaced statute, gargoyle replaced statue. the vikings moved in from the north; the goths, huns, magyars, came in from the east; the crescent moon of islam curved upwards from the desert through the pyrenees; african and amerindian civilizations began to prophesy disaster...

christianity and the holy roman empire attempted to restore or retain the equilibrium ... but that was now impossible ... because there were now too many alternatives: too many new kinds of natives: there was the new science of copernicus; there were the natural philosophers; the medical school at salerno; there was the choice of galilee and galileo; pope or emperor; priest or politician; wake or dream ...

and then money (MAMMON) became the centre of this shattered universe: markets, bourgs, bourse, traders, banks, bourgeoisie, taxes, tax-collectors, regulations, fines, prisons, leviathan, navigation, war, commerce, merchants, mercantilism; travel to new lands, explore, exploit, control: the shift of power outwards: spire, spear, arrow, bullet, cannonshot, ship, sail, horse, *the charge of the light brigade*; print, bible, heaven; the conquest of the sky by sun-jet angel missile. no prayer, but purse; no custom anymore but customhouse and curse. marco polo overland to china; the portuguese by stepping stone to africa; columbus to san salvador; looking for power, for powder, gun / powder; converting the grain to gain, unholy grail.

therefore: montezuma collapsed; chitzen itza defeated; geronimo doomed; saschatewa, mohica, esquimaux and ewe whale worshippers are marked with the hex; timbuctu, kumasi, ile-ife, benin working its bronze, zimbabwe ... hearing the future of the avalanche ... disorder, horror of unburial, dischordant skeletones ... caribs moving towards heroin and syphilis, cherokees moving towards the horse, the wesson rifle and the waggon chain; ibo and nago to barracoon and charnel ship; zulus towards soweto and the locomotive tank; masai beyond the elephant to the jumbo jet; caliban to new york, paris, london town ...

IV

so that here in the caribbean we have people without apparent roots; all the result of this dis / traction, this destruction; people without apparent values, or the values of the whip, force, co-erce, the curse of word, the guttural; the culture of materialism, not of equilibrium: fat, flesh, flash, faggot, fire of destruction; not stone, demon, wilderness, harbour, the conflagrations of creation...

extermination of the arawak; the draining of the lake of mexico into red-eyed howling dust bowl...

first 10, then 20; first 20, then 200; first 200 then 2000; first 2000, then 200,000 ... africans, slaves, lucumi, tears ... 200,000, 300,000, 400,000, a million ... tears, tears, lucumi ... a million, 2 million, 3 million, 5 million ... *materialism* ... building hotels, plantation houses, brothels ... 10 million, 20 million, 25 and 30 million ... flight flight fuel tears ... tears tears lucumi ... 30 million, 40 million, 50 million ... the draining of the lake of mexico, destruction of the fountains of the youth ... *lucumi* ... *tears* ... to feed the hungry missile mouth ... *lucumi* ... *tears* ... *tears* ... where are the bison of the prairies, the water spirits of the pacific indians; where are those 50 million africans, torn out of tongue, torn out of mother, torn out of soil and soul ... *"can you expect us to establish houses here, to build a nation here? where will the old men feed their flocks; where will you make your markets..."*

V

for me, the *history* of catastrophe, the coming to grips with a person bitten by those ratchets; that archetypal labourer; ruined by that greed; requires a *literature of catastrophe* to hold a broken mirror up to broken nature

VI **caribbean literature**

on the whole, our literature has so far — with certain exceptions — failed to see itself — *to act itself out* — as omens of catastrophe. one exception to this is the work of wilson harris: e.g. *the palace of the peacock* (1960), *the whole armour* (1962), *the waiting room* (1967), *tutatumari* (1968). the very style which harris uses, especially in these novels — the implosions that literally take place within the books — so that the world of the novel reflects a physio-cultural explosion — are re/enactments of catastrophe. and the result is that you have *fragments* — indeed some of the words in harris's (later) work are actually blown away out of the novel:

> for how could he dare to believe it was *he*, rather than another, whom she dreamt to invest with the blast of memory? was it the surest ricochet of fantasy? had he misread the frame of her lips? was he merely her ironical substitute — SILENCE PLEASE — shattering and loud like the ornamental cultivation of the deaf, hammer of deity, consciousness?
>
> A famine of spirits blazed in their very facile resemblances whether skin, leaf, petal, brow, eye, lake. And even as he beheld her — or thought he beheld her in a glimmering crowd of stars — he was doubly conscious of her withdrawal into his ignorance of her naked material, immaterial proportions. She had just crossed a dent and crack in sky or

> pavement, hesitated, caught, forced to struggle: bent forward abruptly, like a woman in the fields, intent on a furrow and plant — the terrestrial root and model of which she had herself half-driven, half-ground into him until it almost seemed to grip him like her hallucination and plea, elongated heel, spur, compulsive arch, half-branch, half-step, inverted privilege of community to which he clung...

the important thing here is not simply the sense of the disordered world — that's common to most modern novels — but the apperception and demonstration of it through the technique and language of the work. orlando patterson, the sociologist of slavery, not surprisingly gets close to it from time to time in his first two novels *the children of sisyphus* (1964) and *an absence of ruins* (1966); and so does lindsay eseoghene barrett and andrew salkey in *song for mumu* (1967) and *the late emancipation of jerry stover* (1968) respectively. and as well as in harris, it is most acutely there in the work of george lamming, with his very fine sense of history and his very grand sense of the movements of man, mass and time within history. see especially *the emigrants* (1954) and then read *natives of my person* (1972).

these authors and their instances provide at least OMENS — their work, we might say, are the controlled symptoms — *intimate participation* — of/in the art of the literature of catastrophe. but in general caribbean literature has been concerned with fragments rather than with wholes and certainly with fragments rather than with broken wholes. its main concern has been with the peasant and with the autobiographical development of the artist — his or her own faustian personality; so that out of the peasant experience have come the literal and literary individualists mackay, mittelholzer, austin clarke...

and then there has been the novel of the movement of the peasant into the urban ghetto frustration: the work of roger mais and orlando patterson, earl lovelace and wick williams, comes here to mind...

or the movement of the peasant, or the artistic perception, into bourgeois debility or fear or confusion: alienation from the "roots": mittelholzer, selvon's "the cane is bitter," austin clarke's "griff," patterson's *an absence of ruins*, salkey's *escape, kelly* and *the late emancipation*, and certainly the novels of garth st. omer...

this can often lead to a certain romantical confrontation with the roots, as in sylvia wynter's *the hills of hebron* (1962) and john hearne's *land of the living* (1961).

the disillusionment with this often leads to the cycle of exile, further foreign alienation, a desire to return to a lost and unattainable innocence (mackay's *banana bottom*, lamming's *of age and innocence* and *season of adventure*) leading to further rootlessness and disassociation as in the work of v.s. naipaul: his *guerrillas* (1975) being the summation of this experience so far.

this is why i said elsewhere that our literary criticism is really meaningless unless it is grounded in historical psychoanalysis; because what our writers are witnesses of — thanks to their especial sensibilities and powers of expression — is the effect of cultural catastrophe on the west indian mind and action: that movement from false root to no root; from aggressive assertion to alienation; from child to exile: are aspects of a pattern; effects of the forces of the explosion of catastrophe which i've been talking about. and the point of our literature is that we are describing spectres on a scale of value/movement, without being aware of the total graph or plan. it is this which accounts for our persisting literary characteristic (which is also our persisting cultural characteristic), the contradiction, the dichotomy, the paradox: paradox of style and theme; contradiction of position; dichotomy of sensibility; the intellectually plural in a static and divided world: innocents (like derek walcott) dreaming of corruption; islanders, (like eric roach) dreaming of an exile; exiles (like lamming) dreaming of an island home.

so we have lyric slavery, romantic violence, rape as survival rhythm, peace as a hollow silence, howl's opposite. so that as writers, supposedly objective perceivers of the probe and problem, we remain trapped in the maelstrom of frustration, trapped and imprisoned within the detonations of our own fragmented worlds. so that in the end, the final joke and paradox, (no wonder, then, that some of us begin to emulate the literature of the existentialist absurd), our themes and style become a celebration of the broken word and world; *cul de sac indulgences*; lacking in historical perspective and therefore lacking in a cultural shape and hope: a threshold, exist into self/community. we *accommodate* ourselves, therefore, to our own catastrophe; and so we re*in*force, not force our psyches *out* of it.

nor have our literary critics, our historians, or our model-makers seen this point. for most of these gentlemen and compañeros, the frustrated products of west indian socio-culture are the result of personal frustration, personal moral failure of fibre; or have been marked up against our "philistine society": as if the plantations on which we live are wholes, rather than fragments of much larger holes; as if our history begins here, rather than with the ancestors; as if we were (are) always and only geological islands.

what i am saying within this tidal metaphor of historical and cultural equilibrium/disequilibrium, is that the nature of our catastrophe, the effects we feel, have ancient, subterranean but identifiable sources; that our condition: frustration, exploitation, underdevelopment, slavery, colonialism; *our very sense of self and literature itself*; stems from the original empire on which we impinge, from which the metaphors of our public and official language flow

VII

to create X/SELF: a literature of subversive underdevelopment: from MAMMON of UNPROSPERO: to its creative op- posite: NAM, SYCORAX, MABRAK

VIII

X/Self

prologue

rome burns
and our slavery begins

herod herodotus the tablets of law are broken
the soft spoken
whips are uncoiled on the rhine on the rhone on the tiber
severus the unlocked tiger
of wounds; lacerate me

syracuse is a white rumble of desolation
the train drifts slowly here, slowly
as the last lava of the volcano

nicosia smells of garlic and greeks
makarios and ships, bells and the grey tunics
of guns

there is no sun
in alexandria: date palms and gourds
in the desert; the islamic hosts are arising:
scimitar, saracen, saladin
my companions of the curved cross

the bosporus awaits cannon, tennyson,
salonika, and the dead sea shells of the dardanelles

the stones of venice are cold
gondolas to king arthur's knights bring the jews
in at evening with soft wet step and shadows
under their eyes: they have sold othello the moor

for a pillar of salt

the tribes the tribes are arising like mulled wine
there are no olives in the camp of the visigoths
vercingetorix, the arvernin creole chieftain
has met che, has met young doctor castro
liberators are being guillotined from heaven along the
        ho chi minh trail

caesar's daughter is pompey's wife
what a wedding what a knife
julia, my long gowned token television star

the sky has been cut into square blue holes in the
    ruined colosseum
and there are no laws left: aaron hammurabi dracon

sparks of horses' hooves make stars along the adriatic:
the franks pour into gaul
the lime trees are broken down
hadrian's wall known only to the precursors of the
        textile industry

o bordeaux o engine driving manchester eternal winter
        of niagara falls

where is the iron of hercules
the balanced apples of hesperides
atalanta atalanta my dappled darling da'ta
which races have you run

to seed to spoor to speechless broken spider?

rotundas topple the architecture of your corner:
little jack horner: the colossus of rhodes: the pretorian
        guardian and jupiter
up the hill

they are destroyed by leaks, eked out by whispers
the beguiles of women and the new among the 'nancy
        intellects

who brought from carthage the sister
of the desert: aloes and muslim, aphrodisiacs
for emperors

they wheel high over the desert, over tunis and tripoli,
        over timbuctu and chad

over lagos, ile-ife, ibadan and the markets of abomey

vultures wheel far out over the whisper of hirohito
over the ch'ing dynasty, over the manichures who created
        the great wall of china

cry babylon
galileo is free
far far across the lake of galilee
the aztecs wheel around their painted sticks

IX

in the first place there are plenty of names which many of you may not be too familiar with; some names are vaguely familiar: that is done on purpose; and some, although you know them, you would not expect to meet them in this context. for instance, "he balanced apple of hesperides" is not exactly right, is it; but then, you see, colonial caliban is not supposed to get it right ... but those names there at the corner of your mind ... they are supposed to startle certain memories and fears...

or again, observe how ("you taught me your language") the classical reference is sometimes distorted (?) into something "other"; as in

atalanta atalanta
my dappled darling daughter
which races have you run
to...

something else ... *to seed* ... or whatever; and i'm not sure that girl shouldn't be called atlanta ... and then the poem goes on to talk about the "anansi intellects"; which, in a way, is a long way from classical atlanta / atalanta; though *connected*, you see, since both atalanta and anansi are folk figures ... and i'm also suggesting that as the poem unfolds, that we begin to educate, or rather de-educate ourselves into the meaning of these name / words and provide them — as the calypsonian would — with metaphorical relevance for us. i mean, if t.s. eliot had written this poem, helen gardner, for instance, would have been there to provide you with a glossary of terms and meanings (as indeed gordon rohlehr and maureen warner lewis have done with *masks* and *rights* and *islands*) ... in this poem, all the name /words, all the names and crypto-names, have one thing in common: they are all connected with imperial rome ... herod, for example, was a colonial monarch within the pax romana; just as vercingetorix (he is invoked also in derek walcott's "junta") is what i have called a creole: a native gaul who had been acculturated, to some degree at least, into the roman system of civilization. severus was the first african to have become a roman emperor: another example of the nature of imperial rome and of the fusion and erosion of cultures which that empire made possible ... so that severus, with an effect similar to christ, later, within roman thought, becomes the "unlocked tiger": with the kind, too, of jungle associations that we find in *islands* and sparrow's "congo man"

the use of time, too, in the poem, is significant. i'm using time here not in a linear, chronological sense, but time as *continuum*; so that time, in the poem, doesn't go tick-tock-tick-tock-tic-tic-tic, as in a clock, and with the logic of a clock so that 4 bc must come before 1066 and 1066 before 1492 or what have you; but time here operates at any point in "time" and in its own space, as in a dream. so that richard nixon is julius caesar, presiding over national scandals and his wife (caesar's wife) can discover herself in a black glittered television star...

or take the use of the metaphorical bosporus: the famous straits of history, pivotal to europe, asia, asia minor/africa; pivot around which change wheels: the catastrophes which inaugurate culture-changes, which inaugurate the falls of empires which inaugurate the new lives of revolutions. here in the poem, the atomic bosporus: geological omen: creates for itself the history that will be created around it:

> the bosporus awaits cannon, tennyson
> and the charge of the light brigade

similarly the *gondolas of venice* ... venice, with its renaissance materialism, what some scholars have called humanism, is haunted by shakespeare's othello — at least we can put it this way in the time-continuum ... but with this metaphorical connection we can go even further and condense the image of the gondola, described by that same romantic tennyson of the bosporus into his other vehicular image — the *barge* of "morte d'arthur...." so that the venetians now become tennysonian figures, as the bosporus has already become — the poem here being inhabited or haunted by him — so that we have venice, moors, jews, galilee, the bible, and the whole exploratory/ exploiting imperial age from shakespeare to english-speaking tennyson, metaphorically imposed upon this base, to create the movement of the poem. so that by using time in this very free /associative manner, all kinds of suggestions, eye-corner ghosts of historical memory and meaning, become possible; which i do not think would be possible at all if one were writing "linear" poetry or prose (linear poetry which is prose). but here every word that is used, acquires unto itself a whole burden of meaning and connectivity and as you probe into the experience which is the poem; as you become increasingly aware of its world, so do the word/name: images: begin to disclose the history of them/selves:

> the stones of venice are cold
> gondolas of king arthur's knights
> bring the jews (dews) in at evening
> with soft wet step and shadows under their eyes
> they have sold othello the moor
> for a pillar of salt

and then, after explaining several kinds of disequilibrium *within* empires, causes of their decay ("who poisoned aristophanes, who blinded homer ... brought the four-legged ships to troy"): we observe the far more fundamental cosmological revolution which takes place as the result of this; that is, in fact, an omen or consequence of the disequilibrium: the new cosmology being a cultural catastrophe to the older order (*"who planted the sun in copernicus"*) where the ordered, singing spheres of the ancients, made of clinking glass, are replaced with the explosive centre of light and heat, metal of gold, atom of possibility, a technological furnace: leading to telescope, gunpowder, rocket-blast off, intercontinental probe by prow, ballistic missile: physics, physic, psyche all changing their shape and order because of this. but the discovery of the sun was a disaster for the medieval world: leading to its "progressive" product of new vices (voices): *inquisition, crusade, conquistador*: developments which were really little more or began as really little more than stabilizlng passions: how to control belief; how to recover christ; how, in fact, to control the NEW

and so, in the poem, towards its end, we come to the image of the vultures: opposite of eagles. they come to preside over the dead and/or exploited empires of the world, scavengers of exploration, flying as far as the limits of imperialism permit: beyond abyssinia to india, beyond india to china, from the centre of africa to america

> far far across the lake of galilee
> the aztecs wheel around their painted sticks...

even this image of the aztecs isn't as "far-fetched" as it would first seem ... they in a sense invented the maypole — they had something similar. sometime ago there was a report from israeli scholars that they had found connections between the culture of the ancient hebrews and that of the aztecs; and i must report that the language spoken by the luo people around lake victoria, as it's still called: people who occupy the lake shores between uganda and kenya speak a language very similar to central american amerindian; and at the university of nairobi, the decorative motifs on the buildings are very similar to amerindian motifs. and those of you who buy those mexican bead necklaces must know, by now, that you can buy similar bead necklaces in east africa ... so that the connections are there, and not only in metaphor. the metaphors, in fact, merely seek out the natural and ancient connections within the time-continuum . . .

IX

christine mercantilism

the next poem is called "mont blanc." and here i want to show how the concept of equilibrium and disequilibrium is discussed geographically. i use a geological monument now to describe the sense of cultural equilibrium

mont blanc is, to me, the centre of europe. it is their holy mountain: this hub of white around which european history revolves, the folk mythology surrounding this mass — (and don't forget that mt. blanc, as queen of the alps, is enormous) and i'm not thinking of simple spin-offs like yip-e-dee-i-dee-i-da and the legend of st. bernard...

now, as long as mt. blanc is "passive," "static," a white glacial statue, resting in its own state of equilibrium, everything else around the mountain, naturally, remains in place; also in its state of equilibrium. but when the mountain of history becomes "active," as it were; as mt. blanc "rises," as it were, and becomes "illuminated," as it were; so do the areas around it *sink* and *become* darker; shift away or lean towards; begin to slide and flow, as it were, in a counter-movement of equilibrium: the steppes running from russia, the rhone and the rhine and the danube; the caspian and the adriatic, la manche and the mediterranean; the lowland of the scheldt; even the cold blue fiords of scandinavia, the mountains of the moon and the sahara ... they all move, alter, shift, change...

but this movement of reactive disequilibrium does not stop there; does not, cannot halt or stabilize itself until we reach its total opposite: the black man's mountain holy mound of africa, kilimanjaro: also the hub of histories: civilizations and plains, valleys, lakes and watercourses: the wheel of the world's animals in its shadow; but agrarian, you see, not industrial. so that metaphorically, kilimanjaro is the atomic or electrical, the cultural "opposite" or "other" of mt. blanc; so that what effects mt. blanc affects the other mountain as in a psychic mood or mirror; so that if there is equilibrium, the mountain forces remain silent in their dream of balance; if there is dis/stress, the effects begin to show in plant and animal around the holy axles; although since mt. blanc is the industrial furnace, missile-oriented, the initiative for change has (so far) usually come from that north of the world: even when hannibal crossed the alps, even when othello captured desdemona; even when shylock was demanding his pound of christian flesh. the alteration of initiative has started only in our time: *when mozambique exploded in the heart of portugal...*

but in terms of the poem, rome (MT. BLANC) is a symbol of materialism; while kilimanjaro, its opposite, is a symbol of the spirit; so that rome's disequilibrium, followed by europe's expansion (the expansion being europe's response to the disequilibrium; the attempt, that way, to restore the balance) affects kilimanjaro in that christine materialism begins to affect the spiritual resources of africa and so africa also begins to become increasingly materialistic — as discussed in *masks* — the corruption of the tribe by bribe; the corruption that became the trade in human flesh of slaves. but even wider than this, it is a poem about europe's effect of underdevelopment, as walter rodney puts it, upon the entire naked spread-out world.

mont blanc

rome burns
and our slavery begins

in the alps
oven of europe
glacier of god
chad's opposite

industry was envisioned here in the indomitable glitter

it out proportions the parthenon
the colosseum is not to be compared with it
nor dome, nor london bridge, bernini bronze nor marble
there is more wealth here than with the bankers of
        amsterdam
more power than in any boulder dam of heaven

volt, crackle and electricity it has invented
buchenwald, nagasaki and napalm

it is the frozen first atomic bomb

its factories blaze forth bergs and avalanches
its unships sail down rhine, down rhone, down po,
down danube
to the black sea dead to the world; to the red sea of
isaias

without it, the sahara would have been water
genoa would have been a finchal of the esquimos
latvium carthage tunis would have been dolphin towns
columbus would have sailed south along the congo's
rivers

but being immobile here
more permanent than pope or charlemagne

it has burnt rome
but preserved europe

as it rises
chad sinks

and the green brown of africa crumbles

2

and out of the ground
these men with black faces
they frighten me

they tell of coal
of gaols underground where they may follow the
fathoms of vulcan

they have discovered an ancient city of forests
older than the dinosaur or the ice age

they chip it into black blocks of lamplight
and it warms us with a sun more distant than our
        mother's star

it is this that breathes from their faces: star winds:
        wrinkles of inner darkness

but it is not equiano, it is not paul
robeson, it is not othello the moor

they live beyond the mountain in green apertures
where they have not yet hidden the neutron
they will worship gods that make them smile
that allow them to welcome the stranger
that will make them easily prisoner

but these are the miners of empire
they burn, they eat the land
they vomit it up
they leave lakes of desolation; plantations of dark and
        dead plankton

ceaselessly ceaselessly, clocks ticking to mesh, they
        destroy, they destroy
they do not care; they have cruelled their faces of fear
of the plague, of the ark, of the aardvark

fresh from the bellows
they smile seeds of colonies
they sow islands
shanty towns rise and rust in their oxides
they confound the outnumbered elders

of sarawak, of samarkand, of benin city

there is the new noise of foundries
fords, cadillacs, locomotive triumph

there are explosions of gas, rocket fire,
blitzkrieg of satellites departing through their own light

and all this benignly

all this beneficiently
from the dream of the moon-
faced mountain

white oracle
white order
white ruler
white ships

the image of these ships of trade and intrusion, coming from the "crack" of *masks:*

this was at last the last;
this was the limit of motion;
voyages ended;
time stopped where its movement began;

horizons returned inaccessible.
here at last was the limit;
the minutes of pebbles drop-
ping into the hourless pool.

hands reached into water;
gods nudged us like fish;
black bottomless whales that we worshipped.
o new world of want, who will build the new ways,

the new ships?

X

the visibility trigger

and now, finally, i'd like to take you to the poem i've been building towards; the poem which attempts to illustrate the effect of imperialism not on europe, now, but on the *victims of imperialism*: "the visibility trigger: a poem for kwame nkrumah and the leaders of the third world."

to begin i must explain certain images and concepts. in addition to the notion of equilibrium and disequilibrium, you will notice that the poems about europe "move a lot"; there are these explorators, always in motion. and i characterize that particular kind of culture, a missile culture: its symbols are the castle, spear, arrow, gothic cathedral spire; skyscraper, and now the missile itself: cape kennedy ... intercontinental ballistic ... moonshot, star-struck rocket ... it is, you will note, very aggressive, and it *feeds*, as i said in one of those poems there, on its own light. it needs, because of the great concentration of power within it, it needs to consume its surroundings. when you see that rocket go up, you will see a vast surrounding area, constantly devastated by its blast. in the same way, when europe expands, as europe becomes powerful and imperialist, she has to feed that power; feed herself on that power; and to obtain enough fuel for this, she has to burn/consume an increasingly wide area; first in its own neighborhood (wars in europe) then increasingly further and further afield: exploration into colonialism: into our black space

now these areas — of exploited black space — are also the areas of what is commonly called subsistence culture: where they are concerned — and by choice, certainly not necessarily by *need* (greed) — with stability/equilibrium rather than with progressive disequilibrium. so that just as the symbol of the expansionist is the missile, so the symbol of the subsistence exploited cultures become the circle, hole or target: so that there is this obscure but fatal built-in attraction between the two fields or forces: shot and shot at; arrow to its target; mt. blanc and kilimanjaro. and so the main problem for such subsistence cultures is naturally defence: how to develop armours and strategies against aggression: the quite natural problem of the vulnerability of the target. and what i'm saying here doesn't only apply to whole vast continental complexes such as africa or parts of amerindia; but to small particular units such as our own contemporary folk culture. here people say, for instance, that the "problem" of caribbean folk is that it has been discovered by intellectuals, commercialized and so destroyed; and they blame the "intellectuals" for both the discovery and the "destruction." *leave the culture alone*, is their sooth saying: at least this was their grito until recently. suddenly there has been this change; this sudden pride in roots: roots, rasta, reggae, etc. but thats only because these forms have suddenly become internationally and fashionably "successful" and denotes a change in our national status. but the "problem" of protection still remains; that very international success contains its own danger; the danger of absorption and appropriation; unless we can move from being shell-less snail to cultural (national) hedgehog or armadillo

but this is the form and nature of the culture: and its subsistence symbol is the circle: with africa its chief subsistence source and model. the drums are round, its dancers dance a circle; the villages and their houses: also round, though this shape is changing (superficially?); though the compound, don't you see, remains; and the elders sit in their circle and the farm. surround the villages in dispositions like wheels; and time is a wheel: ancestor, spirit, child...

in the poem, you will find that the images that have to do with the intruder, the invader man from the north, suggest the missile; and that these missile images (prow, put-put, landing) slowly insinuate themselves — rather, sharply insert themselves — into the complex of the circle: bowl calabash cycle of elders: until there is clash, confusion, shape loss and finally destruction — or possibly these. for the poem also goes on to celebrate the circle's subsistence survival...

the visibility trigger
a poem for kwame nkrumah and the leaders of the third world

and so they came up over the reefs
up the creeks and rivers
oar prong put-put
hack tramp silence

and i was dreaming near morning

i offered you a kola nut
your fingers huge and smooth and red
and you took it
your dress makola blue

and you broke it into gunfire

the metal was hot and jagged
it was as if the master of bronze
had poured anger into his cauldron
and let it spit spit sputter
till it was red blue black in my face

it was as if a maggot
had slapped me in the belly
and i had gone soft like the knead of my wife's bread

i could hear salt leaking out of the black hole of kaneshie
i could hear grass growing around the edges of the
        green lake
i could hear stalactites ringing in my cave of vision
bats batting my eyes shut
their own eyes howling like owls in the dead dark

and they marched into the village
and our five unready virginal elders met them

bowl calabash oil carafe of fire silence

and unprepared and venerable
i was dreaming mighty wind in trees
our circles talismans: round hut round village cooking
        pots

the world was round and we the spices in it
time wheeled around our memories like stars;
yam cassava groundnut sweetpea bush

and then it was yams again

birth child hunter warrior
and the breath which is no more

which is birth which is child which is hunter which is
 warrior which is
breath that is no more

and they brought sticks rods roads bullets straight
 objects

birth was not breath
but gaping wound

hunter was not animal
but market sale

warrior was child
that is no more

and i beheld the cotton tree: guardian of graves rise
 upward from its monument of grass
crying aloud in its vertical hull
calling for crashes of branches vibrations of leaves

there was a lull of silver

and then the great grandfather, gnashing upwards from
 its teeth of roots
split down its central thunder
the stripped violated wood crying aloud its murder, the
 leaves' frontier signals alive with lamentations

and our great odoum
triggered at last by the ancestors into your visibility

crashed into history

Select Bibliography

Primary Sources

For a full account of Brathwaite's published prose and poetry, 1948-1986, with details of sites of first publication, variant and / or ammended versions, recordings, reviews, editing etc, the reader is directed to *EKB: His Published Prose & Poetry 1948-1986* by Doris Monica Brathwaite, (Savacou Cooperative, Jamacia, 1986), and her *A descriptive and chronological bibliography of the work of Edward Kamau Brathwaite*, published by New Beacon in 1988. The Primary Sources section of this Select Bibliography draws considerably on those sources.

Collections of Poetry:

Rights of Passage (London: OUP, 1967)
Masks (London: OUP, 1968)
Islands (London: OUP, 1969)
The Arrivants: A New World Trilogy (London, OUP, 1973)
Days & Nights (Mona, Jamaica: Caldwell Press, 1975)
Other Exiles (London: OUP, 1975)
Black & Blues (Havana: Casa de Las Americas, 1976; Benin, Nigeria: Ethiope Publishing Co. 1978).
Mother Poem (London, OUP, 1977)
Soweto (Mona, Jamaica: Savacou, 1979)
Word Making Man (Mona, Jamaica: Savacou, 1979)
Afternoon of the Status Crow (Mona, Jamaica: Savacou, 1982)
Sun Poem (London: OUP, 1982)
Third World Poems (London, Longman, 1983)
Jah Music (Mona, Kingston, Jamaica: Savacou, 1986)
Visibility Trigger (Belgium, Cahiers de Louvain, 1986)
X/Self (London: OUP, 1987)
Sappho Sakyi's Mediations (Mona, Jamaica: Savacou, 1990)
Shar/Hurricane Poem (Mona, Jamaica: Savacou, 1990)
Middle Passages (Newcastle, Bloodaxe Books, 1992)

Poems-into-prose:

DreamStories (London: Longman, 1994)
The Zea Mexican Diary (Madison: University of Wisconsin Press, 1994)
Trench Town Rock (USA: Lost Roads Publishers, 1994)
Barabajan Poems (Kingston, Jamaica; New York: Savacou North, 1994)

Plays:

Four Plays for Primary Schools (London: Longman, 1964)
Odale's Choice (London, Evans, 1967)

Literary/Cultural Criticism — books:
Caribbean Man in Space and Time (Mona, Jamaica: Savacou, 1974)
Contradictory Omens (Mona, Jamaica: Savacou, 1979)
Jamaica Poetry: A Checklist (Mona, Jamaica: Savacou, 1979)
Barbados Poetry: A Checklist (Mona, Jamaica: Savacou, 1979)
Kumina (Mona, Jamaica: Savacou, 1982)
The Colonial Encounter: Language (Mysore, India: University of Mysore Press, 1984)
History of the Voice: The Development of Nation Language in Anglophone Caribbean Poetry (London; Port of Spain: New Beacon, 1984)
Roots: essays in Caribbean Literature (Havana, Casa de Las Americas, 1986; new edition, Ann Arbor Paperbacks, University of Michigan Press, 1993)

Literary/Cultural Criticism — major essays
'Sir Galahad and the Islands', *Bim* 25, 1957, 8-16
'The Controversial Tree of Time', *Bim* 30, 1960, 104-114
'The new West Indian novelists', *Bim* 31, 1960, 199-210 [part I] 32, 1961, 271-280 [part II]
'Roots', *Bim* 37, 1963 10-21
'*Kyk-over-al* and the Radicals', *New World Quarterly* (Guyana Independence issue), May 1966, 55-57
'Jazz and the West Indian Novel', *Bim* 44 ,1967, 275-284 [part I]; 45, 1967, 39-51 [part II] and 46, 1968, 115-126 [part III]
'The Caribbean Artists Movement', *Caribbean Quarterly* 14, 1968, 57-59
'Caribbean Critics', *New World Quarterly* 5: 1-2, 1969, 5-12
'West Indian prose fiction in the sixties', *Caribbean Quarterly* 16: 4, 1970, 5-17
'Creative Literature of the British West Indies during the period of Slavery', *Savacou* 1, 1970, 46-73
'Rehabilitations: a study of Paule Marshall's *The Chosen Place, the Timeless People*', *Bim* 51, 1970, 174-184
'Timehri', *Savacou* 2, Sept. 1970, 35-44
Introduction to Melville J. Herskovits, *Life in a Haitian Valley* (New York: Doubleday/Anchor, 1971), v-viii
'Art and Society: Kapo a Context' in *Jamaica Folk Art* (Kingston: Institute of Jamaica, 1971) 4-6
Introduction to Roger Mais, *Brother Man* (London: Heinemann, 1974), v-xxi
'Race and the Divided Self', *Caribbean Studies* 14:3, 1974, 127-139
'The African Presence in Caribbean Literature', *Slavery, Colonialism and Racism*, (ed.) Sidney Mintz (New York: Norton & Co., 1974), 73-109
'The Love Axe/l: developing a Caribbean aesthetic 1962-74', *Reading Black: essays in the criticism of African, Caribbean & Black American Literature* (ed.) Houston A. Baker (Cornell: Cornell University, Africana Studies and Research Centre, 1976), 20-36
'Houses in the West Indian Novel', *Literary Half-Yearly* 17, 1976, 111-121

'Resistance Poems; the voice of Martin Carter', *Caribbean Quarterly* 23: 2-3, 1977, 7-23

'English in the Caribbean' in *English Literature: Opening Up the Canon* (eds.) Leslie Fiedler and Houston A. Baker (Baltimore: Johns Hopkins University Press, 1981), 15-53

'Gods of the Middle Passage', *Caribbean Review* 11:4, 1982, 18-19, 42-44

'Dionne Brand's *Winter Epigrams*', *The New Voices* 11:22, 1983, 23-38

'A.J. Seymour: *'And deserving of his country's honour"*, *AJS at 70* (ed.) Ian McDonald (Georgetown: private publication, 1984), 58-62

'Helen and the Tempest-Negre: Rene Depestre's *A Rainbow for the Christian West*', *Caribbean Quarterly* 30:1, 1984, 33-47

Introduction to Rex Nettleford, *Dance Jamaica* (New York: Grove, 1985), 7-11

'Metaphors of Underdevelopment: A Proem for Hernan Cortez', *New England Review* 7:4, 1985, 453-476

'*Dance Jamaica* (review)', *Jamaica Journal*, 18:4, November 1985-January 1986, 46-51

'Poetry Presentation', transcription of a talk to the Fifth Annual Conference of West Indian Literature, College of the Virgin Islands, 1986, in Jackson, J. and Allis, J.B., eds *West Indian Poetry: Proceedings of the Fifth Annual Conference on West Indian Literature* (College of the Virgin Islands, St Thomas, 1989), 153-182

'The Unborn Body of the Life of Fiction: Roger Mais' Aesthetics with special reference to *Black Lightning*', *Journal of West Indian Literature* 2:1, 1987, 11-36

'History, the Caribbean Writer, and X/Self' in Davies, G. And Maes-Jelinek, H. eds, *Crisis and Creativity in the New Literatures in English* (Amsterdam; Atlanta: Rodopi, 1990), 23-45

'Pam Mordecai's *Journey Poem*', *Caribbean Quarterly* 36: 1-2, 1990, 127-140

'Ala(r)ms of God — Konnu and Carnival in the Caribbean', *Caribbean Quarterly* 36, 1990, 77-107

'John the Conqueror', *Foundations of a Movement: A tribute to John La Rose on the Occasion of the 10th International Book Fair of Radical, Black and Third World Books* (London: John La Rose Tribute Committee, 1991), 20-23

'The Mighty Sparrow — Slinger Francisco', *The New Voices* XX:39/40, 1992, 110-129

'Caliban's Garden', *Wasafiri* 16, 1992, 2-6

'Newstead to Neustadt', *World Literature Today* 68:4, Autumn 1994, 653-660

History — Books and Major Essays:

'Dialect and dialectic: a review of *How Europe Underdeveloped Africa* by Walter Rodney', *ASAWI Bulletin* no 6, 1973

The People Who Came [Books 1-3] (London: Longman, 1968-72; new edition 1990-1992)

Folk Culture of the Slaves in Jamaica (London; Port of Spain: New Beacon,

1970)
The Development of Creole Society in Jamaica, 1770-1820 (Oxford: The Clarendon Press, 1971)
'Submerged Mothers; Militant Black Women in Historical Perspective', *Jamaica Journal* 9: 2-3, 1975, 48-49
Our Ancestral Heritage: a Bibliography of the English-speaking Caribbean (Kingston, Jamaica: Carifesta Jamaica, 1976)
Wars of respect: Nanny, Sam Sharpe and the Struggle for People's Liberation (Kingston, Jamaica: Agency for Public Information, 1977)
'Caliban, Ariel and Unprospero in the conflict of creolization: a study of the slave revolt in Jamaica 1831-32', in Rubin, V. and Tuden A., (eds.) *Comparative prespectives on slavery in the New World plantation societies* (New York: New York Academy of Sciences, 1977, 41-62)
'Rebellion: anatomy of the slave revolt of 1831/1832', *Jamaican History Society Bulletin* 8:4, 1981, 60-96
'Caribbean Woman During the Period of Slavery', *Caribbean Contact*, May 1984, 2, 13 [part I]; June 1984, 13-14 [part II]
'World Order Models — A Caribbean Perspective', *Caribbean Quarterly* 31, 1985, 53-63

As Editor:

Iouanaloa: Recent Writing from Saint Lucia (Castries, Saint Lucia: UWI, Dept. of Extra-Mural Studeis, 1963)
New Poets from Jamaica: An Anthology (Mona, Jamaica: Savacou, 1979)
Dream Rock: A Collection of Poems (Kingston, Jamaica: Information Service, 1987)
Savacou, nos 1-14/15, 1970-1979. Initially as co-editor with Kenneth Ramchand, then as general editor/publisher, overseeing guest editors, special issues, etc.

Interviews:

James, Sybil, 'Edward Brathwaite Answers Questions on his Poem *Rights of Passage*', *Journal of English Teachers* (Jamaica) IV: 2/3, 1977, 17-35
Gilkes, Michael, 'Barbados heading for revivial of African Cultural Traditions', *Caribbean Contact*, February 1979, 10-11
Searle, Chris, 'Message to Grenada' *Race & Class* XXII:4, 1981, 387-394
Korley, Nii Laryea, 'Brathwaite Home Again', *West Africa* no.3627, March 1987, 514-515
Brown, Stewart, 'Interview with Edward Kamau Brathwaite', *Kyk-over-al* 40, December 1989, 84-93
Brown, Stewart, '"Writing in Light": an interview with Edward Kamau Brathwaite', *Planet* 75, June/July 1989, 58-66 [an edited version of the *Kyk-over-al* interview, above]
Mackey, Nathaniel, 'An Interview with Edward Kamau Brathwaite', *Hambone* 9, Winter 1991, 42-59
Smilowitz, Erika, 'Interview with Edward Kamau Brathwaite', *The Caribbean Writer* 5, 1991, 73-78
Rigby, Grahame, 'Improvisation & Dreams', *The Page*, Newcastle-upon-

Tyne, June/July 1992, 3

Chang, Victor, (ed.) *Three Caribbean Poets on their Work* (Kingston: Institute of Caribbean Studies, University of the West Indies, 1993), 1-29

Searle, Chris, *Words Unchained: Language & Revolution in Grenada* (London, Zed Books 1984), 232-239

Discography:

Rights of Passage, London: Argo, PLP 1110/1, 1969

Masks, London: Argo, PLP 1183, 1972

Islands, London: Argo, PLP 1184/5, 1973

Poemas, Havana: Casa de las Americas, 1976

Mother Poem Workshop, London: Association of Teachers of Caribbean and African Literature, 1980

Edward Kamau Brathwaite, an interview with Yolande Cantu, London: British Council, 1980

Atumpan, Washington, D.C.: Watershed Tapes, C-229, 1990

Representation on Anthology records:

The Poet Speaks, 10 (ed.) Peter Orr, London: Argo Records, 1968

Poetry International '69 (ed.) Peter Orr, London: Argo Records, 1969

Poets of the West Indies Reading Their Own Works, (ed.) John Figueroa, New York: Caedmon, 1971

An Evening of International Poetry (First International Book Fair of Radical and Third World Books), London Alliance Records, 1982.

Secondary Materials

Books and Critical essays on, or substantially referring to, Brathwaite's work:

Aidoo, Ama Ata, 'Akan and English', *West Africa* 2677, 21 September 1968, 1099.

Aiyejina, Funso, 'The Death and Rebirth of African Deities in Edward Brathwaite's *Islands*', *World Literature Written in English* 23:2, 1984, 397-404

Aribisola, Karen King, '*The Arrivants*: Brathwaite's Elemental Directive' in *Black Culture & Black Consciousness*, (ed.) Ernest N. Emsanyounu (Ibadan: Heinemann, 1987), 129-140

Asein, Samuel Omo, 'The concept of form: a study of some ancestral elements in Brathwaite's trilogy', *African Studies Association of the West Indies Bulltetin* 4, 1971, 9-38

Asein, Samuel Omo, 'Symbol and Meaning in the Poetry of Edward Brathwaite', *World Literature Written in English* 20:1, Spring 1981, 96-104.

Asein, Samuel Omo, (ed.) *Comparative Approaches to Modern African Literature* (Ibadan: Ibadan University Press, 1982)

Ashcroft, Bill; Griffiths, Gareth and Tiffin, Helen, *The Empire Writes Back* (London, Routledge, 1989)

Baugh, Edward, 'Review of *Rights of Passage*' *Bim* 45, 1967, 12 -14

Baugh, Edward, 'Review of Masks' Bim 47, 1968, 209-211

Baugh, Edward, *West Indian Poetry 1900-1970: A Study in Cultural Decolonisation* (Kingston, Jamaica: Savacou, 1970)

Baugh, Edward, 'Questions and Imperatives for a Young Literature', *Humanities Association Review*, vol 24, Winter 1973, 13-24

Baugh, Edward, 'The West Indian Writer and his Quarrel with History', *Tapia*, 25th Febraury 1977, 6/7 and 27th February 1977, 6/7

Baugh, Edward, (ed.) *Critics on Caribbean Literature* (London: Allen & Unwin, 1978)

Baugh, Edward, 'Edward Brathwaite as Critic: some Preliminary Observations', *Caribbean Quarterly* 28:1/2, 1982, 66-75

Baugh, Edward and Morris, Mervyn, (eds.) *Progressions: West Indian Literature in the 1970s* (Mona, Jamaica: University of the West Indies, 1990)

Best, Curwen, 'Affecting and Interpreting the Tone that Smiles', in Royden Salick, (ed.) *The Comic Vision in West Indian Literature* (St. Augustine, Trinidad: University of the West Indies, 1993), 148-158

Best, Curwen, 'Text, Tradition, Technology: Crossover and Caribbean Popular Culture', in Stewart Brown, (ed), *The Pressures of the Text: Orality, Texts and the Telling of Tales* (Birmingham: Centre of West African Studies, University of Birmingham, 1995), 75-82

Bloom, Valerie and Bloom, Douglas, 'The Development of Caribbean Dialect Poetry', *Cambridge Journal of Education* 14:3, 1984, 21-24

Bodune, Charles A., 'The Black Writer and the Multicultural Caribbean — the vision of Africa in Edward Kamau Brathwaite's *The Arrivants*' in Marlies Glaser and Marion Pausch, (eds.) *Caribbean Writers: Between Orality and Writing*, MATATU No.12 (Amsterdam, Atlanta, Georgia: Editions Rodopi, 1994), 17-34

Breiner, Lawrence A., 'Tradition, Society, the Figure of the Poet', *Caribbean Quarterly* 26:1/2, 1980, 1-12

Breiner, Lawrence A., 'Lyric & Autobiography in West Indian Literature', *Journal of West Indian Literature* 3:1, January 1989, 3-15

Breiner, Lawrence A., 'The Other West Indian Poet', *Partisan Review* 56:2, 1989, 316-320

Breiner, Lawrence A., 'Edward Kamau Brathwaite', in Lindfors, B. and Sander, R., (eds.), *Dictionary of Literary Biography* Vol. 135: *Twentieth-Century Caribbean and Black African Writers* (Detroit, London: Bruccoli Clark Layman, 1993), 8-28

Brown, Beverly E., 'Mansong and Matrix: A Radical Experiment' in *A Double Colonization: Colonial and Post Colonial Women's Writing*, (ed.) Petersen K. and Rutherford A. (Aarhus, Denmark: Dangaroo Press, 1986), 68-79

Brown, Lloyd W., *West Indian Poetry* (Boston: Twayne Publishers, 1978)

Brown, Stewart, 'A Rainbow Sign', in *Poetry Review* 72:4, 1983, 59-61

Brown, Stewart, 'Dreadtalk: Caribbean Poetry Now', *Planet* 53, 1985,

70-80

Brown, Stewart, 'Middle Passages', *Poetry Wales* 29:1, 1993, 56-58

Brown, Stewart, (ed.) *The Pressures of the Text: Orality, Texts and the Telling of Tales* (Birmingham: Centre of West African Studies, University of Birmingham, 1995)

Brown, Stewart, '"Writin in Light": Orality-thru-typography, Kamau Brathwaite's Sycorax Video Style', in Stewart Brown, (ed.), *The Pressures of the Text: Orality, Texts and the Telling of Tales* (Birmingham: Centre of West African Studies, University of Birmingham, 1995) 125-136

Brunner, Charlotte, 'The Meaning of Caliban in Black Literature Today', Comparative Literature Studies 13:3, 1976, 240-253

Burnett, Paula (ed.), *The Penguin Book of Caribbean Verse in English* (Harmondsworth: Penguin, 1986)

Burton, Richard, 'Derek Walcott and the Medusa of History' in *Caliban* III:2, 1980, 3-48

Busia, Abena P.A., 'Long Memory and Survival: Dramatizing the *Arrivants* Triology', *World Literature Today* 68:4, Autumn 1994, 741-746

Calder, Angus, 'Walcott's "The Schooner Flight" and Brathwaite's "Nametracks": Two Short Verse Narratives' in *Short Fiction in the New Literatures in English: Proceedings of the Nice Conference of the European Association for Commonwealth Literature and Language Studies*, (ed.) Bardolph, Jacqueline (Nice: Faculty des Lettres & Sciences Humaines, 1989), 109-119

Carruth, Hayden, 'Poetry Chronicle', *Hudson Review* 27, Summer 1974, 308-320

Chamberlin, J. Edward, 'Speaking in Tongues: The Language of West Indian Poetry,' *Brick* 26, Winter 1986, 14-20

Chamberlin, J. Edward, 'Myself Made Otherwise: Edward Kamau Brathwaite's *X/Self*, *Carib* 5, 1989, 19-32

Chamberlin, J. Edward, *Come Back To Me My Language: Poetry and the West Indies*(Chicago: University of Illinois, 1993)

Chang, Victor, (ed.) *Three Caribbean Poets on their Work* (Kingston: Institute of Caribbean Studies, University of the West Indies, 1993)

Cobley, A.G. and Thompson, A. (eds.),*The African-Caribbean Connection: Historical and Cultural Perspectives* (Bridgetown, Barbados: Dept of History, University of the West Indies, Cave Hill and the National Cultural Foundation, 1990

Collier, Gordon, 'Artistic Autonomy and Cultural Allegience: Aspects of the Walcott-Brathwaite Debate Re-examined', *The Literary Half-Yearly* 20:1, 1973, 80-96

Connor, William, 'Edward Brathwaite's Symbolic Use of Water Imagery in *The Arrivants: A New World Trilogy*', *Literary Half-Yearly* XXI:2, 1980, 13-21

Cooper, Carolyn, *Noises in the Blood: Orality, Gender and the 'Vulgar' Body of Jamaican Popular Culture* (London: Macmillan, 1993)

Coppleston, Fenella, 'Review of *Mother Poem*', *P.N. Review* 89, 19:3, January/Febuary 1993, 61

Cudjoe, Selwyn R., *Resistance and Caribbean Literature* (Amhurst: Ohio University Press, 1980)

Coulson, Sheila, 'Roots', *Jamaica Journal* 21:3, 1988, 52/3

D'Aguiar, Fred, 'Lines with their knots left in: *Third World Poems* by Edward Kamau Brathwaite and *Midsummer* by Derek Walcott', *Wasafiri* 1:2, 1985, 37-38

D'Costa, J., 'The Poetry of Edward Brathwaite', *Jamaica Journal* 11:3, 1968, 24-28

Dabydeen, Cyril, 'Review of *Middle Passages', World Literature Today* 67:2, Spring 1993, 425-6

Dash, Michael, 'Edward Brathwaite' in Bruce King, (ed.) *West Indian Literature* (London: Macmillan, 1979), 210-227

Dash, Michael, 'Review of *The Visibility Trigger* and *Jah Music*', *The Journal of West Indian Literature* 1:2, 1987, 87-90

Dathorne, O.R., *Dark Ancestor: The Literature of the Black Man in the Caribbean* (Lousiana State University Press, 1981)

Davies, Carol Boyce, and Elaine Savory Fido, (eds.) *Out of the Kumbla: Caribbean Women and Literature* (Trenton, N.J.: Africa World Press, 1990)

Dawes, Kwame, 'Christianity in *Islands*: An Introduction' in Jackson, J. and Allis, J.B. (eds.), *West Indian Poetry: Proceedings of the Fifth Annual Conference on West Indian Literature* (St. Thomas, U.S.V.I.: College of the Virgin Islands, 1986), 195-200

Dayan, Joan, 'Who's Got History? Kamau Brathwaite's "Gods of the Middle Passage"', *World Literature Today* 68:4, Autumn 1994, 726-732.

Edmundson, Belinda, 'Race, Tradition and the Construction of the Caribbean Aesthetic', *New Literary History: A Journal of Theory and Interpretation* 25:1, Winter 1994, 109-120

Fido, Elaine Savory, 'Spectrum and Prism: The Language of Contemporary Caribbean Anglophone Poetry', *Bim* 28:69, 1985, 73-78

Fido, Elaine Savory, 'Africa in the Caribbean: The Literary Case', in *The Africa-Caribbean Connection*, (eds.) Cobley, Alan G. and Thompson, Alvin (Bridgetown, Barbados: Dept of History, University of the West Indies, Cave Hill and the National Cultural Foundation, 1990), 123-143

Fiet, Lowell, (ed.) *West Indian Literature and its Political Context* (Rio Piedras, Puerto Rica: Sargasso, 1988)

Fraser, Robert, *A Critical Review of Edward Brathwaite's Masks* (London: Rex Collings, 1981)

Gikandi, Simon, 'E.K. Brathwaite and the Poetics of the Voice: The Allegory of History in *Rights of Passage*', *Callaloo* 14:3, 1991, 727-736

Gilmore, John, 'Seeing with both eyes: the poetry of Edward Kamau Brathwaite', The New Bajan, January 1988, 14-15

Glissant, Edouard, *Caribbean Discourse* [trans. M. Dash], (Charlottesville: University of Virgina Press, 1989)

Glaser, Marlies and Marion Pausch, (eds.) *Caribbean Writers: Between*

Orality and Writing, MATATU No.12 (Amsterdam, Atlanta, Georgia: Editions Rodopi, 1994)

Gowda, H.H. Anniah, 'Edward Kamau Brathwaite: A Profile', *Literary Half-Yearly* 23:2, 1982, 40-46

Gowda, H.H. Anniah, 'Creation in the Poetic Development of Kamau Brathwaite', *World Literature Today* 68:4, Autumn 1994, 691-696

Grant, Damian, 'Emerging Image: The Poetry of Edward Brathwaite', *Critical Quarterly* 12:2, 1970, 186-192

Griffith, Paul, '*Mother Poem*: Art and National Consciousness' in Baugh and Morris, (eds.), *Progressions: West Indian Literature in the 1970s* (Mona, Jamaica: Dept of English, University of the West Indies, 1990)

Griffiths, Trevor R., 'This Island's Mine: Caliban and Colonialism', *The Yearbook of English Studies* 13, 1983, 159-180

Habekost, Christian, *Verbal Riddim: The Politics and Aesthetics of Afro-Caribbean Dub Poetry* (Amsterdam, Atlanta, Georgia: Editions Rodopi, 1993)

Hoppe, John K., 'From a Common Root: Revolutionary Vision and Social Change in the Poetry of Brathwaite and Chinweizu', *Journal of Caribbean Studies* 8:1/2, 1990, 89-104

Hoppe, John K., 'From Jameson to Syncretism: The Communal Imagination of American Identity in Edward Brathwaite's *The Arrivants*', *Weber Studies: An Interdisciplinary Humanities Journal* 9:3, Fall 1992, 92-105

Huggan, Graham, 'Opting out of the (Critical) Common Market: Creolization and the Post-Colonial Text', *Kunapipi* vii:1, 1989, 27-40

Irele, Abiola, 'The Return of the Native: Edward Kamau Brathwaite's *Masks*', *World Literature Today* 68:4, Autumn 1994, 719-725

Ismond, Patricia, 'Walcott v Brathwaite', *Caribbean Quarterly* 17:3/4, 1971, 54-71

Jackson, J. and Allis, J.B. (eds.), *West Indian Poetry: Proceedings of the Fifth Annual Conference on West Indian Literature*, (St. Thomas, U.S.V.I.: College of the Virgin Islands, 1986)

James, Cynthia, 'The Unknown Text', *World Literature Today* 68:4, Autumn 1994, 758-764

James, Louis (ed.), *The Islands in Between* (London: OUP, 1968)

James, Louis, 'Caribbean Poetry in English — Some Problems', *Savacou* 2, 1970, 78-86

James, Louis, 'A Caribbean Poet Questing', Third World Quarterly 10:1, 1988, 334-337

James, Sybil, 'An Approach to the Teaching of *Rights of Passage* to Students Pursuing a Course in Caribbean Literature in Teachers' Colleges in Jamaica', in *Journal of English Teachers (Jamaica)* vi:2/3, 1977, 1-17

Kadir, Dejal, (ed.) *World Literature Today* 68:4, Autumn 1994 (special issue on Kamau Brathwaite, winner, 1994 Neustdat International Prize for Literature)

Kellman, Anthony, 'A Historical and Musical experience: Edward Kamau

Brathwaite's *X/Self*, *Trinidad New Voices* 16:32, 1988, 88-94
Kellman, Anthony, 'A Rich Plural Heritage as a Tool for Survival: Edward Kamau Brathwaite's *X/Self*, *Callaloo* 11:3, Summer 1988, 645-648
Kellman, Anthony, 'Projective Verse as a Mode of Socio-linguistic Protest', *Ariel* 21:2, 1990, 45-57
Kemoli, Arthur, 'The Theme of the Past in Caribbean Literature', *World Literature in English* 12, November 1973, 304-325
King, Bruce, (ed.), *West Indian Literature* (London: Macmillan, 1979)
King, Bruce, (ed.), *The New English Literatures* (London: Macmillan, 1980)
King, Bruce, 'Walcott, Brathwaite and Authenticity', in Bruce King, (ed.) *New English Literatures* (London, Macmillan, 1980)
Knowles, Roberta and Smilowitz, Erika, (eds.), *Critical Approaches to West Indian Literature* (St Thomas, U.S.V.I.: College of the Virgin Islands, 1981)
Korley, Nii Laryea, 'Brathwaite: Home Again', *West Africa* v. 3627, 16 March 1987, 514-5
Kubayanda, Josaphat, *The Poet's Africa* (Westport, Conneticut: Greenwood Review Press, 1990)
Lucie-Smith, Edward, 'West Indian Writing', *London Magazine* 8:4, 1968, 96-102
Mackey, Nathaniel, 'Edward Brathwaite's New World Trilogy', *Caliban* 3:1, 1979, 58-88
Mackey, Nathaniel, 'Other: From Noun to Verb', *Representations* (University of California) 39, Summer 1992, 51-70
Mackey, Nathaniel, 'Wringing the Word', *World Literature Today* 68:4, Autumn 1994, 733-740
Martini, Jurgen, (ed.) *Missile and Capsule* (Bremen: Caribbean Festival of the Arts, 1980)
Martini, Jurgen, 'Literary Criticism and Aesthetics in the Caribbean, 1: E.K. Brathwaite', *World Literature Written in English* 24:2, 1984, 373-383
Mathurin, Lucille, 'Creative Authenticity: a review of Edward Brathwaite's *The Development of Creole Society in Jamaica 1770-1820*', *Savacou* 5, 1971, 115-120
Maxwell, Marina, 'Towards a Revolution in the Arts', *Savacou* 2, 1970, 19-32
Maxwell, Marina, 'The Awakening of the Drum: A Review of *Masks*', *New World Quarterly* 5:4, 1971, 39-45
McDougall, Russell, 'Something Rich and Strange in the Poetry of Edward Kamau Brathwaite's *The Arrivants*' in *(Un)Common Ground: Essays in Literatures in English*, (eds.) Taylor, a. and McDougall, R. (Adelaide:CRNLE, 1990), 63-74
McWatt, Mark, 'The preoccupation with the past in West Indian Literature', *Caribbean Quarterly* 28: 1&2, 1982, 12-19
McWatt, Mark, (ed.) *West Indian Literature and its Social Context* (Cave Hill, Barbados: University of the West Indies, 1985)
McWatt, Mark, 'The Two Faces of Eldorado: Contrasting Attitudes towards History and Identity in West Indian Literature', in Mark

McWatt, (ed.) *West Indian Literature and its Social Context* (Cave Hill, Barbados: University of the West Indies, 1985), 33-47

Moore, Gerald, 'West Indian Poet', *Transition* 7, 1967, 62-3

Moore, Gerald, *The Chosen Tongue* (London: Longman, 1969)

Moore, Gerald, 'Confident Acheivement', *Journal of Commonwealth Literature* 7, 1969, 122-124

Moore, Gerald, 'Use Men Language', *Bim* 15:57, 1974, 69-76

Moredecai, Pam, 'The Image of the Pebble in Brathwaite's *Arrivants*', *Carib* 5, 1989, 60-70

Morgan, Mary, *A Gathering of Threads* (Kingston, Jamaica, 1991)

Morgan, Mary, 'Highway to Vision: This Sea Our Nexus', *World Literature Today* 68:4, Autumn 1994, 663-668)

Morris, Mervyn, 'Niggers Everywhere: Edward Brathwaite, *Rights of Passage*', *New World Quarterly* 3:4, 1967, 61-65

Morris, Mervyn, 'This Broken Ground: Edward Brathwaite's Trilogy of Poems', *New World Quarterly* 23: 2/3, 1977, 91-103

Morris, Mervyn, 'Some West Indian Problems of Audience', *English* 16: 94, Spring 1967, 127-131

Nanton, Phillip, 'Making Space for Orality on its Own Terms', in Stewart Brown, (ed.), *The Pressures of the Text: Orality, Texts and the Telling of Tales* (Birmingham: Centre of West African Studies, University of Birmingham, 1995), 83-90

Nelson, Emmanuel S., 'Black America and the Anglophone Afro-Caribbean Literary Consciousness', *Journal of American Culture* 12: 4, 1989, 53-58

Ngugi wa Thiong'o, *Homecoming: Essays on African and Caribbean Literature, Culture and Politics* (London: Heinemann, 1972)

Ngugi wa Thiong'o, 'Kamau Brathwaite: The Voice of African Presence', *World Literature Today* 68:4, Autumn 1994, 677-682

Nixon, Rob, 'Caribbean and African Appropriations of *The Tempest*', *Politics and Poetic Value*, (ed.) Robert von Hallberg (Chicago: University of Chicago Press, 1987), 185-206

O'Callaghan, Evelyn, *Woman Version* (London: Macmillan, 1993)

Omotoso, Kole, *The Theatrical into Theatre: a Study of the Drama and Theatre of the English-speaking Caribbean* (London: New Beacon, 1982)

Pagnoulle, Christine, 'The "Voice" of E.K. Brathwaite into French: Grappling with the Untranslatable', *Le Language et l'Homme* 23:3, December 1988, 245-252

Pagnoulle, Christine, 'Labyrinth of Past/Present/Future in Some of Kamau Brathwaite's Recent Poems', *Crisis and Creativity in the New Literatures in English: Cross/Cultures*, (eds.) Davis, Geoffrey and Maes-Jelinek, Hena (Amsterdam: Rodopi, 1990) 449-466

Panel Discussion, 'History in E.K. Brathwaite and Derek Walcott', in *The Commonwealth of Letters* 1:1, June 1989, 3-14

Paquet, Sandra Pouchet, 'Foreward' to Kamau Brathwaite, *The Zea Mexican Diary* (Madison: University of Winconsin Press, 1993), v-xi

Parker, Michael, 'His Island's Voice: Kamau Brathwaite's *Middle Pas-*

sages', *Times Literary Supplement*, 27 November 1992, 27
Pattanayak, Chandrabhanu, 'Brathwaite: Metaphors of Emergence', *The Literary Criterion* 17:3, 1982, 60-68
Pearn, Julie, *Poetry in the Caribbean* (London: Hodder and Stoughton, 1985)
Perrier, Paulette, 'Harmattan: Whose Ancestor am I?, *Journal of Black Poetry* 1:17, 1973, 22-24
Peterson, Kirston Holst, and Anna Rutherford, (eds.) *A Double Colonisation: Colonial and Post-Colonial Women's Writing* (Mundelstrup, Denmark: Dangaroo Press, 1986)
Pollard, Velma, 'Other Exiles', *Caribbean Quarterly* 23: 2/3, 1977, 91-103
Pollard, Velma, 'Language in the Poetry of Edward Brathwaite', *World Literature Written in English* 19:1, 1980, 62-73
Pollard, Velma, 'The Dust — Tribute to the Folk', *Caribbean Quarterly* 26:1/2, 1980, 41-48
Povey, John, 'The Search for Identity in Edward Brathwaite's The Arrivants', *World Literature Written in English* 27:2, 1987, 275-289
Questel, Victor D., 'Blues in Caribbean Poetry', *Kairi* 78, 1978, 4-6
Ramchand, Kenneth, *An Introduction to the Study of West Indian Literature* (London: Nelson, 1976)
Ramchand, Kenneth, 'Parades, Parades: Modern West Indian Poetry', *Sewanee review* 87:1, 1979, 96-117
Ramchand, Kenneth, 'The Fate of Writing', *Caribbean Quarterly* 28: 1/2, 1982, 76-84
Ramchand, Kenneth, *Acts of Possession: The New World of the West Indian Writers*, The ninth Eric Williams Memorial Lecture, (Port of Spain: Bank of Trinidad and Tobago, 1991)
Risden, W., 'Masks', *Caribbean Quarterly* 14:1/2, 1968, 145-147
Rodriguez, Emilio Rodriguez, 'Oral Tradition and Recent Caribbean Poetry' in Marlies Glaser and Marion Pausch (eds.) *Caribbean Writers: Between Orality and Writing*, MATATU No.12, (Amsterdam, Atlanta, Georgia: Editions Rodopi, 1994), 1-16
Rohlehr, Gordon, 'The Historian as Poet', *The Literary Half-Yearly* XI:2, 1970, 171-178
Rohlehr, Gordon, 'Islands', *Caribbean Studies* 10:4, 1971, 173-202
Rohlehr, Gordon, 'West Indian Poetry: Some Problems of Assessment, *Bim* 14:54, 1972, 80-88 [part 1]; 14:55, 1972, 134-143 [part 2]
Rohlehr, Gordon, 'Afterthoughts', *Bim* 14:56, 1973, 227-232
Rohlehr, Gordon, 'The Creative Writer and West Indian Society', *Kaie* 11, August 1973, 48-77
Rohlehr, Gordon, 'History as Absurdity', in *Is Massa Day Done?* (ed.), Coombes, Orde, (New York, Doubleday/Anchor, 1974), 69-109
Rohlehr, Gordon, 'A Carrion Time', *Bim*, 15:58, 1975, 92-109
Rohlehr, Gordon, 'Bridges of Sound: An Approach to Edward Brathwaite's 'Jah'', *Caribbean Quarterly* 26:1/2, 1980, 13-31
Rohlehr, Gordon, 'Background Music to *Rights of Passage*', *Caribbean Quarterly* 26:1/2, 1980, 32-40
Rohlehr, Gordon, 'Songs of the Skeleton — a poetry of Fission', *Trinidad*

and Tobago Review, [Part 1: 'Petit Careme'], 1980, 12-13; [Part 2 'Divali'], 1980, 10, 15, 20

Rohlehr, Gordon, *Pathfinder: Black Awakening in The Arrivants of Edward Kamau Brathwaite* (Port of Spain, Trinidad: private publication, 1981)

Rohlehr, Gordon, 'Metaphors of Making: Art, Craft and the Creative Process in Brathwaite's Poetry', in Knowles, Roberta and Smilowitz, Erika, (eds.), *Critical Approaches to West Indian literature* (St Thomas, U.S. V.I.: College of the Virgin Islands, 1981), 71-94

Rohlehr, Gordon, 'Megalleons of light: Edward Brathwaite's *Sun Poem*', *Jamaica Journal* 16:2, 1983, 81-87

Rohlehr, Gordon, 'The Problem of the Problem of form', Caribbean Quarterly 31:1, 1985, 1-52

Rohlehr, Gordon, 'Songs of the Skeleton: Part III: Flowers of the Harmattan: Brathwaite's *Black & Blues* Examined', in Jackson, J., and Allis, J.B., (eds.), *West Indian Poetry: Proceedings of the Fifith Annual Conference on West Indian Literature* (St Thomas, U.S.V.I.: College of the Vrigin Islands, 1986), 201-217

Rohlehr, Gordon, 'Rohlehr on Brathwaite' in Markham, E.A. (ed.), *Hinterland: Caribbean Poetry from the West Indies and Britain* (Newcastle-upon-Tyne: Bloodaxe, 1989), 109-116

Rohlehr, Gordon, Introduction to *Voiceprint: An Anthology of Oral and Related Poetry from the Caribbean*, (eds.), Brown, S., Morris, M., and Rohlehr, G., (Harlow: Longman, 1989), 1-23

Rohlehr, Gordon, 'Gordon Rohlehr talks to E.A. Markham about Edward Brathwaite's *X/Self*', *Artrage* 18, Autumn 1989, 27-29

Rohlehr, Gordon, 'The Rehumanisation of History: Regeneration of Spirit, Apocalypse and Revolution in Brathwaite's *The Arrivants* and *X/Self*, in his *The Shape of That Hurt: and other essays* (Port of Spain, Trinidad: Longman, 1992), 248-292

Rohlehr, Gordon, 'Dream Journeys', 'Introduction' to *DreamStories* (Harlow: Longman, 1994), iii-xvi

Rohlehr, Gordon, 'Dream Journeys', *World Literature Today* 68:4, Autumn 1994, 765-774

Note: many of the articles by Gordon Rohlehr listed above are included in two recent collections of essays:

Rohlehr, Gordon, *My Strangled City and Other Essays* (Port of Spain, Trinidad: Longman, 1992)

Rohlehr, Gordon, *The Shape of That Hurt: and other essays* (Port of Spain, Trinidad: Longman, 1992)

Reiss, Timothy J., 'Reclaiming the Soul: Poetry, Autobiography, and the Voice of History', *World Literature Today* 68:4, Autumn 1994, 683-690

Saakana, Amon Saba, *The Colonial Legacy in Caribbean Literature* (London: Karnak House, 1987)

Sail, Lawrence, 'Poetry Chronicle II (*X/Self*)' *Stand* 29:2, Spring 1988, 73-74

Salick, Royden, *The Comic Vision in West Indian Literature* (St. Augustine, Trinidad: University of the West Indies, 1993)

Savory, Elaine, 'Wordsongs & Wordwounds/Homecoming: Kamau Brathwaite's *Barbajan Poems*', *World Literature Today* 68:4, Autumn 1994, 750-757

Searle, Chris, *Words Unchained: Language & Revolution in Grenada* (London, Zed Books, 1984)

Senanu, K.E., 'Brahwaite's Song of Dispossession', *Universitas* 1, 1969, 59-63

Slemon, Stephen, and Tifin, Helen, (eds.), *After Europe: Critical Theory and Post Colonial Writing* (Mundelstrup, Denmark: Dangaroo Press, 1989)

Thomas, Kathryn, 'Sunken Treasure' [Review of *Middle Passages*] *CRNLE Reviews Journal* (Australia) 1, 1994, 142-145

Thomas, Sue, 'Sexual Politics in Edward Brathwaite's *Mother Poem* and *Sun Poem*', *Kunapipi* IX:1, 1987, 333-43

Torres-Saillant, Silvio, 'The Trials of Authenticity in Kamau Brathwaite', *World Literature Today* 68:4, Autumn 1994, 697-707

Walcott, Derek, 'Tribal Flutes: Review of *Rights of Passage*', *Sunday Guardian Magazine* (Trinidad), 19 March 1967, 2-3

Walcot, Derek, 'What the Twilight Says: An Overture', *Dream on Monkey Mountain and other plays* (New York: Farrar, Strauss and Giroux, 1970), 3-40

Walmsley, Anne, 'Dimensions of Song', *Bim* 13:51, 1970, 152-167

Walmsley, Anne, *The Caribbean Artists Movement 1966-1972: a Literary and Cultural History* (London: New Beacon, 1992)

Walmsley, Anne, 'Her Stem Singing: Kamau Brathwaite's *Zea Mexican Diary*', *World Literature Today* 68:4, Autumn 1994, 747-749

Warner-Lewis, Maureen, 'Odomankoma 'Kyrema Se'', Caribbean Quarterly 19:2, 1973, 51-99

Warner-Lewis, Maureen, *Notes to Masks* (Benin, Nigeria: Ethiope, 1977)

Warner-Lewis, Maureen, 'Image and Idiom in Nationalist Literature: Achebe, Ngugi and Brathwaite' in *Studies in Commonwealth Literature* (eds.), Breitenger E. amd Sander R., (Tubingen: Narr, 1985), 105-114

Warner-Lewis, Maureen, 'The meaning of religious metaphor in Edward Brathwaite's Islands', in Jackson J., and Allis, J. B., (eds.), *West Indian Poetry: Proceedings of the Fifth Annual Conference on West Indian Literature* (St Thomas, U.S.V.I.: College of the Virgin Islands, 1986), 183-194

Warner-Lewis, Maureen., *E. Kamau Brathwaite's Masks: Essays and Annotations* (Kingston, Jamaica: Institute of Caribbean Studies, University of the West Indies, 1992)

Weinstein, Norman, 'Jazz in the Caribbean Air', *World Literature Today* 68:4, Autumn 1994, 715-718

Wilson-Tagoe, Nana, 'Tradition and the Creative Imagination: The Poetry of Christopher Okigbo and Edward Brathwaite' in Assein, S.O., (ed.), *Comparative Approaches to Modern African Literature* (Ibadan:

Ibadan University Press, 1982), 133-152

Wilson-Tagoe, Nana, 'The Backward Glance: African Continuities as Gateways to Definition in Caribbean Writing: Harris, Lamming and Brathwaite Re-examined' in Emanyonu, (ed.), *Black Culture and Black Consciousness* (Ibadan: Heinemann, 1987), 143-154

Wilson-Tagoe, Nana, 'Edward Brathwaite: Poems', in *A Handbook for Teaching Caribbean Literature*, (ed.), Dabydeen, David (London: Heinemann, 1989) 105-115

Index of works by Brathwaite cited

Acknowledgements

Acknowledgement is gratefully made to the University of Michigan Press for permission to quote from *Roots*; and to Oxford University Press for permission to quote from other works by Brathwaite.

Notes on Contributors

Stewart Brown lectures at the Centre of West African Studies, University of Birmingham. He has published many essays on aspects of African and Caribbean literature and contemporary British Poetry, as well as three collections of his own poetry, most recently *Lugard's Bridge* (Seren, 1989). He is the editor of several anthologies of Caribbean writing, including *New Wave: Contemporary Caribbean Short Stories* (Heinemann, 1991) and — with Ian McDonald — *The Heinemann Book of Caribbean Poetry* (1992). He also edited the collection of critical essays, *The Art of Derek Walcott* (Seren, 1991).

J. Edward Chamberlin is professor of English and comparative literature at the University of Toronto. He has published widely on nineteenth and early twentieth century literature, contemporary poetry, and aboriginal rights. His books include *The Harrowing of Eden: White attitudes towards Native Americans* (1975), *Oscar Wilde's London* (1987), and most recently *Come Back to Me My Language: Poetry and the West Indies* (University of Illinois Press, 1993). He is poetry editor of *Saturday Night Magazine.*

Glyne A. Griffith lectures at Buckell University, Lonisbury, USA. He was a lecturer in the Department of English at the University of the West Indies for several years. He recently completed his doctorate on contemporary critical theory and West Indian literature.

Louis James is Professor of Victorian and Modern Literature at the University of Kent at Canterbury. He has taught at various universities in Africa, the USA, the Caribbean and the Far East. He has published widely in the areas of nineteenth century literature and popular culture, and on Commonwealth literature, particularly writing from Africa and the Caribbean. His books include *Fiction for the Working Man* (1963), *Print and People* (1976), *Jean Rhys* (1978) and he edited the first collection of critical essays on Caribbean literature in English to be published, *The Islands In Between* (1968). In 1990 he produced *Writers from the Caribbean*, a reader's guide published by the Book Trust.

Bridget Jones is Senior lecturer in the Department of Modern Languages, Roehampton Institute, University of Surrey. From

1964-1982 she lectured in the Department of French at the University of the West Indies, Jamaica. She has published many essays on Caribbean writing in French and wrote a critical introduction to Simone Schwarz-Bart's *The Bridge of Beyond* (Heinemann 1982). She translated an edition of Pierre Clitandre's novel *Cathedral of the August Heat* for Readers International (1987). Her own poems have been published in several magazines and a selection was included in the anthology *Jamaica Woman.*

Nathaniel Mackey teaches at the University of California, Santa Cruz. He is the author of two books of poetry, *Eroding Witness* (University of Illinois Press, 1985) and the *School of Udhra* (City Lights Books, 1993). He is also the author of an ongoing prose work, *From A Broken Bottle Traces of Perfume Still Emanate,* of which two volumes have so far appeared, *Bedouin Hornbook* (Callaloo Fiction Series, 1986) and *Djbot Baghostus's Run* (Sun and Moon Press, 1993). He is editor of the literary magazine *Hambone.*

Mervyn Morris is a reader in West Indian Literature at the University of the West Indies, Jamaica. In addition to many essays on aspects of West Indian writing, he has published four books of his own poetry, most recently *Examination Centre* (New Beacon Books, 1992). He has also edited several anthologies of Caribbean writing, including *The Faber Book of Caribbean Short Stories* (1990). In 1992 he spent several months as Visiting Writer in Residence at the South Bank Centre in London.

Gordon Rohlehr is Professor of West Indian Literature at the University of the West Indies, Trinidad. He co-edited (with Stewart Brown and Mervyn Morris) *Voiceprint,* an anthology of oral and related poetry from the Caribbean (Longman, 1989) and he has published several books of criticism, including *Pathfinder: Black Awakening in the Arrivants of Edward Kamau Brathwaite* (1981), *Calypso and Society in Pre-Independence Trinidad* (1990) and in 1992 Longman Trinidad published two volumes of his essays 1969-90, *My Strangled City and other essays* and *The Shape of that Hurt and other essays.*

Elaine Savory (Fido) was Senior lecturer in the English Department at the University of the West Indies, Barbados, from 1974 until 1990 and now divides her time between New York and Barbados. She has written widely on African Caribbean literature, particularly on women's writing and on theatre and drama. She co-edited *Out of the Kumbla,* a collection of essays on Caribbean women and literature, with Carole Boyce Davies (1990). She recently published a collection of poems, *Flame Tree Time* (Sandberry Press, Jamaica, 1993).

Anne Walmsley is a free-lance writer, working in London. She was a teacher in Jamaica in the early 60s and spent several years as Caribbean Editor for Longman. She also worked in Kenya and Nigeria and was for some time Africa Researcher for *Index on Censorship.* She has published widely on Caribbean art and literature, edited two acclaimed schools anthologies of Caribbean writing, *The Sun's Eye* (Longman 1968, new edition 1989) and — with Nick Caistor — *Facing the Sea* (Heinemann 1986). In recent years she has been involved in research on The Caribbean Artist Movement, of which she was an active member. She complied *Guyana Dreaming: The Art of Aubrey Williams* (Dangaroo Press, 1990) and in 1992 her major documentary history *The Caribbean Artists Movement 1966-1972: A Literary and Cultural History* was published by New Beacon Books.

Maureen Warner-Lewis is a Senior Lecturer in the Department of English, University of the West Indies, Jamaica. She had previously taught and undertaken field research in Trinidad and Nigeria. In 1989-90 she spent a year in the Department of African and Asian Languages and Literature at the University of Florida in Gainsville, on a Fullbright Research Fellowship. She has published many articles on African and Caribbean literature, history and linguistics. She edited the *African Studies Association of the West Indies Bulletin* between 1970 and 1980. Her books include *Notes to Masks* (1977, revised edition 1992), *Garvey: Africa, Europe and the Americas* co-edited with Rupert Lewis, and *Guinea's Other Sons: The African Dynamic in Trinidad Culture* (The Majority Press, 1992). *Yoruba Songs of Trinidad* was published in 1994 by Karnak House.